W9-AGQ-055

Praise for previous editions of

QUICK ESCAPES®
MINNEAPOLIS/ST. PAUL

"This book, a must-have for summer travel, does everything but pack your suitcase for you."

—*The Maplewood Review* (Maplewood, Minn.)

". . . Well-balanced, with lodging choices for both families and couples and activities that keep both culture vultures and tree-huggers happy."

—*Star Tribune* (Minneapolis, Minn.)

Help Us Keep This Guide Up to Date

Every effort has been made by the author and editors to make this guide as accurate and useful as possible. However, many things can change after a guide is published—establishments close, phone numbers change, facilities come under new management, etc.

We would love to hear from you concerning your experiences with this guide and how you feel it could be improved and kept up to date. While we may not be able to respond to all comments and suggestions, we'll take them to heart and we'll also make certain to share them with the author. Please send your comments and suggestions to the following address:

The Globe Pequot Press
Reader Response/Editorial Department
P.O. Box 480
Guilford, CT 06437

Or you may e-mail us at:
editorial@GlobePequot.com

Thanks for your input, and happy travels!

QUICK ESCAPES®

MINNEAPOLIS/ST.PAUL

21 WEEKEND GETAWAYS
IN AND AROUND THE TWIN CITIES

FOURTH EDITION

Mark R. Weinberger

The
Globe
Pequot
Press

GUILFORD, CONNECTICUT

The prices and rates listed in this guidebook were confirmed at press time. We recommend, however, that you call establishments before traveling to obtain current information.

Interior photo credits: pp. 1, 5, 62, 84: courtesy of the Minnesota Historical Society; pp. 12, 27, 34, 48, 74, 87, 96, 109, 130, 146, 189: courtesy of the Minnesota Office of Tourism; p. 23: courtesy of the Minneapolis Park Board; p. 120: photo by Carla Arneson; p. 151: courtesy of Jane O'Reilly; p. 159: photo by J. Hertel; courtesy of the Wisconsin Division of Tourism; pp. 174, 209: p. 201: courtesy of the Wisconsin Dells Visitor and Convention Bureau; p. 223: courtesy of the Iowa Division of Tourism; p. 226: courtesy of the Iowa Film Office; p. 241: courtesy of Arnold's Park Amusement Park; p. 251: courtesy of Amana Colonies Convention and Visitors Bureau.

Maps by M. A. Dubé except where noted otherwise.

ISBN 0-7627-3023-4
ISSN 1547-8777

Manufactured in the United States of America
Fourth Edition/First Printing

*To my children and newest travel companions,
Matthew and Alexandra.*

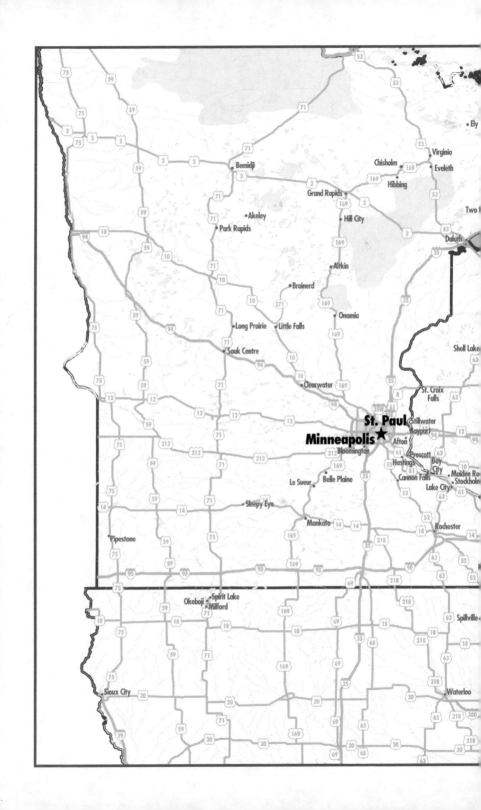

CONTENTS

INTRODUCTION

When we Minnesotans travel, some of us pack bags and head to magnificent, far-off, adventuresome places, saving what's close to home for that infamous and proverbial rainy day. Other persons pack up and head to the cabin on every free weekend, and local attractions simply become landmarks along the way. And some of us rarely travel, considering it too costly or time consuming.

Here are twenty-one quick escapes in and around Minneapolis/St. Paul designed to change those habits and bring traveling closer to home. Most of the destinations are fewer than 250 miles from the Twin Cities to keep driving to a minimum and take enjoyment to the maximum. Each itinerary outlined offers something for everyone, including options to let you customize your escape.

I went on my first trip when I was six months old when my parents took me along for a vacation on the north shore of Lake Superior. Since then I have returned to that magnificent lake at least once a year, and sometimes more. But back in the late 1990s, while researching a bicycling book, I spent many days exploring other parts of Minnesota that I had never visited or had only passed through on my way somewhere else. From these trips I gained a new appreciation for the variety of geography that Minnesota has to offer. From the rolling hills and endless prairie views of southwestern Minnesota to the narrow valleys and steep bluffs of the southeast to the glacial mounds that dot the countryside of the west central part of the state, I found incredibly diverse landscapes. Minnesota may not have mountains or oceans, but it has a unique geography that just might surprise those who embark on weekend escapes round the state.

This region abounds in history, interesting architecture, bike trails, the arts, restaurants, resorts, and state parks. Within 250 miles of the Twin Cities you can camp under the stars or stay in a fine hotel, bike or go for a carriage ride, paddle a canoe or relax on a paddle wheeler, try your hand at churning butter or order it—drawn—for your lobster, learn the art of bonsai or visit fine-art museums, or simply walk among pine forests that have no counterparts.

Traveling the upper Midwest at its best means following back roads, distant church spire to distant church spire; visiting river towns, woods, farm communities, and local diners; understanding boom-and-bust economies; and appreciating changing seasons, local legends, area history, and traditions. Of course there are the lakes, at least 12,000 of them in Minnesota alone, but don't worry—you don't have to be a boat enthusiast or even don a bathing suit to enjoy them. And it doesn't have to be summer, either. A drive along the North Shore in September or a midwinter stay in a B&B can be spectacular. And where else does the water change color with the seasons? The icy blue waters of winter give way to a molten sunlight-warmed hue in the summer and then reflect orange and crimson by fall.

In fact, if there's one single underlying theme to this region, it is water. From Great Lakes to trickling headwaters, there's water in every form but salt water. (But, hey, if you followed the Mississippi long enough, you'd encounter that, too.)

What to Bring

One of the amazing things about our climate is the ability for temperatures to change as much as fifty degrees overnight. Admittedly that's rare, even in the winter, but it means that when you're traveling here you need to be prepared. This is especially true if you head north of the Twin Cities. Things to consider:

- Bicycle, lock, and water bottle
- Cooler/picnic basket
- Journal
- Backpack
- Folding chairs (for parades)
- Compass
- Seasonal clothing
- Warm jacket (even in July)
- Binoculars
- Camera and film
- Walking shoes
- Rain gear
- Bathing suit
- Personal items

Permits and Rentals

The itineraries in this book take you to, or near, more than twenty Minnesota state parks. All Minnesota state parks require a vehicle permit. Daily and annual passes are available; however, I would recommend that you purchase an annual pass. If the timing is right, purchase your pass after October 1. The passes are good through the calendar year; purchased after October 1, the pass is valid through the end of the next calendar year.

This region offers splendid camping in national forests, state forests, state parks, and private campgrounds, from primitive sites to full hookups and bathhouses, so you may want to give the camping experience a try. Fortunately you don't have to own the gear. The following businesses rent the equipment you will need:

Brambillas, 550 Valley Park Drive, Shakopee (952–445–2611; www.brambillas.com), sells, rents, and services several makes and models of motor homes. Rental rates depend on the size and make of the vehicle, but a weekly cost for a family of four would average about $950. Gas, mileage, and insurance are extra.

Pleasureland RV Center, Inc., Thirty-seventh Avenue and Division Street, St. Cloud (320–251–7588 or 800–862–8603; www.pleasureland rv.com), rents a variety of motor homes. Weekly rates for a 24-footer start at $1,200; gas and mileage are extra.

AARCEE Recreation, 2910 Lyndale Avenue South, Minneapolis (612–827–5746; www.aarceerental.com), has everything you need for camping, from sleeping bags to tents. A tent for four costs about $40 for a weekend. If you want a few more amenities, consider a tent trailer; they cost from $265 to $415 a week. Skis and snowshoes are also available for rental seasonally or by the weekend.

MINNESOTA
ESCAPES

A Historical and Cultural Getaway within the Twin Cities

There's No Place Like Home

2 Nights

In the chronological scheme of things, first there was Fort Snelling, then there was Pig's Eye, and then there was St. Anthony Falls. Pig's Eye changed its name to St. Paul when it became a city, and St. Anthony Falls merged with another community to become Minneapolis. Today Minneapolis and St. Paul are affectionately known as the "Twin Cities," but situated, for the most part, on the opposite banks of the Mississippi River, they are anything but the same.

☐ Living History

☐ Museums

☐ Concerts

☐ Theater

Although both cities have a strong industrial heritage—St. Paul took the lead early in steamboat transportation and river trade, and Minneapolis led the nation as a flour milling center—both spawned famous families like the Pillsburys, Hills, Ordways, and Daytons, and both are very pretty cities with ancient public park systems and numerous suburbs that continue to grow, the two cities are more like distant cousins.

Minneapolis, the "City of Lakes," has always been more industrially advanced than St. Paul. It's hard to know whether this economic edge caused more change or simply allowed for it, but even from a distance, with its towering ice-blue skyscrapers and sprawling downtown, Minneapolis looks like a modern metropolis. And St. Paul, made of red brick and limestone on terraced hillsides, looks like the old, elegant capital city it is. If St. Paul had a nickname, it would be the "City of Charm." The attitude of newer, better, faster seems to work in Minneapolis, but in St. Paul life is a little more laid-back, a little slower paced. Minneapolis has more hotels, more restaurants, and more shopping, but St. Paul seems to have more time.

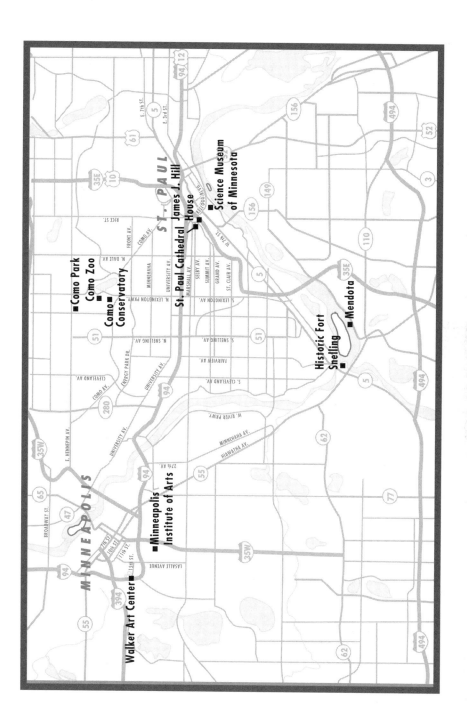

With this sense of time, St. Paul also has a strong sense of its own history. Old buildings are rarely torn down; most are restored for new use, like the old courthouse. And others, such as the St. Paul Public Library, opened in 1917, are still today what they were originally built for decades ago.

For many reasons river towns are popular getaway destinations these days. River towns capture the essence of a gentler age, offer refuge from big cities, and provide the romance that seems to be missing in a hustle-and-bustle life. How soon we forget that Minneapolis and St. Paul are our original river towns. Even the first lock and dam on the Mississippi are right here! And these cities, despite their huge populations, still have main streets, historic inns, and quaint restaurants.

Together, Minneapolis and St. Paul offer an incredible collection of activities, combining the historic with the new, the traditional with the avant-garde, and great buildings with the great outdoors. Between the two cities there are nearly fifty theaters and more than one hundred museums (some dedicated to a single ethnic community), offering a cultural mecca that could actually take years' worth of weekends to tour. And each city offers a change of pace from the other—a getaway in itself.

Day 1 / Morning

Eat a hearty breakfast and include a picnic lunch as you pack your bags and head off to tour Minneapolis and St. Paul. Follow I–494 or State Highway 62 to State Highway 55 and then follow the signs to **Historic Fort Snelling,** which is "about five minutes and 175 years away," as they like to say there.

In its heyday Fort Snelling was a frontier outpost, a bustling dock, and an economic and social center. The fort was built at the confluence of the Mississippi and Minnesota Rivers, and there was a time when everyone coming into the area would have stopped there. Today this living history museum sits at the confluence of Highway 55 and I–494, and it's easy to sail right past en route to work or more distant attractions. This time, follow the brown HISTORIC SITE signs to the interpretive center and Fort Snelling.

As you take your self-guided tour, chat with the costumed "residents" and let them take you back in time to experience fort life in 1827. The women in the barracks quilt, mend, cook, and wash clothes, making a visit to the commandant's house feel, even to the tourist, like a reprieve from life on the frontier. Mrs. Snelling brought to the fort many fine furnish-

The Round Tower at Historic Fort Snelling

ings, as well as servants, in an effort to preserve a more aristocratic lifestyle on the remote river bluff.

Some of the soldiers drill, while others work in the sutler's store and blacksmith shop or stand guard at various posts. As you wander building to building, the distant lilt of a military tune from a tin whistle will remind you how lonely fort life must have been.

Be ready to accept a musket and drill with the men, excavate with archaeologists, dance the Virginia reel, or partake in theatrical vignettes. The entertainment is always changing, and every day has a different theme. If you visit often enough, you'll watch history change before your very eyes: The *interpreted* year will soon be 1838; rumor has it the men are in for a new general as well as new uniforms. Open May through October, Monday through Saturday 10:00 A.M. to 5:00 P.M., and Sunday noon to 5:00 P.M. Admission: adults $6.00; seniors over 62, $5.00; children 6 to 15, $4.00; children under 6 are free. Maximum household rate $12.00. Call (612) 726–1171 or visit www.mnhs.org.

LUNCH: Enjoy your quick picnic lunch at one of the picnic tables near the parking area—there is still a lot of historic ground to cover!

Afternoon

In order to move ahead in time, you must backtrack to State Highway 55 and follow it east across the Mendota Bridge. Follow the brown HISTORIC SITE signs that direct you to Highway 13 north, down into the river valley and to the **Sibley, Faribault,** and **Dupuis homes.**

It is now the mid-1800s, and the future Twin Cities are underway. The site is small but fascinating. The houses and trading post in Mendota were built out of local limestone block with the help of soldiers from Fort Snelling. The structures once faced the open river, but the river has since shifted, the woods have filled in, and the modest dwellings appear to be facing a forest wall, like little children being punished in the corridor of a school from a bygone era.

A visit here allows a new understanding of life in the days of Minnesota Territory. You'll hear a little historic gossip and make links between John Stevens (of the Stevens house in Minnehaha Park), the sutler's store at Fort Snelling, early Minnesota politics, and more. Fort Snelling was the social hub, and Henry Sibley (the state's second governor) and his wife visited the fort on many occasions. In the winter, when the river froze over, they would walk across for parties and gatherings.

Allow a little more than an hour for the tour. The site is open from May through October; tours leave between 10:00 A.M. and 3:30 P.M., except on Sunday, when they're between noon and 3:30 P.M. The site is closed Tuesdays and Wednesdays. Admission: adults $4.00; seniors $3.50; children 5 and older, $2.50; children under 5 are free. Call (651) 452–1596.

Minnesota baby boomers probably remember looking at Casey the gorilla in a cage in the original WPA zoo building and sitting on the rock-hard back of Toby, the giant Galapagos tortoise, possibly not knowing he was alive, but they may not realize that 1997 marked the hundredth anniversary of the **Como Zoo.** The zoo got its start when Como Park received three deer as a gift and had to put a fence around them.

Today the zoo has a magnificent collection that includes lions, Siberian tigers, gorillas, orangutans, polar bears, giraffes, and always a baby something. Traditionalists will enjoy the "Sparky the Seal Show" and, like many, prefer the grizzly and Kodiak bears to the exotic animals. The zoo is not the only attraction in Como Park, however. The world-famous historic **Como Conservatory,** hailed as a "horticultural castle," has attracted botanists, gardeners, newlyweds (for wedding photos), and sightseers since 1915. The all-glass domed building looks like a summer ice palace, and even small children are intrigued.

To enjoy Como Park, backtrack across the Mendota Bridge to State Highway 5 east, which turns into West Seventh Street in St. Paul. Turn left onto Snelling Avenue and continue about 4 or 5 miles to Midway Parkway (directly in front of the state fairgrounds) and turn right. Follow Midway Parkway for 0.5 mile into Como Park. Parking for the conservatory and Como Zoo will be on your left. The park and zoo are free; the conservatory costs $1.00 for adults and 50 cents for children. Call (651) 487–8200.

Evening

DINNER AND LODGING: From the Como Zoo backtrack to Snelling Avenue and go left. Continue on Snelling Avenue until it intersects with I–94. Follow I–94 east to the Fifth Avenue exit, which takes you into downtown St. Paul. Follow Fifth Avenue to Market Street. Take a right on Market and then a left into the circle drive of the **St. Paul Hotel,** 350 Market Street. Parking ramps surround the hotel, but if you choose one of the fine packages, you will have complimentary valet parking.

The Dinner Package offers a deluxe room for one night, a $100 food and beverage credit, and turn-down services at night for $249 per couple. The rooms are exceptional, and as a member of Historic Hotels of America, the hotel's ambience is unsurpassed. The staff is wonderfully helpful, the concierge is especially knowledgeable about what there is to do, and your dinner in **The St. Paul Grill,** often written up as "the best restaurant in the Twin Cities," will be superb. The hotel is located directly across the street from the **Ordway Music Hall,** so you may want to time your stay at the hotel with an evening concert. Call (651) 292–9292 or visit www.stpaulhotel.com.

After dinner stroll through **Rice Park** in front of the hotel, or consider a carriage ride through **St. Paul's Cultural Corridor.** Step out of the hotel and look toward Fifth and Market Streets for the handsome Amish-built carriages, the Percheron draft horses, and their snappily dressed drivers. The thirty-minute tour, for two to four people, runs on a first-come, first-served basis for $35. The carriages are at your service from 6:00 to 11:30 P.M., weather permitting, mid-April through September, and on weekends only in October and from Thanksgiving through New Year's

Eve. The carriages can be reserved for special occasions by calling **Lindell Carriage,** (651) 438–3452.

Day 2 / Morning

BREAKFAST: Enjoy a leisurely breakfast in your room, or dine in the hotel restaurant. Breakfasts run anywhere from continental (about $5.00) to the Cafe California Breakfast that includes an omelette, seasonal berries, muffins or toast, and juice ($9.00).

You can easily make a day of one good museum and a stop for lunch, so get an early start in order to allow for much more, and then begin your day of discovery in St. Paul at the **Science Museum of Minnesota,** 120 West Kellogg Boulevard on the river bluff. Leave your car at the hotel; the museum is only a couple of blocks away.

No matter what good things you have heard about the museum, you will be in awe. At first glance it may seem as if it's for children—like a giant playhouse where the toys are real—but adults quickly find themselves building, manipulating, and pondering and then asking the knowledgeable staff all kinds of questions. There are hands-on experiments for building bridge trusses, making clouds, and extracting DNA. You can touch a tornado, study a mummy, identify birds and fossils and dinosaurs, play music simply by going up and down the stairs, or learn about the Hmong culture of Southeast Asia through their art and a full-scale dwelling. A new addition to the museum is an exhibit from the Museum of Questionable Medical Devices, which was formerly located in Minneapolis. This unique 325-piece collection contains examples of medical quackery, including a hip reducer with large rolling pins for removing fat from thighs and a phrenology machine that is supposed to read a person's personality from bumps on the head. The Science Museum allows hands-on use of some of the machines.

And then there's the **William L. McKnight–3M Omnitheater and IMAX Dome,** the first retractable dome in the United States, with an 89-foot semispherical movie screen that makes you feel as if you're in outer space, the middle of the ocean, a volcano, or the sky, depending on the theme of the presentation. The movies run about forty-five minutes; it's a good idea to get in line about twenty minutes before the performance, at least on weekends. The screen is designed for all to see, but upper middle seats offer the best viewing.

LUNCH: It will be lunchtime before you know it, and you'll be hungry long before you're ready to leave, but fortunately everything is fun at the

Science Museum, including lunch. Stop by the **Chomp Eatery,** a snack bar near the dinosaurs; eat at **Elements,** a full-scale restaurant upstairs; or just grab a cup of coffee at the **Omni Coffee Shop** near the theater. The museum is open June through December, Monday through Saturday 9:30 A.M. to 9:00 P.M. and Sunday 10:00 A.M. to 7:00 P.M., with reduced hours from January through the first week of June. Admission is charged; ticket prices range from $8.00 to $13.50 for adults and from $6.00 to $10.50 for children ages 3 to 12 and seniors over 65, depending on the exhibit or combination package chosen. Wheelchair accessible. Call (651) 221–9444; TDD (651) 221–4585; www.smm.org.

Afternoon

From the Science Museum return to your car. Follow St. Peter Street (on the east side of the St. Paul Hotel) north to West Seventh Street and go right to West Fifth Street. Take another right and continue to John Ireland Boulevard (in front of the Minnesota History Center) and go left, at all times driving toward **St. Paul Cathedral.** The cathedral sits at the junction of Selby and Summit Avenues; you can't miss the impressive copper dome (replaced in 2003) looming over the neighborhood. Park free across from the cathedral. (Time Sunday visits for about 2:00 P.M. to avoid masses held at 10:00 A.M. and 5:00 P.M.)

Tours are available, but no information will do justice to the awe-inspiring sensation of standing in the center and looking straight up into the dome. Almost as breathtaking is the view from the cathedral's front steps, looking down the hill to the city of St. Paul.

One block over from Selby Avenue is **Summit Avenue** (the streets converge in front of the cathedral). Summit Avenue is the most prestigious street in Minnesota. House styles include massive Italianates, Victorians, you name it. And most have equally impressive carriage houses.

Summit Avenue is home to the **James J. Hill House** (it looks like one of his railroad stations), the **Governor's Mansion,** and the **University Club.** It's also the street where a young F. Scott Fitzgerald once lived and wrote *Tender Is the Night.* (The best stretch is from Cathedral Hill west to Snelling Avenue.) Pick up Summit Avenue and continue away from downtown. Take a left at Dale, go 1 block to Grand Avenue, and go right.

Shopping on **Grand Avenue** can consume a whole day. From Dale west to Fairview Avenue, and tapering off on either end, Grand Avenue is full of antiques stores, gift shops, art galleries, restaurants, and coffee shops from the offbeat to the classic, including ethnic shops specializing in everything from Irish imports to locally made Hmong textiles and crafts.

DINNER: Since you're already roaming around on Grand Avenue, you might as well stay for dinner. And it's a safe bet you'll find something to please your palate along this vibrant urban corridor. For a uniquely Minnesota dinner, stop at **Tavern on Grand,** 656 Grand Avenue; (651) 228–9030. The walleye is the Minnesota state fish, and under the restaurant's listing in the phone book, the line "Famous for Walleye" says it all. This mild-tasting fish causes hundreds of thousands of Minnesotans to flock to our abundant lakes from mid-May through the coldest days of winter, and Tavern on Grand has a reputation for preparing it to perfection. If dining on our state fish doesn't interest you, the restaurant has a full menu, or you could cross the street and walk west about 1 block to **Dixies on Grand,** 695 Grand Avenue; (651) 222–7345. Dixies specializes in southern cooking and has an excellent selection of dishes from the South.

LODGING: To head to Minneapolis for the night, backtrack to Snelling Avenue and go left (north) on Snelling to I–94 west. Take the Eleventh Street exit to **Doubletree Suites,** 1101 La Salle Avenue, about 6 blocks down on your left. Doubletree Suites is smaller than most of the hotels downtown and focuses on personalized service, which includes a gift of homemade chocolate chip cookies upon your arrival. Although it's a little off the beaten path, it's only 1 block off Nicollet Avenue, and the hotel's free shuttle will take you anywhere in the downtown area. The rooms are spacious, and each has a wet bar, refrigerator, and microwave oven. Upgraded suites offer oversize whirlpool tubs, turn-down service, and chocolates on your pillow. Rates vary, depending on amenities and the season. An executive-level suite for two starts at about $150 and includes breakfast in the hotel's restaurant, **The Cafe Luxx.** Phone (612) 332–6800.

Evening

End your day with an evening in the Cafe Luxx, enjoying a cocktail and listening to live jazz. The cafe features many favorites, such as Ginger Commodore, Debbie Duncan, and the Bruce Henry Trio.

Day 3 / Morning

BREAKFAST: Select whatever you like from the breakfast buffet served in the cafe. Choose from eggs, bacon, sausage, potatoes, muffins, and pastries. A beverage is also included.

Doubletree Suites is only a few blocks from your first Minneapolis destination, the **Walker Art Center.** Follow La Salle Avenue about 4 blocks south to Fifteenth Street. Take a right on Fifteenth Street, cross Hennepin and Lyndale Avenues, and continue past the front of the museum. (The Walker and the Guthrie Theater share an entrance at 725 Vineland Place.) Wind to Kenwood, to the left, and continue to the parking lot near the conservatory; pay as you enter.

Start your tour in the **Cowles Conservatory,** which is especially delightful in the fall and winter; it provides a break from the cold and a tropical tunnel to the museum and theater. One of the most popular rooms in the conservatory houses the *Standing Glass Fish,* a stunning 22-foot-tall creation of hundreds of glass "scales."

Continue your tour outside and proceed through the **Minneapolis Sculpture Garden.** The garden, a collaborative effort of the Minneapolis Park and Recreation Board and the Walker Art Center, opened in 1988 on the old grounds of the Armory Gardens. The Sculpture Garden is like a visual and cerebral amusement park; it spans eleven acres and includes forty works of modern art, from cast bronze nudes and abstract sculptures to the local favorite by Claes Oldenburg and Coosje van Bruggen, *Spoonbridge and Cherry,* a 51-foot sculpture of a spoon topped with a 1,200-pound cherry fountain.

The Walker Art Center began in 1879 as the private collection of Thomas Barlow Walker and became the first public art gallery in the Upper Midwest. In 1940, under the Work Projects Administration, it became an arts center and has grown from there. Today the Walker displays modern and contemporary art from its large permanent collection and hosts many unique temporary exhibits as well as music, dance, and film events.

The Walker galleries will take you on an artistic trek through various movements and expressions, teach you its visual vocabulary, and show you that everything around you, from a cafe street scene to a cartoon, can be art.

The Minneapolis Sculpture Garden is open daily from 6:00 A.M. to midnight. Cowles Conservatory is open Tuesday through Saturday 10:00 A.M. to 8:00 P.M. and Sunday 10:00 A.M. to 5:00 P.M., with extended hours that coincide with performances at the Guthrie Theater. Both the garden and the conservatory are free. Phone (612) 370–3996. The Walker Art Center is open Tuesday, Wednesday, Friday, and Saturday from 10:00 A.M. to 5:00 P.M., Thursday 10:00 A.M. to 9:00 P.M., and Sunday 11:00 A.M. to 5:00 P.M. Wheelchair accessible. Admission: adults $6.00; seniors and chil-

Minneapolis Sculpture Garden

dren 12 to 18, $4.00; children under 12 are free. Admission is free for everyone on Thursday and the first Saturday of each month. Phone (612) 375–7622; TDD (612) 375–7585; www.walkerart.org.

LUNCH: Before you leave stop for lunch at the **Gallery 8** restaurant, where the museum literally continues: Black-and-white photographs adorn the walls, and there's a great view of the Sculpture Garden. The food selection is limited, but everything in Gallery 8 is made daily on the premises, and the menu changes regularly. There is always a choice of soup (the cream of potato is excellent; $2.50); a hot entree, from ratatouille to roast turkey and dressing (about $7.00); sandwiches; breads; great desserts like vanilla cheesecake and brownies; and beer and wine by the glass. The restaurant is open Tuesday through Sunday 11:00 A.M. to 4:00 P.M.

Afternoon

To finish up your weekend, return to the front of the Walker Art Center and take a right onto Hennepin Avenue, heading south. Take a left on Twenty-fourth Street and follow it all the way to the **Minneapolis Institute of Arts** at 2400 Third Avenue, a total trip of about 2 miles. Turn right on Third Avenue to the far end of the building and park, for free, in the ramp.

Here the Minneapolis Institute of Arts and the **Children's Theatre Company** share an entrance on Third Avenue. The Minneapolis Institute of Arts houses a comprehensive collection of artwork, one of the top ten in the nation, with ancient to contemporary pieces representing numerous cultures. Three of the institute's most famous and valuable pieces are the Chinese *Jade Mountain,* considered to be the largest piece of historic carved jade in the Western Hemisphere; the Roman nude *Doryphoros,* or *Spearbearer,* in marble, dating from the first century B.C.; and the Ife head, in terra cotta, dating from the twelfth to fourteenth century in Ife, present-day Nigeria.

Other magnificent exhibits include works by Rembrandt (including the prized *Lucretia*), Monet, van Gogh, and Picasso; tapestries; sculptures; and the renowned Period Rooms of decorative arts. Open Tuesday through Saturday 10:00 A.M. to 5:00 P.M., Thursday and Friday until 9:00 P.M., and Sunday 11:00 A.M. to 5:00 P.M. Admission is free; donations are encouraged. Wheelchair accessible. Phone (612) 870–3131; www.artsmia.org.

The museum has two options for hungry visitors. **ArtsBreak by D'mico & Sons** is a coffee shop that also serves pastries and desserts and is open during museum hours. **ArtsCafe by D'mico & Sons** features Neopolitan-style pizzas, Italian sandwiches, and gourmet salads. Hours for ArtsCafe are Tuesday through Saturday 11:00 A.M. to 2:30 P.M. and Sunday 11:00 A.M. to 3:00 P.M.

There's More

Minneapolis

The Ard Godfrey House, Central Avenue and University Avenue Southeast, between the Riverplace and St. Anthony Main complexes, is the oldest historic residence in Minneapolis. Run by the Women's Club of Minneapolis, the house has been completely restored and contains many original furnishings. First floor is wheelchair accessible. Open June through September, Friday through Sunday noon to 3:30 P.M., and by appointment. Admission: adults $2.00; seniors $1.00; students 6 to 18, 50 cents. Call (612) 870–8001.

Frederick R. Weisman Museum, 333 East River Road (612–625–9494), is one of the newest additions to the Twin Cities' cultural array—and its skyline! Uniquely shaped and clad in sculptural stainless steel, the museum overlooks the Mississippi on the campus of the University of Minnesota and houses the university's extensive art collection. Open Tuesday, Wednesday, and Friday 10:00 A.M. to 5:00 P.M., Thursday 10:00 A.M. to 8:00 P.M., and Saturday and Sunday 11:00 A.M. to 5:00 P.M. Admission is free. Wheelchair accessible.

Music and Theater. Orchestra Hall, 1111 Nicollet Mall (612–371–5656), features the Minnesota Orchestra, a series of Pops concerts, and other performances. There's also the Children's Theatre Company, 2400 Third Avenue; (612) 874–0500, ext. 104. Delightful performances all year long include classics such as *The Prince and the Pauper* and fantasies such as *Peter Pan*. Rush tickets, as available, are offered fifteen minutes before the performances at discount prices. The Guthrie Theater, 725 Vineland Place (612–377–2224), has been bringing literary classics to its semicircular stage for more than thirty years. Charles Dickens's *A Christmas Carol* is a holiday tradition. Wheelchair accessible; ASL and audio description are available. Free outdoor concerts at the Lake Harriet Bandshell, Lake Harriet Parkway (612–661–4800), occur evenings throughout the summer.

The *Stone Arch Bridge* was built by the Minneapolis Union Railway Company in 1863. Abandoned and recently restored, it is now a pedestrian bridge that offers a panoramic view of St. Anthony Falls. You can reach it via the Heritage Trail on either side of the river; the easiest access is just down from St. Anthony Main.

Trolley and Carriage Rides. River City Trolley Rides offers a fun way to tour the city. Purchase a two-hour pass and ride the trolley as a tour, or buy an all-day pass and use it as transportation. The trolley boards every twenty minutes at the Minneapolis Convention Center, the Walker Art Center, and St. Anthony Main and takes you on a full loop down First Avenue and up Nicollet Mall. Open early May through late October, Tuesday through Sunday and holidays 10:00 A.M. to 4:00 P.M.; closed Monday. Fares: adults $10.00; seniors 65 and over and children 2 to 12, $5.00. All-day pass is $15.00. Call (612) 204–0000; www.rivercitytrolley.com.

There are three restored trolleys running on the mile-long stretch of track from Lake Harriet to Lake Calhoun that was once part of the Como-Harriet Line. The trolleys run regularly from May 24 through Labor Day, 6:30 P.M. to dusk on weeknights, 1:00 P.M. to dusk on Saturday, and 12:30 P.M. to dusk on Sunday. All rides cost $1.00, but children under 3 are free. Call (651) 228–0263 for more information.

Nicollet Island Carriage runs seasonally on Nicollet Island. Fares range from $5.00 per person for fifteen minutes on "standby" to $75.00 an hour for reserved rides.

St. Paul

The Alexander Ramsey House, 265 South Exchange Street; (651) 296–8760. Home of Minnesota's first governor, the house contains many furnishings and belongings of the Ramsey family. Open mid-April through December, Tuesday through Saturday 10:00 A.M. to 3:00 P.M. Admission: adults $6.00; seniors 65 and over $5.00; children 6 to 15, $4.00; children younger than 6 get in free. Call for reservations.

The **F. Scott Fitzgerald Walking Tour** retraces the steps of the author who captured the 1920s in novel form. Maps are available through the Minnesota Historical Society; (651) 296–6126.

The James J. Hill House, 240 Summit Avenue; (651) 297–2555. Tour the railroad magnate's massive Victorian mansion at 240 Summit Avenue every half hour, Wednesday through Saturday 10:00 A.M. to 3:30 P.M. Admission: adults $6.00; seniors $5.00; children 6 to 15, $4.00.

Landmark Center, 75 West Fifth Street; (651) 292–4355. This building, built at the turn of the twentieth century, was once the Federal Courts Building. Today it houses the Minnesota Museum of American Art, featuring permanent and changing displays in several media, and the Schubert Piano Museum. The building also stands as a museum itself for the sheer beauty of its construction. The center is open Monday through Friday 8:00 A.M. to 5:00 P.M., Thursday until 8:00 P.M., Saturday 10:00 A.M. to 5:00 P.M., and Sunday 1:00 to 5:00 P.M. The museums have separate hours. The art museum requests donations.

The Minnesota Children's Museum, 10 West Seventh Street; (651) 225–6000; www.mcm.org. The museum is geared for children from infancy through age 10, with lots of hands-on exhibits, weekly events, and occasional visits from literary characters such as *The Cat in the Hat*. Open Monday through Sunday 9:00 A.M. to 5:00 P.M., until 8:00 P.M. on Thursday; closed Monday from Labor Day to Memorial Day. Admission: ages 3 through 59, $5.95; 60 and older $3.95.

The Minnesota History Center, 345 Kellogg Avenue; (651) 296–6126. This modern museum (visible from the steps of St Paul Cathedral) displays the essence of Minnesota's history, from birch-bark canoes to local rock-star memorabilia. Open Tuesday 10:00 A.M. to 8:00 P.M., Wednesday through Saturday 10:00 A.M. to 5:00 P.M., and Sunday noon to 5:00 P.M. Admission is free; donations are encouraged.

Music and Theater. The Park Square Theatre in the Hamm Building, 408 St. Peter (651–291–7005; wwwparksquaretheatre.org), has brought classic drama and comedy (and even an occasional musical) to the stage for twenty-five years. The season runs from mid-January through August; performances are held Thursday through Sunday. Depending on age and seating, tickets range in price from $19 to $25. The Ordway, 345 Washington Street (651–282–3000; www.ordway.org), features performances by the St. Paul Chamber Orchestra, the Minnesota Opera, the Schubert Club, and the St. Paul Series of the Minnesota Orchestra, as well as traveling groups, musicals, and Broadway plays.

Riverboat Cruises. Padelford Packet Boat Co., Pier 1; (651) 227–1100; www.padelfordboats.com. Choose from two Mississippi River excursions: Fort Snelling or the St. Anthony Mill District. Boats depart daily from either Harriet Island (across the river from downtown St. Paul) or Boom Island (in Minneapolis) at noon and 2:00 P.M. Memorial Day weekend through Labor Day. Fares: adults $12.00; seniors $10.00; children 5 to 12, $6.00.

St. Paul Gangster Tours depart from the Wabasha Street Cave (south on Wabasha, across the bridge). Tour gangster hideouts and hot spots one Saturday each month from noon to 2:15 P.M. Admission: adults $20; seniors $19; children 6 to 15, $17. Call (651) 292–1220 for reservations; www.wabashastreetcaves.com.

Winter Alternatives

Music. For the fastest tropical getaway, try the Como Conservatory for midwinter *Music Under Glass,* Thursdays at noon in January and February, with paid admission to conservatory. Call (651) 487–8200, ext. 5.

Special Events

January to February. The St. Paul Winter Carnival; (651) 223–4700. Begun in 1886, the festivities include ice sculptures, sporting events, multicultural activities, snow sculptures, and the Grand Day and Torchlight Parades.

March. The St. Patrick's Day Parade, St. Paul; (651) 887–7052.

May. Festival of Nations, Civic Center, St. Paul; (651) 647–0191. Includes a bazaar, food booths, and dances and music of various ethnic groups.

June. The Stone Arch Festival of Arts, Main Street, Minneapolis; (612) 378–1226. Includes food, music, and art.

July. Annual Minnesota Heritage Festival, Nicollet Island and Main Street, Minneapolis; (612) 673–5123. Includes ethnic music, a lumberjack show, food, living history, and historic train rides.

Taste of Minnesota, Harriet Island, St. Paul; (651) 772–9980 or (651) 291–5600; www.tasteofmn.org Features food vendors, outdoor entertainment, and nightly fireworks.

July to August. The Minnesota Orchestra Viennese Sommerfest, 111 Nicollet Mall, Minneapolis; (612) 371–5656 or (800) 292–4141. Features the music of the great composers—Strauss, Mozart, Schubert, Suppé, and Dvořák—and guest conductors. Free outdoor concerts and food concessions on the Plaza, renamed Marktplatz for the event. Admission charged for concerts in Orchestra Hall.

August to September. The Minnesota State Fair, Minnesota State Fairgrounds, St. Paul; (651) 642–2200; TTY (651) 642–2372; www.mnstate fair.org. One of the country's largest state fairs offers live entertainment, rides on the midway, food, equipment, livestock and handicraft exhibits, and demonstrations.

September. Annual European Oktoberfest, Main Street on the riverfront, Minneapolis; (612) 673–5123. Food, dancing, and crafts.

November. The Night We Light, Rice Park, St. Paul; (651) 224–9122. Includes a laser show and a synchronized lighting of the park and downtown buildings.

November to December. The Holidazzle Parade, Minneapolis; (612) 616–SNOW. Floats sparkle with Christmas lights every night starting at 6:30 P.M. The parade takes about a half hour and travels down the Nicollet Mall from Thirteenth Street to Fifth Street.

December. Capital New Year, Rice Park, St. Paul; (651) 290–9054. A New Year's Eve party featuring performing arts.

Other Recommended Restaurants and Lodgings

Minneapolis

Buca Di Beppo, 1204 Harmon Place; (651) 638–2225. A lot of fun is served along with southern Italian family-style cuisine in a bustling basement locale. This is a restaurant to share with friends; the portions are so large, they easily serve three to four people. Favorites include chicken cacciatore, chicken or veal marsala, and ravioli. The garlic mashed potatoes are *deliziosi!* Dinner, from appetizer through dessert (such as the fabulous tiramisu), averages about $23 per person. Open Monday through Friday 5:00 to 10:00 P.M., Saturday 4:00 to 11:00 P.M., and Sunday 4:00 to 10:00 P.M.

Cafe Havana, 119 Washington Avenue North; (612) 338–8484. Specializing in Cuban cuisine, the cafe serves delicious, authentic Latin American food in an intimate setting. Specialties include fish, steaks, chicken, and ribs served with plenty of black beans, rice, and fried plantains. Entrees range from $11 to $24. Open Tuesday through Saturday 5:00 P.M. to 1:00 A.M.

Four Points Sheraton Metrodome, 1500 Washington Avenue; (612) 333–4646. Near the University of Minnesota, it has a restaurant, bar, pool, workout room, and whirlpool suites. A standard room for two is about $100 a night. Bed-and-breakfast rates are also available.

The Hyatt, 1300 Nicollet Mall; (612) 370–1234; www.minneapolis. hyatt.com. The Hyatt has a pool, two restaurants, access to an athletic club, and is connected to the Minneapolis Convention Center and downtown shops and restaurants via the skyway system. A standard room for two runs about $135 a night; packages are available.

The Hyatt Whitney Hotel, 150 Portland Avenue; (612) 339–9300. Perched on St. Anthony Falls, the hotel is a renovated flour mill that is now renowned for its accommodations and cuisine. Deluxe rooms start at

$125; rooms with a view are more. Dining delights in the elegant, intimate Whitney Grill include beef tenderloin, scallops, salmon, and lamb. Entrees range from $25 to $30. The restaurant is open from 6:30 A.M. to 10:00 P.M. Monday through Saturday and for Sunday brunch from 10:00 A.M. to 2:00 P.M.

Lucia's, 1432 West Thirty-first Street; (612) 825–1572; www.lucias.com. Combining talent, great recipes, and local and organic ingredients whenever possible, Lucia's has been serving the Twin Cities exquisitely creative food since 1985. Located in the heart of Uptown, Lucia's restaurant and wine bar, with its canopied windows, hardwood floors, tin ceilings, and accents of gold and cobalt blue, provides a perfect ambience for a wonderful dinner—or just dessert—and good conversation. The menu changes constantly but always includes a meat, poultry, fish, and vegetarian entree. Dinner entrees range from pasta with vegetables, herbs, and pine nuts (about $12) to seven-hour leg of lamb with dried apricots, currants, and couscous (about $20). Lucia's also features a tempting tray of ever-changing desserts (about $5.50 a serving) and a large selection of wine and imported beers. Open Tuesday through Friday for lunch from 11:30 A.M. to 2:30 P.M. and for dinner from 5:30 to 9:30 P.M. (until 10:00 P.M. on Friday and Saturday). On Sunday brunch is served from 10:00 A.M. to 2:00 P.M. and dinner from 5:30 to 9:00 P.M. Smoking is permitted in the bar only.

The Nicollet Island Inn, 95 Merriam Street, Nicollet Island; (612) 331–1800. (Restaurant, 612–331–3035.) Built in 1893 as a door and sash factory, it is now a charming place to spend the night ($125 to $160 per night) and an elegant place in which to eat. The inn is famous for its award-winning Sunday brunch that includes pasta dishes, fish dishes, pastries, and omelettes and eggs Benedict made to order. The desserts alone are worth the $22 per person. Some rooms have views of St. Anthony Falls; the dining room has a view of quaint Main Street.

St. Paul

The Cafe Latte, corner of Victoria Street and Grand Avenue; (651) 224–5687. Located in the charming commercial area known as Victorian Crossing, the building isn't very old, but it is in the heart of the historic district. Service is cafeteria-style, and the menu includes a variety of soups, breads, salads, individual pizzas, and desserts. (No matter where you dine in the Twin Cities, it's worth driving to Cafe Latte for dessert.) High tea is also offered. Two people can eat very well for less than $18.

Cossetta's, 211 West Seventh Street; (651) 222–3476. A third-generation family restaurant and deli, it has been in the same neighborhood since 1914. The restaurant serves its award-winning pizzas and mostacciolo cafeteria-style in classic Italian surroundings: Salamis, cheeses, garlic braids, and loaves of bread are on display. Several pictures of the old neighborhood adorn the wall. The market is open Monday through Saturday 8:30 A.M. to 10:00 P.M., Sunday 10:00 A.M. to 9:00 P.M. The restaurant is open Monday through Saturday 11:00 A.M. to 10:00 P.M., Sunday 11:00 A.M. to 9:00 P.M., closing an hour earlier in the winter.

The Covington Inn, 100 Yacht Club Road, Pier 1, Harriet Island; (651) 292–1411; www.covingtoninn.com. The inn is housed at the end of a fifty-some-year-old towboat moored on the Mississippi River. It is open all year and has four rooms, including the Pilot House Suite, with private baths and fireplaces. Rooms range from $150 to $235 per night.

Dakota Jazz Club & Restaurant, 1010 Nicollet Avenue, (612) 332–1010; www.dakotacooks.com. Emphasizing Minnesota ingredients, the Dakota combines the ordinary with the different for extraordinary results: Minnesota brie and apple soup, which is remarkably good, or ravioli stuffed with butternut squash and caramelized onions, sautéed with fresh sage and black walnuts. Jazz music seven nights a week. Open Monday through Saturday from 4:00 P.M.; dinner is served Monday through Thursday 5:30 to 10:30 P.M., until 11:30 P.M. on Friday and Saturday (the bar is open until 1:00 A.M.). On Sunday the Jazz Brunch is served from 10:00 A.M. to 2:00 P.M., dinner 4:00 to 9:30 P.M.

Radisson Hotel, 11 East Kellogg; (651) 292–1900. These excellent accommodations include an indoor pool, spa, and the Carousel Restaurant that rotates for a panoramic view of the city. Rates range from $90 for a standard room to about $300 for a whirlpool, champagne, chocolates, and a full breakfast for two.

Vintage, 579 Selby Avenue; (651) 222–7000. Once a crumbling edifice, this beautifully restored redbrick Victorian duplex now houses one of the newest restaurants in the Twin Cities. Vintage is known for serving specialty wines by the glass (hence the name) and featuring a different vineyard or region monthly. Seafood is the specialty, but the menu is varied; lunch entrees are anything from a grilled salmon sandwich ($9.00) to Alaskan halibut in a curried clam broth with a mushroom and crab salad (about $24.00). Open Monday through Friday 11:30 A.M. to 1:00 A.M.,

Saturday and Sunday 10:30 A.M. to about midnight.

W. A. Frost & Co., 374 Selby Avenue; (651) 224–5715; www.wafrost.com. Set in the historic Cathedral District, the restaurant has ambience and an incredible antique bar. Outdoor seating is offered in the summer; fireplaces glow in the winter. Dinner entrees include seafood, steaks, and pastas; average price is $20. Open Monday through Saturday 11:00 A.M. to 2:00 P.M. and 5:00 to 10:30 P.M., Friday and Saturday until 11:30 P.M. Sunday brunch is served from 10:30 A.M. to 2:00 P.M.

For More Information

ArtTown OnLine; www.mnonline.org/artsentertainment/arttown.

Festival and Heritage Foundation, 332 Minnesota Street, Suite 102E, St. Paul, MN 55101; (651) 223–4700 or (800) 488–4023.

Greater Minneapolis Convention and Visitors Association, 400 Multi Foods Tower, 33 South Sixth Street, Minneapolis, MN 55402; (612) 661–4700; www.minneapolis.org.

The Minnesota Historical Society, 345 Kellogg Boulevard West, St. Paul, MN 55102; (651) 296–6126 or (888) PAST–FUN; www.mnhs.org.

The Minnesota State Board of Arts; (651) 215–1600.

The Mississippi Mile Events Hotline (covers activities along the Mississippi River from I–35 to Plymouth Avenue); (612) 673–5123.

St. Paul Convention and Visitors Bureau, 55 East Fifth Street, Suite 102, St. Paul, MN 55101; (651) 297–6985; www.stpaulcvb.org.

A Recreational Getaway within the Twin Cities

Make a Day of It!

1 Day

There are more than 22 lakes within the Twin Cities proper, tens of miles of river flowing through them, and about 200 parks. The park system in each dates back over a century and remains a primary focus in city development to this day. From swimming to skiing, there are myriad activities to choose from in every season, and some of the best are free. One of the most popular outdoor activities today is bicycling, and the increasing number of paved trails, especially the conversion of abandoned railroad grades to interconnected miles of paved zero-grade trails, makes the sport even more appealing.

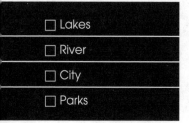

☐ Lakes

☐ River

☐ City

☐ Parks

As the idea sweeps across the nation, it is worth noting that paved bike paths aren't new to Minnesota. In fact, aside from having more miles of paved bike paths following abandoned railroad grades than any other state in the country, Minnesota has had paved bike paths for over twenty-five years, since the first ones went in around the Chain of Lakes in Minneapolis. Most avid bicyclists have ridden the Paul Bunyan Trail near Brainerd or the Root River Trail near Lanesboro, but even some of the most ardent pedalers aren't familiar with **The Grand Rounds,** part of the Minneapolis Park System, right at our doorstep.

The Grand Rounds refers to the 37-plus miles of the just-about-contiguous biking and walking trail system that starts in north Minneapolis, north of Victory Memorial Boulevard; travels along Shingle Creek; follows Minneapolis parklands around the Chain of Lakes, through Minnehaha Park, and along the Mississippi River; and then heads downtown, across the Hennepin Avenue Suspension Bridge to Nicollet Island and Main Street. It continues, eventually connecting with East River Road. For more information go to www.minneapolisparks.com. There is also a short trail, originally designed for commuters, that follows the railroad bed from the north

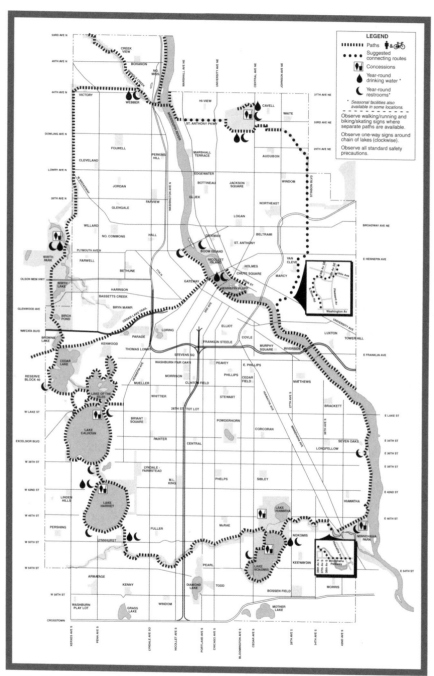

The Grand Rounds, Minneapolis

courtesy of the Minneapolis Park Board

side of Cedar Lake down Hennepin Avenue into downtown. Other routes offer links to St. Paul, Hidden Falls, and Fort Snelling State Park.

Biking the Grand Rounds is a thrilling way to spend a day, a wonderful workout, and, especially during fall color, a fabulous way to sightsee. Biking the whole thing is a serious undertaking, but you could start just about anywhere on the route and make a day of it by enjoying the nearby sights, feeding the ducks, wandering public gardens, stopping to eat, and then backtracking to your car. Depending on where you live, with a little extra research and a willingness to bike on the roads here and there, you may not even need your car!

So grab a friend or two and your bike lock (after all, this is the city), and hit the trail. If biking isn't your idea of a good time, try the parallel walking paths or opt for other outdoor activities offered by the park systems in both Minneapolis and St. Paul. You'll find yourself enjoying these cities in a way you never thought possible.

Morning

An especially good ride, without biking the entire Grand Rounds, is the portion from the **Chain of Lakes** area to **St. Anthony Falls.** This section offers great scenery, including views of the grand mansions near the lakes, places to eat, and access to numerous historic sites.

The east side of **Lake Calhoun** is an ideal place to start. Park in the lot at the intersection of Lake Street and Thomas Avenue, across from the **Calhoun Beach Club,** and continue south on your bike to **Lake Harriet.** The route around the Chain of Lakes goes counterclockwise, so keep this in mind as you're pedaling. Also keep in mind that the speed limit throughout the park system is 10 miles per hour, and you must "sound off" if you pass another bicyclist. Keep to the east side of Lake Harriet and you won't have to bike all the way around the lake to continue on the route without riding on the streets. If you're already thirsty, stop at the **Lake Harriet Concession Stand** for a drink and a box of the world's best popcorn (they use real butter). After your snack, the **Lake Harriet Rose Gardens,** the second oldest public rose garden in the United States, are just a little farther on and worth the stop.

Around Fifty-second Street the path winds east toward **Lake Nokomis.** Be careful here, too, to avoid riding in circles around the lake. There are actually two trails, one that goes around Lake Nokomis and one that continues westward to **Minnehaha Park.** For now the paths are discernible by their age and condition; the path around the lake is brand new—follow the older one.

The path gets a little tricky as you near Minnehaha Park. You have to wind for a few blocks on the residential streets from Forty-seventh Street, crossing Thirty-sixth, Thirty-seventh, and Thirty-eighth Avenues to Minnehaha Parkway, and then cross Hiawatha Avenue to get to the park. The path resumes immediately across the street on the north side of the park near the painstakingly restored pale yellow **Longfellow House** that is home to the Hospitality Center and the Trailhead Interpretive Center for the Minneapolis Park System. Stop in for free brochures and regional park maps or a chat with the on-site naturalist.

Minnehaha, a Dacotah word meaning "laughing water," was once a celebration site for the Dacotah Indians. Today it is a celebrated park enticing families, bicyclists, and history buffs, so lock up your bike and hike its grounds on the numerous paths and boardwalks. Stop on the bridge overlooking the falls and let the gentle rush of the water lull you as the serenity of our own "Central Park" takes hold. (Some visitors even kick off their shoes and step across on the rocks.) You'll quickly understand why **Minnehaha Falls** is the most photographed site in the state of Minnesota.

The charming, amber-colored Victorian "Princess" train depot was last used officially in 1963, although locals can recall the circus trains unloading there and the traditional march of the animals as recently as the mid-1980s. The restored depot, complete with stationmaster, is now part of the **Minnesota Transportation Museum,** housing an interpretive center so thorough that it even offers classes in American Morse telegraphy. The depot is open Sunday and holidays, Memorial Day to Labor Day, 12:30 to 4:30 P.M. Admission is free. Call (651) 228–0263.

Another delightful surprise in the park is the **John H. Stevens House,** aka the birthplace of Minneapolis. Originally located in downtown Minneapolis, in 1896 the house was put on rollers and moved, with the help of 10,000 schoolchildren, to Minnehaha Park, where it sat idle for nearly one hundred years until restoration officially began in 1983. It was in this house that the Minneapolis public schools were founded and where Minneapolis got its name (narrowly escaping being called "Minne*ha*polis," the city of laughing water). Open from May through October, Saturday and Sunday 1:00 to 5:00 P.M. Admission: adults $2.00; children 12 to 18, $1.00; children under 12 free. Call (612) 722–2220.

All the other sights in the park are free. The park is open year-round, but the refectory is open May through October only, Monday through Saturday 9:30 A.M. to 9:00 P.M. and Sunday 10:30 A.M. to 9:00 P.M. Call the refectory at (612) 370–4939. Call (612) 661–4800 for general park information. Call (612) 661–4827 or visit www.byways.org for specific bike trail information.

NOTE: At the far end of the parking lot that runs parallel with Hiawatha is access to the bike trail that goes to Fort Snelling.

At the east end of Minnehaha Park is the entrance to **Lock and Dam #1.** The trail is navigable by bike, but you must go down (and back up) a steep hill. At the lock and dam the route turns north along the Mississippi River. If you were impressed by the beauty of the lakes and the lush foliage along Minnehaha Creek, you will be overwhelmed by the scenery along the river, especially in the fall.

The stretch along the river from Minnehaha Park to St. Anthony Falls is about 5 miles, running parallel to West River Road. Downtown, just behind the post office, a circular ramp will take you up onto the **Hennepin Avenue Suspension Bridge.** Follow the bridge most of the way across the river to Wilder Street and take a right onto **Nicollet Island.** Go left to Main Street and follow the signs for the **Heritage Trail.** The trail takes you along Main Street; park your bike in one of the bike stands and stretch your legs.

LUNCH: After thirty years, **Pracna on Main,** 117 Main Street Southeast, deserves special recognition for its early efforts in helping to revitalize Main Street. With its incredible bar—serving twenty draft beers—and intimate atmosphere right on the riverfront, Pracna remains a fun and popular place to eat. The extensive sandwich menu features just about everything, from a hamburger to a Reuben or even a charbroiled tuna steak. Prices range from $8.00 to $10.00. Dinner entrees include pastas, steaks, and fish and range from $14 to $21. Open daily 11:30 A.M. to 1:00 A.M., still serving the eggs Benedict that made them famous from 11:30 A.M. to 2:00 P.M. on Saturday and Sunday. Call (612) 379–3200.

Afternoon

Continue on the Heritage Trail. It crosses the river on the **Stone Arch Bridge,** an old abandoned railroad bridge built by magnate James J. Hill in 1863 and then restored for pedestrians and bikers just a few years ago. Pause and take in the incredible view, from the university to the skyscrapers and beyond.

Park pathway

If you don't feel up to retracing your pedaled steps, opt for the shorter route home on the **Cedar Lake Trail,** down Hennepin Avenue and past the Dunwoody Institute to the north side of Cedar Lake. Follow the bike path south, across the southern edges of Cedar Lake and Lake of the Isles, to your car on the east side of Lake Calhoun.

There's More

Baseball. The St. Paul Saints, member of the Northern League, offer the classic outdoor baseball experience. Their season runs from Memorial Day through Labor Day. Games are played at Midway Stadium, 1771 Energy Park Drive, St. Paul. Admission is charged. Call (651) 644–6659.

Bike Rentals. Calhoun Rental, 1622 West Lake Street, Minneapolis; (612)

827–8231; www.calhouncycle.com. Bike rentals from about $6.00 an hour to $25.00 a day.

Biking. St. Paul has the Grand Rounds route and numerous other bike paths. Call (651) 266–6400 for maps and more information.

Golf. Phalen Golf Course, 1615 Phalen Drive, St. Paul (651–778–0424), has eighteen holes, a shop, and clubhouse. Highland 18-hole Golf Course, 1403 Montreal, St. Paul (651–695–3776), has a driving range and putting green. Highland 9-hole Golf Course, 1797 Edgcumbe Road, St. Paul (651–695–3708), is good for beginners. Theodore Wirth Golf Club, 1301 Theodore Wirth Parkway (763–522–4584), has a nine-hole and an eighteen-hole course with a clubhouse, practice greens, and rentals.

Ice-skating. Parade Ice Garden, 600 Kenwood Parkway, Minneapolis; (612) 370–4846. Indoor skating all year; rental skates available. Adults $4.50; seniors and children under 18, $4.00. Phone for times; open skating can be preempted by hockey tournaments.

Sailing Lessons. The Minneapolis Park and Recreation Board offers sailing lessons for adults and children at the beginner and advanced-beginner levels. Adult lessons are offered at both Lake Calhoun and Lake Harriet in the evenings; children's lessons are at Lake Harriet in the mornings and early afternoons. All classes meet at the refectories at each lake. These are group lessons with no more than fifteen people per class and about four people per boat. The boats used are 14-foot Lidos. In 2003 four two-and-a-half-hour lessons were $65 for children and $88 for adults. Rates are reduced for residents of the city of Minneapolis. Registration begins mid-May. Call (612) 661–4875.

Winter Alternatives

Cross-country Skiing. There are 18 miles of groomed trails in Fort Snelling State Park, State Highway 5 and Post Road; (612) 725–2389. The City of St. Paul has 10K of groomed trail in Phalen Park and beginning-level trails at Highland 9-hole Golf Course; (651) 266–6400.

Downhill Skiing. Como Ski Center, Como Park, St. Paul; (651) 488–9673. A ski slope that's great for beginners, with tow ropes, lessons, rentals, and a chalet.

Ice-skating. Many of the parks in Minneapolis have ice-skating rinks with warming houses. Call (612) 370–4900.

Sights. Minnehaha Falls is definitely worth the stop in the dead of winter. The frozen falls are literally time standing still.

Sliding. Theodore Wirth Park, Plymouth and Glenwood Avenues, Minneapolis; (612) 661–4800. Tubing on the golf course; chalet and rentals available.

Special Events

May. Thai Two On 5K Walk/Run. Benefits the American Lung Association. Registration fee.

July. Walking tours, Minnehaha Park. Sunday 2:00 P.M. and 4:00 P.M. A fee is charged.

The Minneapolis Aquatennial; (612) 331–8371; www.aquatennial.org. Includes the Grand Day Parade, milk-carton boat races, duck races, sand sculpture competition, fireworks, and the Torchlight Parade.

September. St. Paul Classic Bike Tour; (651) 290–0309; www.spnec.org.

October. The Twin Cities Marathon; (763) 287–3888; www.twincities marathon.org.

Other Recommended Restaurants

Near the Chain of Lakes

Concession stands at Lake Calhoun, Lake Harriet, Lake Nokomis, and the refectory at Minnehaha Park offer great hot dogs, popcorn, and ice-cream cones.

Famous Dave's, 4264 Upton Avenue South, Minneapolis; (612) 929–1200. Famous-recipe barbecue ribs and chicken are offered along with other items, including sandwiches and hamburgers. Entree prices range from $6.00 to $18.00. A children's menu is available. Open Sunday through Thursday 11:00 A.M. to 9:00 P.M., until 10:00 P.M. on Friday and Saturday.

Near Minnehaha Park

Bridgeman's Embers America, 4757 Hiawatha Avenue, Minneapolis; (612) 721–6433. Breakfast, lunch, dinner, and ice-cream specialties are served; prices range from $2.00 to $8.00. Open Sunday through Thursday 7:00 A.M. to 10:00 P.M., until 11:00 P.M. on Friday and Saturday.

Cap's Grille, 5000 Hiawatha Avenue, Minneapolis; (612) 722–2277. Cozy and adorned with neon, toys, and trinkets, Cap's has been voted as having the "best ribs" and the "best pork chops." Sandwiches and hamburgers average $6.00 to $7.00. Open Tuesday through Friday 11:00 A.M. to 9:00 P.M., Saturday and Sunday 7:30 A.M. to 9:00 P.M.

Dairy Queen Brazier, 4740 Minnehaha Avenue, Minneapolis; (612) 721–5400. Offerings include hamburgers, hot dogs, and famous ice-milk confections. Open daily February through October.

Near the University of Minnesota

Bullwinkle's Saloon, 1429 Washington Avenue South, Minneapolis; (612) 338–8520. The restaurant serves its famous Coney Island hot dog with cheese (about $2.50) in addition to burgers, salads, and other sandwiches ($3.50 and up). Open Monday through Saturday 11:00 A.M. to 1:00 A.M.; Sunday hours depend on the televised sports games.

Grandma's Saloon and Grill, 1810 Washington Avenue, Minneapolis; (612) 340–0516. Decorated with neon signs, antiques, and odds and ends, Grandma's has one of the most eclectic and unique interiors and one of the most extensive menus in the Twin Cities. There is a separate bar and pool hall upstairs. Serving salads, sandwiches, pastas, steaks, and especially good hamburgers, prices range from $7.00 to $19.00. Open daily 11:30 A.M. to 10:30 P.M., until 11:30 P.M. on Saturday and 9:00 P.M. on Sunday.

Sgt. Preston's, 221 Cedar Avenue, Minneapolis; (612) 338–6146. The original sandwich bar. If you don't design it yourself, you can choose from nearly twenty sandwiches on the menu. Other specialties include homemade soups, chilis, and desserts, and it is famous for its large selection of ales on draft. Sandwich prices average between $7.00 and $8.00. Outdoor seating is available in the summer. Happy hour held Monday through Friday 3:30 to 6:30 P.M. Open daily 10:30 A.M. to closing.

Near St. Anthony Falls

The Aster Cafe, St. Anthony Main; (612) 379–3138. Scones, bars, cookies, soups, sandwiches, beer, and flavored coffees are served in an open, casual atmosphere great for chatting or playing the piano in the corner. Open Monday through Thursday 7:30 A.M. to 10:00 P.M., Friday and Saturday 9:00 A.M. to 11:00 P.M., and Sunday 10:00 A.M. to 4:00 P.M., with reduced hours in winter.

For More Information

Minneapolis Park & Recreation Board, 400 South Fourth Street, Minneapolis, MN 55415–1400; (612) 661–4800.

Minnesota Office of Tourism, 121 Seventh Place East, St. Paul, MN 55101–2112; (651) 296–5029 or (800) 657–3700; www.explore minnesota.com.

Mississippi National River and Recreation Area, 175 East Fifth Street, Suite 418, St. Paul, MN 55101; (651) 290–4160.

St. Paul Parks, 300 CHA-25 West Fourth Street, St. Paul, MN 55102; (651) 266–6400.

The Brainerd Lakes Area

At the Lake

2 Nights

The Brainerd Lakes area, about a 50-mile radius of lakes and North Woods surrounding Brainerd, has been drawing tourists for more than one hundred years. The earliest visitors (and summer-only residents) were from Kansas. They came north by train, to beat the heat of the dry plains, and were met at the depots by horse-drawn wagons. The north shore of Bay Lake is still referred to as the Kansas City Colony. Modern tourists follow some of the same old train routes, but today they're riding bicycles.

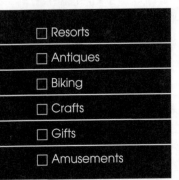

☐ Resorts

☐ Antiques

☐ Biking

☐ Crafts

☐ Gifts

☐ Amusements

During the 1940s big bands came to places such as Bar Harbor. In the 1960s there was a surge in sales of private cabins; the 1970s saw the rise in interest in the racetrack and brought tons of young tourists; and the 1980s and 1990s brought condos, fewer family resorts, more private homes, and a lot more golf.

Today there are more than one hundred resorts and an additional fifty-plus places to stay, such as campgrounds, hotels, and B&Bs (sixty-five of which remain open in the winter); more than 450 holes of golf within 35 miles of Brainerd; several public beaches and lake accesses; the Paul Bunyan Bike Trail; the Brainerd International Raceway (BIR); a multitude of amusements; an incredible number of fine restaurants; too many gift shops to count; and dozens of antiques stores.

The Brainerd Lakes area is the beginning of the North Woods, an ideal spot to visit. It's so close that you can leave after work on Friday, feel like you've been gone for a week, and be back in your routine by Monday morning.

Day 1 / Morning

Brainerd is about 150 miles north of the Twin Cities. U.S. Highway 10 north is the old standard route and is easy to pick up in St. Paul. I–494 to I–94 west

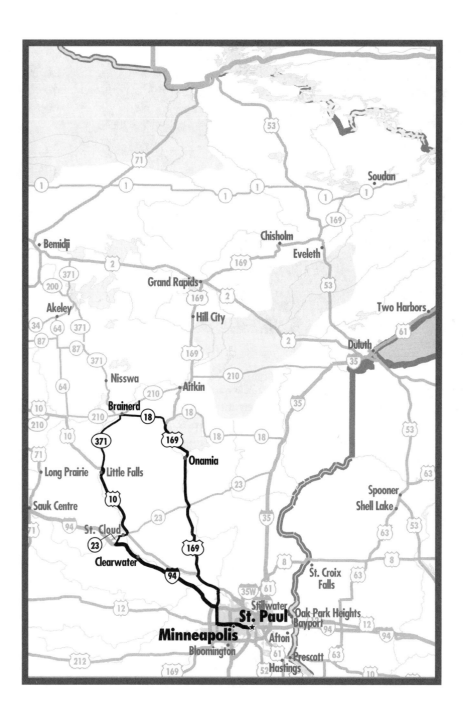

Paul Bunyan Bike Trail

(cutting east to Highway 10 at Clearwater) is a fairly efficient route.

Either way, Highway 10 turns into State Highway 371 just north of Little Falls, and you'll end up passing **Camp Ripley**, about 25 miles south of Brainerd, within a couple of hours. Camp Ripley is an active military training base, and the **Minnesota Military Museum** there is worth the stop. Turn left at the tank (you can't miss it) between the stone posts, and continue a fraction of a mile across the bridge to the camp's entrance. The exhibits follow Minnesota's military history from the frontier outpost era to the Gulf War. The vehicles, weapons, uniforms, photographs, and paraphernalia will captivate any history buff and intrigue just about everyone else. One very moving display shows the dutiful effort of Colonel E. B. Miller to keep his journal during captivity in a Japanese prisoner of war camp. A Brainerd native, Miller survived the Bataan Death March and then risked his life by writing on every scrap of paper imaginable. He later wrote *Bataan Uncensored*. There is also a display that lists every Minnesotan who has received the Medal of Honor, including Charles A. Lindbergh, who received a special award for his flight to Paris.

Kids (of any age) can try on uniforms and helmets and even buy personalized dog tags as a souvenir.

Allow about an hour for your visit. Open late May through Labor Day, Wednesday through Sunday 10:00 A.M. to 5:00 P.M.; after Labor Day through April, Thursday and Friday 9:00 A.M. to 4:00 P.M. Admission is free, but a donation of $3.00 per adult is suggested. Call (320) 632–7374.

LUNCH: Continue north on State Highway 371 into downtown Brainerd to the **Northwind Grille,** 603 Laurel Street; (218) 829–1551. The grille has an extensive menu that serves breakfast, lunch, and dinner, and you can count on a really good bacon-lettuce-and-tomato sandwich with homemade coleslaw and a milk shake for about $7.00. Park in the lot 1 block beyond Laurel, behind the restaurant. Smoke-free. Open Monday through Thursday 7:00 A.M. to 8:00 P.M., Friday and Saturday until 9:00 P.M., and Sunday until 3:00 P.M. Wheelchair accessible.

Afternoon

Continue north on State Highway 371, and take a left at the old-fashioned water tower. Saved from demolition in the 1970s, the water tower has become a regional landmark and is affectionately referred to as Paul Bunyan's flashlight.

Continue on State Highway 371/210 for a couple of miles, past the strip of franchises and shopping malls, and make a right turn at the lights to follow State Highway 371 north. The stretch to Nisswa is laden with restaurants, grocery and discount stores, boat and dock suppliers, and numerous amusement options; you may want to make a mental note.

If you have the time, follow the highway a few more miles north into **Nisswa,** the area's prime tourist-shopping mecca. Nisswa has several gift and souvenir shops (two of which, **The Totem Pole** and **Zaiser's,** have celebrated their fiftieth birthdays), a candy store, bookstores, antiques stores, a hardware store, an A&W, and other shops.

LODGING: Backtrack down State Highway 371 and take a right on Interlachen Road; the Nisswa Family Fun Center will be on your right, and Schaefer's grocery store will be on your left. Follow Interlachen about 2 miles to a restaurant, Zorbaz, on the Gull Lake Narrows; Lost Lake Road is to your right. Go right about 0.25 mile and watch closely for the Lost Lake Lodge sign on your left. You'll fall in love with Lost Lake Lodge by the end of the secluded driveway.

Lost Lake Lodge (218–963–2681 or 800–450–2681; www.lost lake.com) is the kind of place you can check into and then allow the staff to take over. Full breakfasts and gourmet dinners (including homemade breads from grains ground at their own Lost Lake Grist Mill) are included, making Lost Lake Lodge the smallest American-plan resort in Minnesota. Activities are planned daily for the children, and all guests are welcome to use the watercraft.

The beautifully redone cabins are rustic enough to let you enjoy the woods, but very modern and spotlessly clean so your stay will be a true vacation. The cabins range in size from a cozy one-bedroom unit to the equivalent of a three-bedroom lake home. Most of the cabins have wood-burning fireplaces; one is completely wheelchair accessible. Cabin 11 is a favorite: It sits on the edge of the lake with its own private dock.

A one-bedroom cabin with a living room and a fireplace runs about $290 to $496 per night (plus tax and service charge) during summer months, and that includes two meals for each person for each day: Overnight guests enjoy dinner that night and breakfast in the morning.

Lost Lake Lodge closes for the winter, about mid-October through mid-May.

DINNER: Lost Lake Lodge dining room, of course. Guests are served dinner between 6:00 and 7:00 P.M. Your menu will be a verbal one, starting with a salad selection, then an entree such as Cornish game hen basted with white wine tarragon sauce or sirloin strip. Dessert could be Boston cream pie or a French pastry. The menu changes daily, and no two entrees are ever offered together more than once. Remember, everything is homemade, and you'll be pleased to know that the chef is happy to share his recipes.

Day 2 / Morning

BREAKFAST: The sunshine, a calling loon, or the lap of lake water will probably wake you up, and there's no better way to start your day in the North Woods than with a hearty breakfast. Lost Lake Lodge dining room breakfast is served between 8:00 and 9:30 A.M. Among the many choices are eggs any style, specially spiced Lost Lake fried potatoes, Belgian waffles, French toast, fresh fruits, and even homemade granola. (It's amazing how hungry you can get just breathing in the North Woods air.)

It's worth a trip to the popular **flea market,** held every Saturday from Memorial Day through Labor Day and Sundays, too, on major holiday weekends. Take a right at the intersection of State Highway 371 and Interlachen, stay in the right-hand lane, and follow the stream of cars into the old airfield just a few blocks south. Parking is well organized, and vendors have everything, including antique furniture, fishing lures, handcrafted items, books, and even minidoughnuts.

LUNCH: If you manage to be hungry after a Lost Lake Lodge breakfast (and possibly minidoughnuts), stop for a sandwich or hamburger at **Country Cookin' Cafe** (218–963–3326) on the corner of Main Street in Nisswa. The restaurant opens at 6:30 A.M., only serves breakfast and lunch, and closes by 2:30 P.M. You can get a hamburger and fries for about $5.00, and you won't go out hungry.

Afternoon

Spend your afternoon enjoying what you came for: the peace and quiet and the sights and fragrance of the woods. Take advantage of the well-marked trails that traverse Lost Lake Lodge Resort, take the paddleboat out for a spin, or go for a swim. It's good to work up an appetite here.

DINNER: Lost Lake Lodge dining room.

Evening

Enjoy a walk, a fire in the fireplace (even midsummer nights can be cool), or maybe a group campfire down by the beach.

Day 3 / Morning

BREAKFAST: Lost Lake Lodge dining room.

If you didn't bring your bikes, you can rent some at **TrailBlazer Bikes** ($7.00 per hour or $25.00 per day) in Nisswa, at the south end of town on Main Street; (218) 963–0699. The **Paul Bunyan Bike Trail** is worth the ride, or the walk. It follows the old train bed from Brainerd to Bemidji (eventually) and winds along lakeshores and through the woods. Even for beginning bikers, the virtually nonexistent grade is pleasant. The 32-mile trip from Nisswa (pick up the trail by the old depot at the north end of town on Main Street) to Pine River and back again is manageable in a few hours and even allows you to stop and browse the little towns in between. Bike racks, shops, and snack stops are becoming more and more abundant along the trail.

LUNCH: Until now, after the hunger you've worked up on the trail, you probably haven't needed the **Nisswa Grille,** one of the best restaurants in the lakes area. The Nisswa Grille is the restored Hotel Nisswa, which housed the famous Anthonie's clothing store for years. The new rustic but polished interior invites you in for specialty coffees, wine and beer, home-made gourmet soups, and incredible sandwiches. Hop off your bike, pop it in the rack, and stop in for a focaccia or panini sandwich, pasta special, or mango salad. Vegetarian selections are available. The menu changes daily, the variety is amazing, and you can eat heartily for about $6.00. Then visit the unique clothing and gift shop upstairs. Open daily 7:30 A.M. to 5:00 P.M. Call (218) 963–4717; www.nisswa.com.

Afternoon

For a different, scenic route home, follow County Road 18 east out of Brainerd to Garrison, then turn south on U.S. Highway 169. This will give you a chance to stop in Onamia at the **Mille Lacs Band Indian Museum** across from **Grand Casino Mille Lacs.** The museum displays Ojibwe artifacts, illustrating the history of this Ojibwe community and its two and a half centuries on Mille Lacs Lake. The grounds also include a restored 1930s trading post with additional exhibits; crafts and souvenirs are for sale. Open Memorial Day through Labor Day, daily 10:00 A.M. to 6:00 P.M. From the first Friday in May to Memorial Day and from Labor Day to the last Monday in October, the museum is open Friday through Monday 11:00 A.M. to 4:00 P.M. Admission: adults $6.00; seniors over 62, $5.00; children 6 to 12, $4.00. Wheelchair accessible. Call (320) 532–3632.

There's More

Brainerd

Brainerd International Raceway is just north of Brainerd on State Highway 371; (218) 824–7220; www.brainerdraceway.com. Offers world-class auto races and auto shows.

Crow Wing County Historical Society, 320 Laurel Avenue; (218) 829–3268. Housed in the old sheriff's residence and adjoining jail cells, this museum has five galleries that include American Indian, logging, mining, and railroading exhibits and a tour through two floors of the restored sheriff's quarters. Open Memorial Day through Labor Day, Monday through Friday 9:00 A.M. to 5:00 P.M. and Saturday 9:00 A.M. to 1:00 P.M.; Labor Day through Memorial Day, Monday through Friday 1:00 to 5:00 P.M. and Saturday 9:00 A.M. to 1:00 P.M. Admission: adults $3.00, children and students admitted free.

Pirate's Cove Adventure Golf is just north of Brainerd, State Highway 371; (218) 828–9002. There are eighteen holes to play around ships, waterfalls, and pirate trivia, plus an eighteen-hole "challenge course." There is also a small snack bar. Open seasonally 10:00 A.M. to 11:00 P.M.; admission charged.

Nisswa

Antiques. There are several antiques stores in the Brainerd area. Stop in the Nisswa Chamber of Commerce for a guide to shop locations. The current issue lists more than twenty-five antiques stores from Brainerd west to Motley and northeast to Crosby.

Golf. With more than 450 holes of golf, your best bet is to call the Brainerd Lakes Area Chamber of Commerce at (800) 450–2838 for information. A partial list of resorts with courses includes: Madden's, 8001 Pine Beach Peninsula on Gull Lake; (218) 829–2811 or (800) 247–1040. Sixty-three holes; open April through October. Breezy Point, on Pelican Lake just east of Pequot Lakes; (218) 562–7811 or (800) 432–3777. Thirty-six holes; open May through October. Grand View, on Gull Lake; (218) 963–2234 or (800) 368–1885; www.grandview.com. Fifty-four holes; open from the end of April through October.

Nisswa Caboose and Depot, Main Street in downtown Nisswa. A delightful museum filled with railroad artifacts and pictures of the area and its founders from the early days of the resort community. Open daily 11:30 A.M. to 2:30 P.M. Memorial Day through Labor Day, weekends only until mid-June. Free, but donations are suggested.

Paul Bunyan Nisswa Family Fun Center, corner of State Highway 371 and Interlachen; (218) 963–3545. The center's offerings include a 400-foot waterslide and an in-line skating track. Rentals are available.

Turtle Races, a Nisswa tradition, have been taking place for more than thirty years. They are held every Wednesday at 2:00 P.M. behind the Nisswa Chamber of Commerce on Main Street. If you don't have your own mud turtle, you'd better get there early to "rent" one. A turtle currently runs about $2.00, and you get $1.00 back if you return it at the end of the race. As many as 500 contestants enter; if your turtle does well, it could take a fair chunk of time out of your afternoon . . . or your turtle could head off the wrong way and you'll be done in about five minutes. Call (218) 963–2620 or (800) 950–9610.

Winter Alternatives

Cross-country Skiing. There are more than sixteen trail systems, including the Pillsbury State Forest. Call (800) 450–2838 or (218) 963–2620.

Downhill Skiing. Ski Gull (218–963–4353), about 14 miles north of Brainerd on County Road 77, has fourteen runs for downhill skiing and a chalet.

Snow Reports. Call (800) 450–2838, ext. 475.

Snowmobiling. There are more than 1,200 miles of snowmobile trails, including the Paul Bunyan Bike Trail that converts to a snowmobile trail. Call (800) 450–2838 or (218) 963–2620.

Special Events

January. $100,000 Jaycees Ice-fishing Extravaganza, Gull Lake.

February. Winter Jubilee and Ice-fishing Contest, Nisswa.

May. Manhattan Beach 10K Run, Crosslake.

July. Racing events at BIR, Brainerd. Fourth of July celebrations include a parade and spectacular fireworks (and Art in the Park the following Sunday) in Brainerd, fireworks in Pequot Lakes, and the Freedom Day parade, on the fifth, in Nisswa.

Other events include the Gull Lake Yacht Club Regatta and the Arts and Crafts Festival in Nisswa.

August. Crow Wing County Fair and racing events at BIR, Brainerd. Krazy Days and Annual Corn Feed and Lion's Pork on a Stick, Nisswa.

September. Fall Harvest Days in Nisswa.

October. Fall Color tours, everywhere. Lake Country Tour of Homes, Nisswa.

November. City of Lights and Lighting of the Luminaries, Nisswa.

December. Snowmobile International Race of Champions, Crow Wing County Fairgrounds, Brainerd.

NOTE: For more information on the special events in Brainerd, call the Brainerd Lakes Area Chamber of Commerce at (218) 829–2838 or (800) 450–2838. For more information on the special events in Nisswa, call the Nisswa Chamber of Commerce at (218) 963–2620 or (800) 950–9610.

Other Recommended Restaurants and Lodgings

This is a resort community, so there are myriad resorts, with an equivalent range of prices. Most of the traditional resorts, however, only offer weekly rates in the prime season that runs from mid-June to late August. If your schedule doesn't allow that kind of time, it's still worth a phone call to check out nightly or weekend vacancies.

The Black Bear Lodge and Saloon, State Highway 371 North; (218) 828–8400. The Black Bear is an architectural-award-winning rustic log structure that offers a standard menu of hamburgers, soups, and salads for lunch; prime rib on Friday and Saturday nights; and a Sunday brunch (adults about $10.00; children about $8.00). The dinner menu also includes walleye, shrimp, and pastas; entree prices range from $11 to $20. Open year-round Monday through Saturday 11:00 A.M. to 11:00 P.M., Sunday 9:30 A.M. to 11:00 P.M. (The kitchen closes at 10:00 P.M. during the summer.)

Eagle's Nest, 1516 Poplar, just north of Nisswa on Lower Cullen Lake; (218) 963–2336 or (800) 922–0440; www.eaglesnestnisswa.com. This is a classic resort with rustic housekeeping cabins and a great view of the lake. The cabins rent Saturday to Saturday. A one-bedroom cabin that sleeps up to four people runs between $650 and $840 per week, depending on the season. Aside from the pristine grounds, the fun-filled recreation room, and the spectacular beach and dock area, the resort sits right on the Paul Bunyan Bike Trail. Bikes and boats are available on-site.

The Good Ol' Days, just north of Nisswa on Lower Cullen Lake, Box 358, Nisswa; (218) 963–2478 or (800) 227–4501; www.goodoldaysresort.com.

Located next door to the Eagle's Nest on Lower Cullen Lake, the resort is geared toward young families with its beautiful sandy beach and many children's activities. The old-fashioned white cottages come with microwave ovens, coffeemakers, and a boat. Some have fireplaces. An average two-bedroom cabin rents for about $750 per week in midsummer. Open Memorial Day through Labor Day.

Grand View Lodge, on Gull Lake; South 134 Nokomis, Nisswa; (218) 963–2234 or (800) 432–3788; www.grandviewlodge.com. A fixture on Gull Lake for more than eighty years, Grand View Lodge offers cottages, townhomes, golf packages, weekend specials, and more. A one-bedroom unit, accommodating up to two people on the modified American plan, with two meals daily, use of the pool and nonmotorized watercraft, unlimited golf at The Garden course, and much more, runs between $295 and $355 per night, midsummer. The fabulous Grand View Lodge is on the National Register of Historic Places.

Iven's on the Bay, State Highway 371 North, Baxter, about 6 miles north of Brainerd; (218) 829–9872; www.brainerd.com/iven's. This restaurant provides fine dining in a casual atmosphere, overlooking North Long Lake. Iven's specializes in an array of seafood, from pan-fried walleye (the house specialty) to king crab. Duck, lamb, and steaks are also served. Entrees start at $13. Early dinner specials are served from 5:00 to 5:30 P.M. Open daily year-round. A Sunday brunch is offered from Memorial Day through Labor Day.

Kavanaugh's Resort and Restaurant, on Sylvan Lake, 2300 Kavanaugh Drive Southwest, Brainerd; (218) 829–5226 or (800) 562–7061; www.kavanaughs.com. A family-operated resort with an award-winning restaurant. Amenities include three golf courses, a pool, beach, tennis courts, a gift shop, and access to both hiking and cross-country ski trails. Accommodations include suites, cottages, and villas. Rates vary depending on the season and choice of lodging. A studio condo runs about $155 a night on a prime summer weekend. A minimum stay is usually required.

The Train Bell Resort, 100 Train Bell Road, on North Long Lake in Merrifield; (218) 829–4941 or (800) 252–2102; www.trainbellresort.com. The Train Bell Resort, on North Long Lake just outside Brainerd, right on the bike trail, was once an old hotel. The hotel is the office for today's resort, which includes rustic cabins with lake views (the boathouse sits on the lake) and modern motel units. A two-bedroom cabin, accommodating up to four people, runs about $1,055 per week in midsummer. The Delux Villas (the motel units) are wheelchair accessible and run about $1,220 per week in midsummer.

For More Information

Brainerd Lakes Area Chamber of Commerce, P.O. Box 356, Brainerd, MN 56401–0356; (218) 829–2838 or (800) 450–2838; www.brainerd.com.

Nisswa Chamber of Commerce, P.O. Box 185, Nisswa, MN 56468; (218) 963–2620 or (800) 950–9610; www.nisswa.com.

Duluth

On the Inland Sea

2 Nights

A visit to Duluth is a must. Descending the bluff into the town sprawled along the shore of Lake Superior, the largest body of freshwater in the world, feels like driving down a mountain to the sea. With its cobblestone main street, a downtown that gently recedes to residences as it steps up the hills and spreads north along the shore, and the promenade quality of Canal Park, Duluth feels more like a little European seaport than it does an American industrial city with more than 85,000 residents.

☐ Ships

☐ Parks

☐ History

☐ Architecture

Some of the best attractions are simply a part of everyday life in Duluth. The ancient Lift Bridge in Canal Park that allows barges, ships, and tall sailboats to pass between the lake and the harbor goes up and down as many as sixty times a day and is fascinating to watch over and over again. A freight train still runs regularly, filling barges with taconite and grain. Even the foghorn, sounding its eerie warning audible from the hilltops, is for real.

It's easy to get around Duluth if you remember that Superior is the main street running north and south through town, and that Lake Avenue, running east and west, connects with I–35 and leads to Canal Park and Park Point. Their intersection is midpoint. Beginning there, the avenues number themselves in opposite directions, north and south. It is important to note that some of the lane markings on Superior Street are simply lighter colored bricks and can be fairly tricky to follow.

Don't be fooled by the weather at home when you pack to head north. Duluth can be hot, but no matter what the weather when you leave home, bring warm clothing—enough for the whole weekend. It will be warm in the summer when the sun is shining, but fog can roll in off the lake in less time than it takes to get out of your car, and you'll be shivering just as quickly.

Whether you're jumping from rock to rock along the shore or cruising the harbor on a boat tour, you'll find Lake Superior immensely appealing.

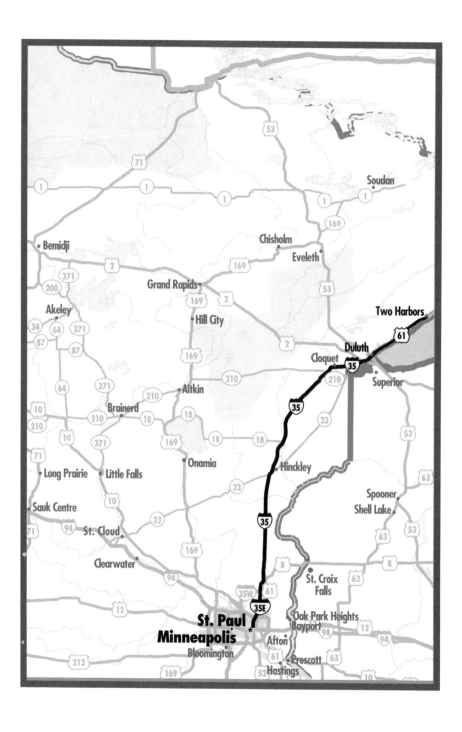

Sites such as the Maritime Museum and Glensheen Mansion can fill an entire day, and hikes through any of the many parks and simple sightseeing will consume a weekend. You'll just have to come back.

Day 1 / Morning

Duluth is a two-and-a-half- to three-hour trip north from the Twin Cities on I–35. You won't need to stop until you reach Duluth, but make a point of pausing in Hinckley to visit the **Hinckley Fire Museum.** Follow the signs on County Road 61. The museum documents the devastation of the fire that destroyed the town more than one hundred years ago. Housed in the restored depot, the museum also includes a refurbished depot agent's apartment from a bygone era. Open May 1 through mid-October, 10:00 A.M. to 5:00 P.M. Tuesday through Saturday and noon to 5:00 P.M. on Sunday. Admission: adults $3.00; seniors 62 and over $2.00; children 6 to 12, 50 cents; children 5 and younger are free. Call (320) 384–7338.

Continue north on I–35 straight into Duluth. The top of the bluff (especially at night) provides a spectacular view of the city and Lake Superior.

LUNCH: For a good culinary introduction to this diverse city, stop at **Bennett's on the Lake,** the restaurant in the lower level of **Fitger's Inn** at 600 East Superior Street. (Parking is available along the street and in several nearby lots, but park in Fitger's underground ramp because this is where you'll be staying.) The Bennetts combine years of experience with their unique style (they use a lot of flavored oils and make their own sauerkraut and potato chips) to bring you a broad selection of menu items, from a grilled chicken sandwich (about $8.00) to pan-seared Atlantic salmon (about $13.00). Bennett's on the Lake also offers one of the finest wine lists in town. Dinner is considered fine dining, and entrees range from capellini with crème fraîche and fresh herbs (about $11) to lamb chops with mint and garlic polenta (about $28). Bennett's overlooks Lake Superior, so be sure to sit outside if weather permits. Open daily 6:00 A.M. to 10:00 P.M., until 11:00 P.M. on Friday and Saturday. The bar is open until 1:00 A.M. Call (218) 722–2829 or (218) 722–DINE; www.bennettsonthelake.com.

Afternoon

The view from Bennett's will lure you to the water's edge. Step down behind Fitger's to **Lakewalk,** one of Duluth's best attractions. Lakewalk is a paved walking path, flanked by the lake, trees, and low hills of an urban park. It also has an adjacent boardwalk for part of its length that leads to **Canal Park,** 1 mile to the right, and to the **Rose Gardens,** about 1.5 miles to the left. Take your time and enjoy this beautiful walk along the shore of Lake Superior, and walk it all the way to the **Lift Bridge.** Be sure to pick up a copy of the *Duluth Shipping News,* which tracks the arrivals and departures of major ships in the harbor. It's a single sheet, covering a few days at a time, that includes a few advertisements and area information. The schedule is free and available at just about any establishment. It's amusing, in these high-tech times, to follow a schedule that reads "expected at Duluth sometime" or "should arrive late Saturday night," but the big ships still depend on winds and currents, and the uncertainty of "when" only adds to the thrill of a ship's arrival. They suddenly appear like magic on the great lake's horizon. (If you're really anxious, though, you can call the Canal Park Museum Boatwatcher's Hotline at 218–722–6489 or check their Web site, www.duluthshippingnews.com.)

Skip a few rocks in the lake, get an ice-cream cone at the red train car, and walk out to the lighthouse, or peruse the many fine gift shops, including antiques stores, in Canal Park. Don't miss the candy store in the DeWitt-Seitz building or the Sievertson Gallery, which features Liz Sievertson's original art, at 361 Canal Park Drive. It will be dinnertime before you know it.

DINNER: Lake Avenue Cafe, 394 Lake Avenue South, in the DeWitt-Seitz Marketplace building in the heart of Canal Park. It has an unassuming cafeteria interior but great food, servers dressed in black and white, original art on the menu covers (they're for sale), and a unique collection of salt and pepper shakers (a different pair for each table). Menu selections include burgers, vegetarian pizzas, fettuccine (with or without sautéed shrimp or chicken), salads, and a really good sundae topped with homemade hot fudge. Main course prices range from $10 to $14. Call (218) 722–2355; www.lakeavenuecafe.com.

LODGING: Fitger's Inn, a landmark in downtown Duluth, is a restored brewery turned into a complex of shops, restaurants, and lodging. (You'll be compelled to browse for a while.) Despite the fact that the lobby used to be the shipping and receiving area, and the rooms were part of the bottling plant, the inn feels like an old-world hotel with its grand lobby and Victorian-style accommodations. The wonderful lake-view rooms and the

The Lift Bridge in Duluth Harbor

inn's ideal downtown location will make your stay exceptionally pleasant. Each of the sixty rooms has something unique about it. Lake-side rooms start at $165 for the Deluxe to $285 for the Lakeside Whirlpool Suites. City-side rooms are less. Wheelchair accessible. Call (218) 722–8826 or (888) FITGERS; www.fitgers.com.

Day 2 / Morning

BREAKFAST: Complimentary coffee, tea, juice, and a selection of homemade rolls are served in the lobby. A full breakfast is available at Bennett's at menu prices, and room service is also available.

No trip to Duluth is complete without a visit to **Glensheen,** the elegant redbrick manor home at 3300 London Road. Built in 1905 on the shore of Lake Superior by Chester Congdon, an iron mine executive, Glensheen was tangled up in a scandal surrounding the death of Chester's daughter, Elizabeth Congdon; became a property of the University of

Minnesota; and was opened as a museum in 1979. Follow State Highway 61 north, along the lake, for about 5 miles (you'll see other signs of Duluth's old wealth in many other homes along this route). Glensheen will be your morning. You'll need a few hours to not only tour the home, carriage house, and gardens, but to also stand on the grounds, look out at the lake, and imagine yourself living there; despite the grandeur of this thirty-nine-room mansion, Glensheen is very welcoming. Glensheen is open daily 9:30 A.M. to 4:00 P.M. May 1 through October 31; Friday through Sunday 11:00 A.M. to 2:00 P.M. November through April. Admission: adults $9.50; seniors 61 and over and children 12 to 15, $7.50; children 6 to 11, $4.50; children 5 and under admitted free. Call (218) 724–8863, (218) 724–8864, or (888) 454–GLEN; www.d.umn.edu/glen.

LUNCH: Return to Duluth proper, stop at **Sir Benedict's Tavern on the Lake,** 805 East Superior Street, and pick up a sandwich and beverage for a picnic at **Park Point.** Once one of those ancient corner gas stations before being converted to a restaurant more than twenty years ago, Sir Benedict's offers a huge variety of sandwiches, soups, desserts, just about everything that can be prepared for takeout, and 197 imported beers. Order a full or half sandwich, choosing from various meat and veggie combinations, and your lunch, with a beverage, will cost you about $7.00. Open daily 11:00 A.M., until 11:00 P.M. Sunday through Tuesday and until 1:00 A.M. Wednesday through Saturday. Call (218) 728–1192.

To get to Park Point (or Minnesota Point, as it has also been called), follow Superior Street to Lake Avenue. Go left on Lake Avenue and through the lighted intersection. Follow Lake Avenue across the Lift Bridge. Park Point is a strip of land that runs 6 miles out into Lake Superior. In most places it is two-lane-road-plus-one-house wide. At the end of the street is a city park complete with playground and beach house. Enjoy your lunch, then enjoy a leisurely stroll along the shore, looking for rocks and "beach glass" worn smooth by the crashing waves.

Afternoon

On your way back into Duluth, stop at the **Lake Superior Maritime Visitors Center** in Canal Park. Operated by the U.S. Army Corps of Engineers, the museum gives an excellent history of the harbor, information on the current shipping activity, artifacts from many ships, and reconstructed ships' cabins. Children are attracted to the ship's wheel in the pilothouse. The museum is open daily 10:00 A.M. to 9:00 P.M. Memorial

Day through Labor Day; reduced daily hours April, May, and September through mid-December; Friday through Sunday 10:00 A.M. to 4:30 P.M. from late December through mid-April. Admission is free. Call (218) 727–2497; www.lsmma.com. Wheelchair accessible.

DINNER: It's hard to pass up **Grandma's Saloon and Grill,** 522 Lake Avenue, Canal Park, with its novel atmosphere—antiques, ornate bar, lots of heavy wood in the walls and trim—and its dependably good menu, but if it's a busy weekend, you may want to put your name on the list before touring the Maritime Museum. Grandma's is especially famous for cheesecake and hamburgers, but the menu includes other sandwiches, pastas, and salads. Prices start at $6.00. Call (218) 727–4192.

LODGING: Fitger's Inn.

Day 3 / Morning

BREAKFAST: Fitger's Inn.

If you are intrigued by trains, or just want to see a good museum, then a stop at the **Depot** at 506 West Michigan Street is a must. The restored 1892 depot, with its turrets and sloping roofs, houses four museums: the **Duluth Art Institute,** the **Duluth Children's Museum,** the **St. Louis County Historical Society,** and, most notably, the **Lake Superior Museum of Transportation.** The Depot is open daily 9:30 A.M. to 6:00 P.M., with reduced hours from September 1 through May 23. Admission: adults $8.00; children 3 to 13, $4.25. Call (218) 727–8025; www.duluthde pot.org. Wheelchair accessible.

LUNCH: For a last spectacular view of Duluth before you head home, stop for lunch at the **Top of the Harbor Restaurant** at the top of the **Radisson Hotel,** 505 West Superior Street. The dining tables sit on the window side of the floor, which rotates a full 360 degrees every seventy-two minutes. The lunch menu is standard American fare that includes salads, sandwiches, and pastas with prices starting at $5.25. Open daily 6:30 A.M. to 10:00 P.M., until 11:00 P.M. on Friday and Saturday. Prices range from $7.50 to $12.00. Seniors 65 and over get 10 percent off the standard menus. Call (218) 727–8981.

There's More

Duluth

Baseball. The Duluth Huskies, a Northwoods League baseball team, have a home-game season that begins in June, at Wade Stadium. Call (218) 786–4909; www.duluthhuskies.com. Located at the corner of Stadium Road and West Second Street; take I–35 to the Forty-eighth Avenue West exit to Grand Avenue to Thirty-fourth Avenue West. Admission starts at $5.00.

Bike and In-line Skate Rentals. Munger Rentals, 7408 Grand Avenue; (218) 624–4814 or (800) 982–2453; www.mungerinn.com. Near the zoo and at the start of the Willard Munger State Trail. Open all year 8:00 A.M. to dusk. Bike and skates rentals cost about $20 for half a day.

Carriage Rides. Canal Park, (218) 729–5873. You'll see the horse-drawn carriages.

Charter Fishing. There are numerous guides and excursions registered with the North Shore Charter Captain's Association. Check with the visitors bureau for more information; (218) 722–4011 or (800) 4DULUTH.

Fon-du-Luth Casino, 129 East Superior Street; (218) 722–0280 or (800) 873–0280; www.fondduluthcasino.com. Open twenty-four hours on weekends; 10:00 A.M. to 2:00 A.M. Monday through Thursday.

Golf. Duluth has two twenty-seven-hole courses, each with views of Lake Superior: Lester Park, East Superior Road and Lester Park Road (218–525–0828), and Enger Park, Skyline Parkway (218–723–3451).

Jay Cooke State Park, State Highway 210, between State Highway 23 and I–35, about 20 miles southeast of Duluth; (218) 384–4610. Jay Cooke State Park was created to protect the northern hardwood forest; it has been naturally preserved for years because the terrain was simply too rugged to log. Although the area lends itself to mountain-biking trails, the manageable William Munger State Trail runs along the north end of the park. Most hiking trails remain rugged, and the clay is extremely slippery when wet, but the scenery is superb. Highlights include a 120-foot-long pedestrian-only swinging suspension bridge that spans the St. Louis River and offers an extensive view of the river's path. Open daily 8:00 A.M. to 10:00 P.M. A vehicle permit is required; no permit is required for bikers.

Lake Cruises. Vista Fleet (218–722–6218; www.vistafleet.com) takes you out on the lake (depending on the waves) and then into the harbor for an up-close view of the ships, the Lift Bridge, ore docks, and harbor activity. About one and a half hours. Vista Fleet departs from DECC Dock on Harbor Drive, on the bayfront. Dinner and lunch excursions are also available. Open mid-May through mid-October. Fares: adults $10.00; children 3 to 11, $5.00.

Lake Superior Zoological Gardens, Grand Avenue and Seventy-second Avenue West; (218) 733–3777; www.lszoo.org. Exhibits include Siberian tigers, snow leopards, kangaroos, and eagles. The grounds include a children's zoo, gift shop, and cafe. Open summer 10:00 A.M. to 6:00 P.M., winter 10:00 A.M. to 4:00 P.M. Admission: adults $6.00; children 4 to 11, $2.50; children 3 and under free.

Train Rides. Follow Superior Street to Grand Avenue to Seventy-first Street West to the Lake Superior and Mississippi Railroad for a ride on a vintage train that runs alongside the St. Louis River. Open weekends only, mid-June through early October. Fares: adults $8.00; children 12 and under, $6.00. Call (218) 624–7549; www.lsmrr.org. Train rides are also available on the North Shore Scenic Railroad, 506 West Michigan Street, Union Depot; ninety-minute, six-hour, and "pizza" train rides are offered. Fares for the shorter route: adults $10.00; children 3 to 13, $5.00. Fares for longer route: adults $18.00; children 3 to 13, $8.00; children under 3 ride free. Fares for the "pizza" ride: adults $17.00; children 3 to 13, $12.00; children under 3 are free. Open Memorial Day through mid-October. For more information call (218) 722–1273 or (800) 423–1273; www.lsrm.org.

Tram Rides. Watch for the signs for the pink-and-blue tram and ride it around Canal Park for free. Duluth's Waterfront Shuttle runs on weekends from early June through Labor Day, Friday and Saturday 11:00 A.M. to 9:00 P.M., Sunday 11:00 A.M. to 8:00 P.M.

The Tweed Museum of Art, 10 University Drive, in the University of Minnesota at Duluth; (218) 726–8222. The museum is tricky to find in the tunnel system that connects the university buildings, but it is worth the effort. The collection includes old masters and contemporary works in several media. A highlight is the Tweed's annual Contemporary Artist Series, dedicated to artists working in the region. Open Tuesday 9:00 A.M. to 8:00 P.M., Wednesday through Friday 9:00 A.M. to 4:30 P.M., Saturday and

Sunday 1:00 to 5:00 P.M. Closed on Monday. Admission is free, but donations are suggested.

Willard Munger State Trail. This bike and in-line skating trail links West Duluth to Jay Cooke State Park in Carlton, 14 miles away. Start the trail at Grand Avenue and Seventy-fifth Avenue West, near Indian Point Park. The St. Louis River and other streams cut through the trail, creating spectacular scenery. This is an especially good route for fall foliage sightseeing.

The **William A. Irvin *Ore Boat*** and the **Lake Superior *Tug*,** 350 Harbor Drive (218–722–7876; www.williamairvin.com), are "floating museums." The *William A. Irvin* was once the flagship of the US Steel fleet, and the tug helped build the Great Lakes Seaway. Open 9:00 A.M. to 6:00 P.M. Sunday through Thursday and 9:00 A.M. to 8:00 P.M. Friday and Saturday, Memorial Day through Labor Day, with reduced hours the rest of the year. Admission: adults $6.75; students and seniors 65 and over $5.75; and children 3 to 12, $4.75. The *Irvin,* aka Ship of Ghouls, offers haunted tours presented by the U of M Duluth Theatre Department during the week of Halloween.

Two Harbors

Split Rock Lighthouse State Park, (218) 226–6377. About an hour north of Duluth on U.S. Highway 61 is the famous Split Rock Lighthouse. A permit is required to enter the park but is not necessary for touring the lighthouse. Tours of the lighthouse, the keeper's home, and fog signal building and entrance to the museum are handled separately, and, if you request it, this fee will include a park vehicle permit during lighthouse hours only. The park, one of the state's finest, is open daily 8:00 A.M. to 10:00 P.M.; the lighthouse is open daily mid-May through mid-October 9:00 A.M. to 5:00 P.M. Tour prices: adults $6.00; seniors 65 and over, $5.00; children $4.00. Park permits are $4.00.

Superior, Wisconsin

Fairlawn Mansion, 906 Harbor View Parkway East; (715) 394–5712. The restored 1890 home of lumber baron Martin T. Pattison has one of the most impressive Victorian interiors available for tour. Ahead of its time, the forty-two-room mansion was built with state-of-the-art plumbing, electricity, and air-conditioning (a large vertical air shaft with fans at the top and bottom circulates the air and is concealed by elaborate stained-glass windows). The home overlooks Lake Superior a few miles south of Duluth on U.S. Highway 53. Open daily 9:00 A.M. to 5:00 P.M. Admission: adults $7.00; students and seniors $6.00; children 6 to 12, $5.00.

Winter Alternatives

Cross-country Skiing. Miles and miles of groomed and ungroomed trails—some of which are lighted—are available. A Minnesota ski pass is required on city trails. Cross-country ski trails are also offered at Spirit Mountain. Call the visitors bureau for more information (218–722–4011 or 800–4DULUTH).

Downhill Skiing. The Spirit Mountain Recreational Area (218–628–2891 or 800–642–6377; www.spiritmt.com) is about ten minutes from downtown Duluth; take exit 249 from I–35. Facilities include twenty-three runs, a snowboard park, instructional classes, a tubing hill, and a large chalet.

Snowmobiling. From 45 city miles to trails that connect with the Willard Munger Trail and the North Shore Trail, Duluth offers a lot of snowmobiling opportunities. Call the visitors bureau for more information (218–722–4011 or 800–4DULUTH).

Special Events

January. John Beargrease Sled-dog Marathon.

February to March. The Ski Challenge, Spirit Mountain.

March. Special art exhibits at the Tweed Museum.

June. Grandma's Marathon.

July. Annual Duluth Open Horseshoe Tournament. Duluth Invitational Regatta.

August. Bayfront Blues Festival. Glensheen Festival of Fine Art and Craft.

September. North Shore In-Line Marathon.

October. Annual Scandinavian Festival, fairgrounds, Superior, Wisconsin.

November. Spirit National Snocross snowmobile races.

November to December. Christmas City of the North Celebration. Duluth Curling Club Ladies Annual Bonspiel.

NOTE: For more information on these and many more special events in Duluth, call the Duluth Visitors Bureau at (218) 722–4011 or (800) 4DULUTH.

Other Recommended Restaurants and Lodgings

Angie's Cantina and Grill, adjacent to the DeWitt-Seitz building in Canal Park, Duluth; (218) 727–6117. Good Mexican food is served in a fun atmosphere. The claim to fame here is "all kinds of margaritas" and thirty-two different kinds of tequila. The chicken and beef fajitas ($11 to $14) stand out among the other Mexican favorites. Outdoor seating with views of Lake Superior and Canal Park is available in the summer. Open daily 11:00 A.M. to 10:00 P.M. and at 8:00 A.M. on Saturday and Sunday for breakfast.

Comfort Suites of Canal Park, 408 Canal Park Drive, Duluth; (218) 727–1378 or (800) 228–5150. Located in the heart of the Canal Park district, Comfort Suites offers a free continental breakfast, free HBO, and a pool. Some suites have whirlpools. Rates depend on the season and view: A lake-view suite, without a whirlpool, in midsummer is about $140 a night.

Crawford House Bed and Breakfast, 2016 Hughitt Avenue, Superior, Wisconsin; (715) 394–5271. Years in the making, the pale blue Greek Revival Crawford House with white trim is a lovely place to spend the weekend. Antiques, lace, and charm best describe the decor. The three main guest rooms have private baths; one has a double whirlpool tub. Common areas include the main-floor parlor and the third-floor billiard room. A full breakfast is included. From $59 for "Lydia's Room" to $89 for "Katherine's Suite."

The Inn on Lake Superior, 350 Canal Park Drive, Duluth; (218) 726–1111 or (888) 668–4352. The inn overlooks the lake and Lakewalk from the heart of Canal Park. A pool and spa are available. Rates vary depending on the season, view, and size of room: A standard lake-side room in midsummer on a weekend is about $175 a night.

The Olcott House Bed and Breakfast, 2316 East First Street, Duluth; (218)

728–1339 or (800) 715–1339; www.olcotthouse.com. Enjoy the city's tremendous wealth and architecture firsthand. Fireplaces, private baths, and candlelight breakfasts are just some of the luxuries offered. Rates run from $125 to $185 per night.

The Pickwick Restaurant, 508 East Superior Street in the Fitger's Complex, Duluth; (218) 727–8901. A family business and in the same location since 1914, it offers a fabulous view of Lake Superior. Pickwick's is known for its charbroiled steaks, seafood, and delicious homemade onion rings. Try the pepper cheeseburger (about $7.00), an excellent choice for lunch, and the lake trout or pike for dinner (about $15.00). If you're really hungry, go for the twenty-ounce porterhouse steak (about $25.00). Open Monday through Saturday 11:00 A.M. to 11:30 P.M.

Radisson Hotel Duluth–Harborview, 505 West Superior Street; (218) 727–8981 or (800) 333–3333. Located downtown with a restaurant that rotates overlooking the harbor. Rates run from $89 to $130 per night.

A Taste of Saigon, DeWitt-Seitz building, Canal Park, Duluth; (218) 727–1598. An incredible list of Vietnamese cuisine with specialties in curry, lemongrass, and cashew dishes offered. Prices range from $6.00 to $12.00. Open 11:00 A.M. to 8:30 P.M. Sunday through Thursday, until 9:30 P.M. on Friday and Saturday.

For More Information

Duluth Convention and Visitors Bureau, 100 Lakeplace Drive, Duluth, MN 55802; (218) 722–4011 or (800) 438–5884; www.visitduluth.com. Open Monday through Friday 9:00 A.M. to 5:00 P.M.

Superior/Douglas County Tourist Information Center, 305 Harbor View Parkway, Superior, WI 54880; (715) 392–2773 or (800) 942–5313; www.visitsuperior.com.

Other bed-and-breakfast inns: Duluth abounds in beautiful inns. Take a look at some of them at www.visitduluth.com/historicinns.

Grand Rapids and the Iron Trail

Home on the Range

2 Nights

Until the discovery of iron ore in the late 1800s, logging was the chief industry in northern Minnesota. Grand Rapids, at the navigational head-waters of the Mississippi River, was the economic hub that served surrounding logging camps. The prospect of steady work in the logging industry attracted many Scandinavian and Slovenian immigrants, and the arrival of the train brought even more.

☐ Forests

☐ Iron Mines

☐ History

☐ Camping

☐ Storytellers

The first shipment of ore left the Mesabi Range in 1892, and northern Minnesota, in a very literal sense, took on a new look. Most of the good timber was gone—land around Grand Rapids looked like a field of stumps. As that city focused on paper milling and other industries, new towns sprang up on the Iron Range and open-pit iron-ore mining was under way. This industry drew even more immigrant settlers. At one time there were forty-three different nationalities represented in the towns on the Iron Range, the majority of whom were Finnish, Italian, Slovenian, and Scandinavian. That diverse heritage is evident in the celebrations and festivals that continue today.

About the same time that Grand Rapids sent its last log drive down the Little Fork River in the late 1930s, the Iron Range hit its heyday. The iron mines of northern Minnesota provided more than 70 percent of the iron ore needed for the war effort and shipped out more than 336 million tons of iron ore between 1941 and 1945.

Today Grand Rapids capitalizes on recreation opportunities on the Mississippi River and the 1,000 lakes in the area and on its claim to fame as Judy Garland's birthplace. For now the Iron Range towns remain indus-trial—seven iron-ore mines are still functioning on the Mesabi Range—and they're just beginning to play up Hibbing as the birthplace of singer

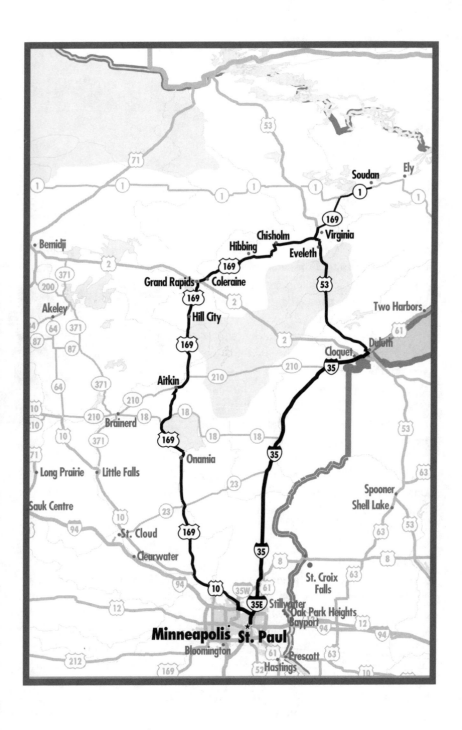

Bob Dylan. There is, however, an increasing interest in the rich ethnic heritage of the range and the important role it has played in Minnesota history. Taking advantage, too, of the long snowy winters in the north, the whole area is becoming more popular as a winter destination.

Day 1 / Morning

Grand Rapids is a three-and-a-half- to four-hour drive from the Twin Cities. Follow U.S. Highway 169 north out of the metropolitan area, past Mille Lacs Lake, through Aitkin and Hill City all the way to Grand Rapids.

The town of Grand Rapids is very manageable: Most attractions are along Pokegama Avenue (U.S. Highway 169), which runs north and south, and U.S. Highway 2, which runs east and west. The roads converge in front of the **Old Central School,** 10 Northwest Fifth Street, one of the highlights of the town. You can't pass up a visit to the school, but after the day's long drive, you may want to save the visit until after lunch.

LUNCH: Just across the street from Old Central School is the **Hometown Cafe,** 18 Northwest Fourth Street; (218) 326–8646. (Park on the street or in the lot near the railroad tracks behind the restaurant.) The Hometown Cafe is a classic small-town diner where everyone knows everyone else—and where they still serve Maid Rites! Everything is made from scratch, and the hot beef sandwich (with "the only real mashed potatoes in town") is a local favorite (about $5.00). That and a slice of homemade pie ($1.95) will hold you all afternoon.

Afternoon

Leave your car in the lot, cross the street, and follow the "Yellow Brick Road" through the gardens and into the school. This magnificent one-hundred-year-old building has been lovingly restored—sparing its beautiful wainscoting, woodwork, and even the blackboards—and now houses a museum, shops, and other businesses. The tall ceilings, transomed doors, and large windows create a light-filled atmosphere in this old building, and the standard classroom fixtures have been used creatively by the building's new tenants. Although the elegant double staircase alone is worth the visit, it will probably lure you upstairs, and with good reason: **The Itasca Heritage Center** is on the second floor. Displays interpret life in Itasca County around the turn of the twentieth century, focusing on family and community life in that era and the impact of the logging and steamboat industries.

There is also a display about Frances Gumm (Judy Garland) and the Gumm family. Sadly, the Ruby Slippers are only replicas, but Oz fans will enjoy seeing them anyway. Open Monday through Friday 9:30 A.M. to 5:00 P.M. and Saturday 10:00 A.M. to 4:00 P.M. Open Sunday in the summer only, noon to 4:00 P.M. Admission: adults $4.00; seniors 55 and over $3.00; children 6 to 12, $2.00. The family rate is $12.00. Call (218) 326–6431.

While you're in town, try to visit the **Children's Discovery Museum** (formerly the Judy Garland Children's Museum), located on U.S. Highway 169 about 1.5 miles south of downtown Grand Rapids. Although this newly opened museum is designed for 3- through 12-year-olds, many of the exhibits should prove interesting for adults. Exhibits include a hands-on art room where children can paint and sculpt; Exchange City, a child-size town square with ten different shops that children pretend to run; River Water Table, a replica of the Mississippi River (which flows through town) that includes a hydroelectric plant and a working dam; Geo-Zoooom, an interactive geography exhibit; River Forest; Tot Park Maze; and Dinosaurs. You may find yourself asking your children if it's time to leave yet instead of the other way around. Open daily 10:00 A.M. to 5:00 P.M., noon to 5:00 P.M. Sunday, closed most holidays. Admission is $5.00 per person over 1 year old. Call (218) 326–1900 or (866) CDM–KIDS; www.cdmkids.org.

The **Judy Garland Museum,** 2227 U.S. Highway 169 South, is located next to the Children's Discovery Museum and contains an extensive collection of Judy memorabilia. The exhibits not only include Dorothy's dress and other costumes and a sword from the witch's castle, but also the carriage that transported Dorothy and friends through Oz (and once belonged to President Abraham Lincoln). Open daily 10:00 A.M. to 5:00 P.M. Admission is $5.00 per person over 1 year old. Call (218) 326–9276 or (800) 664–5839; www.judygarlandmuseum.com.

DINNER AND LODGING: Follow U.S. Highway 169 south for about 15 miles and take a right on Sugar Lake Road. Follow Sugar Lake Road about 5 miles to **Ruttger's Sugar Lake Lodge.** Unlike the historic Ruttger's of Bay Lake, this Ruttger's is one of the newest resorts in the state. Ruttger's Sugar Lake Lodge offers a variety of superb accommodations, including beachside cottages, golf villas, and lodge suites. With warm pine walls, fieldstone fireplaces, and a Southwestern flair to its decor, Ruttger's is the dream cabin you'd build for yourself. Sit down to a fine dinner in Otis' Restaurant in the main lodge. Enjoy the dinner buffet that includes an appetizer and dessert bar (about $19 per person).

Then delight in spending the night in the North Woods; your whirlpool and fireplace await you. A one-bedroom suite in the main lodge is about $225 per night in the summer. Golf and use of motorized boats are extra. Two-night minimum. Rates are slightly reduced off-season. Wheelchair accessible. Call (218) 327–1462 or (800) 450–4555; www.ruttgerssugarlake.com.

Day 2 / Morning

BREAKFAST: Otis' Restaurant offers the standard North Woods fare for breakfast: bacon, eggs, and pancakes.

It's time to enjoy what you came for: the resort itself! Play a round of golf, take a boat out for a spin, rent a bicycle from the resort (about $5.00 an hour), or simply hang out by the pool. This is country club living!

LUNCH: When you're ready for lunch, just wander over to **Jack's Grill.** A true grill, Jack's offers casual dining inside the Sugarbrooke Golf Club next to Ruttger's main lodge. Hamburgers and a selection of sandwiches and soups are available ($5.00 to $10.00).

Afternoon

If you feel like an outing, a trip to the **Forest History Center** will provide a very interesting afternoon. Follow Sugar Lake Road out to U.S. Highway 169 and head north toward Grand Rapids. Take a left on Golf Course Road and follow the state signs to the site. A project of the Minnesota Historical Society, the Forest History Center portrays life in a logging camp as it was at the turn of the twentieth century. The costumed residents make it especially interesting because this era is rarely explored through living history. Featured aspects of the logger's life include a river "wanigan," a floating cook shack and supply boat that accompanied the log drives down the river to the mills; a cabin from the Minnesota Forest Service that dates from the 1930s; and a fire tower that tourists can climb. Interesting exhibits include tools, equipment, a 10,000-year-old stump, and a 1919 Model T used by the Minnesota Forest Service. Open Memorial Day weekend through October 15, 10:00 A.M. to 5:00 P.M. Monday through Saturday and noon to 5:00 P.M. on Sunday. The interpretive building is open Monday through Friday 8:00 A.M. to 4:30 P.M. the rest of the year. Admission: adults $6.00; seniors 65 and over $5.00; children 6 to 15, $4.00. Call (218) 327–4482 or (888) PAST–FUN or visit www.mnhs.org.

Laborer at the Forest History Center

DINNER: Forest Lake Restaurant, 1201 Northwest Fourth Street (U.S. Highway 2), offers fine dining downstairs or family dining upstairs in a rustic log lodge with beautiful views of Forest Lake. The extensive steakhouse menu includes barbecue ribs and fish. Dinners cost from $12 to $22. Open daily, with varied hours for each dining room and the bar. Call (218) 326–3423.

Day 3 / Morning

Get an early start and return to Grand Rapids on U.S. Highway 169 for a fascinating side trip on your way home.

Grand Rapids sits on the western edge of the Mesabi Range, barely included in the Iron Range. As you continue north on U.S. Highway 169 through Grand Rapids, you will embark on the **Iron Trail,** and within 5 miles you will come to the mining town of Coleraine. The terrain suddenly changes as rust-colored hills, in varying sizes, rise up from the earth. These are not true hills, but slag piles or tailings, the displaced rock from the open-pit iron-ore mines.

The one-time wealth is evident in the architecture in the bigger towns like Hibbing and Virginia (the "Queen City of the North"). Even the **Hibbing High School,** on the corner of Eighth Avenue East and Twenty-first Street, now on the National Register of Historic Places, is an opulent display. The building has hand-painted murals, cut-glass chandeliers, and an auditorium with plush seats and a balcony that would rival those in a European opera house. Tours are available during the summer; a small fee is charged. Call (218) 262–0404, (218) 263–3675, or (800) 444–2246.

BREAKFAST: If you didn't eat at Otis' before departing, continue through Hibbing to Chisolm and head straight to the **Sunny Side Cafe,** a neighborhood fixture at 12 West Lake Street, Chisolm's main street. The short stack of delicious pancakes will easily fill you up for $3.50. Each one is the size of a pizza—you can't even find the plate! Omelettes run $4.00 to $7.00. Open Monday through Friday 6:00 A.M. to 3:00 P.M., Saturday and Sunday 6:00 A.M. to 2:00 P.M. Call (218) 254–7444.

After breakfast backtrack to the **Ironworld Discovery Center,** at the base of the 85-foot miner, just off U.S. Highway 169. Ironworld sounds like it should be a place like Six Flags or another novelty amusement park, but instead it is a poignant interpretation of the area's history. There is a play area for small children with a ball crawl, a slide, and a carousel. There is also a well-presented tribute to the Civilian Conservation Corps and an impressive research center connected with the Mormon genealogy service in Salt Lake City, Utah. Numerous ethnic artisans and a gift shop are there, too. None of this is what you'll remember of your trip to Ironworld, though. It all pales against one little trolley ride out to **Mesaba Junction.**

The living history guides at Mesaba Junction take you back in history, though not very far, to a time when the mines were very active and "Locations," or mining-site towns, dotted the range. Ironically, abandoned pit mines create some of the most spectacular, albeit man-made, scenery in the world: craters filled with crystal-clear water with lush forests growing right to the edge of the red cliffs. The beauty is in raw contrast, however, to the life of a mining family, and you will be impressed by the spirit and perseverance of our Minnesota ancestors.

Casey will plink out tunes on the banjo; Gloria, an awe-inspiring professional storyteller, will regale you with memories, sing in Swedish, and even whistle; and Lynn will tell you what it was like to cook for a houseful of men who took turns sleeping on the floor as they worked opposite shifts, or how the children would walk their fathers' lunches to the mines and wait for the men to claim them—the miners were so dirty, the children couldn't recognize their own dads.

The little yellow house, an authentic miner's cottage, was once in **Glen Location.** Houses such as this one are referred to as the "original mobile home," built with sturdy crossbeams and without basements so they could be relocated. Open-pit mining eats away at the earth, so as mines expanded, the towns on their edges had to move frequently. Sometimes this would happen so quickly that a miner had to track down his home at the end of a shift.

At Mesaba Junction children can play old-fashioned games, such as beanbag toss and hopscotch, and climb on some of the massive mining equipment. When you hear the trolley return, hop aboard for the rest of your tour.

LUNCH: There are food concessions ringing the **Pavilion,** where you can get pizza by the slice or a gyros sandwich, but if you're hungrier than that, head to the lower level of the **Ethnic Arts Center** to the **Ethnic Restaurant** and enjoy the buffet. You can select a variety of ethnic foods such as sarma (Yugoslavian cabbage-wrapped meat), pasties (Cornish meat pies), or Swedish meatballs, in addition to soups and desserts. The buffet runs $8.00 to $12.00 a person depending on the featured selections, but there are daily specials and items available a la carte.

Watch the day's schedule of events; you might be lucky enough to catch the troupe of performers dance the polka or present a variety show in the Pavilion. Ironworld Discovery Center is open daily late May through Labor Day 9:30 A.M. to 5:00 P.M. The research center is open all year. Admission: adults $8.00; seniors 62 and over $7.00; students 7 to 17, $6.00; children under 7 free. Wheelchair accessible. Call (218) 254–7959 or (800) 372–6437 or visit www.ironworld.com.

Afternoon

Continue north on U.S. Highway 169 to Virginia, then follow U.S. Highway 53 south and the signs along the southern end of town to the **Mineview in the Sky.** Watch for the giant yellow dump truck perched on the twenty-story pile of rock and drive up the hill toward it. The Hospitality Host, the gentleman in the red beret, is a history buff and glad to offer information and answer questions. The visitor center also has a gift shop that sells handmade quilts, baby clothes, and other crafts made by the senior citizens of the area. The view is of the Rouchleau Mine group, the deepest mine in the area. The pit is nearly 3 miles long. Open daily 8:00 A.M. to 6:00 P.M. Memorial Day through Labor Day. Admission is free. Call (218) 741–2717.

From the Mineview in the Sky, follow U.S. Highway 53 to Eveleth, home of the world's largest hockey stick and the **United States Hockey Hall of Fame,** right off Highway 53 at 801 Hat Trick Avenue.

It's most appropriate for Minnesota, especially northern Minnesota, to have a museum revolving around a winter sport. Where else but here and Canada would tourists ooh and aah over a Zamboni display? It also features an Olympic champions exhibit, a shooting rink, and tributes to honored players. Sports fans will love it! Open year-round Monday through Saturday 9:00 A.M. to 5:00 P.M., Sunday 10:00 A.M. to 3:00 P.M.; closed holidays. Admission: adults $6.00; seniors over 60 and students 13 to 17, $5.00; children 6 to 12, $4.00; children under 6 are free. Call (218) 744–5167 or (800) 443–7825; www.ushockeyhall.com.

You may want to linger along Eveleth's main street full of shops and restaurants, several blocks west of U.S. Highway 53.

Although the Iron Trail continues through more towns, and there are mines nearly as far north as Ely, the drive from Eveleth to the Twin Cities will take about three and a half hours. To head home follow U.S. Highway 53 south to State Highway 33 to Cloquet; pick up I–35 and continue south into the Twin Cities.

There's More

Biking. The Itasca Trail has miles of paved trail from just north of Itasca to Gunn Park. The Suomi Hills Recreation Area has 21 miles of trails, north on State Highway 38 (the Scenic Byway), the Edge of Wilderness National Scenic Byway, near Marcell. Another trail that is a must ride for cyclists is the Mesabi Trail. It will eventually stretch an amazing 132 miles, and as of late 2003 had 66 miles of completed pavement. The longest paved section currently runs from Nashwauk to Eveleth, a 51-mile ribbon of pavement. For more information visit www.mesabitrail.com.

Camping. Chippewa National Forest has several primitive camping sites.

Call (218) 246–2123 for the Deer River region, 15 miles west of Grand Rapids, or (218) 832–3161 for the Marcell region, 25 miles north of Grand Rapids. Birch Cove Resort and Campground (218–326–8754 or 800–382–2498) offers wooded sites for tent camping and recreational vehicle sites with full hookups, 0.5 mile east of U.S. Highway 169, south of Grand Rapids. McCarthy Beach State Park, located at 7622 McCarthy Beach Road on Side Lake, has wooded sites (seventeen with electricity), a sandy beach, fishing piers, and access to both Sturgeon and Side Lakes. A Minnesota State Park vehicle permit is required. Call (218) 254–2411, (612) 296–6157, or (800) 766–6000; TDD (218) 296–5484 or (800) 657–3929.

Golf. Eagle Ridge Golf Course, located on U.S. Highway 169 North about 5 miles north of Grand Rapids, Coleraine (218–245–2217), has eighteen holes, a pro shop, a driving range, food, and a bar. Pokegama Golf Club, 3910 Golf Course Road, south on Highway 169, Grand Rapids (218–326–3444), and Wendigo Golf Club, 750 Golf Crest Drive, south on Highway 169 from Grand Rapids (218–327–2211), have equivalent features. Quadna Hills Golf Course, 17 miles South of Grand Rapids on Highway 169, Hill City (218–697–8444 or 800–422–6649), offers nine holes and rentals. Virginia Golf Course, located on Ninth Avenue South, Virginia (218–741–4366), offers eighteen holes and a restaurant and lounge. Giants Ridge Golf and Ski Resort, Biwabik (218–865–4143 or 800–688–SNOW), has a PGA-sanctioned eighteen-hole course.

Mine Tours. Hill Annex Mine State Park, off U.S. Highway 169 in Calumet, and the Soudan Underground Mine State Park, southwest of Ely off Highway 169 in Soudan, offer tours of their distinctly different mines. Open Memorial Day through Labor Day. A Minnesota State Park vehicle permit is required to enter the parks. Admission is charged for tours. Call the Department of Natural Resources Hill Annex at (218) 247–7215 and the Soudan at (218) 753–2245, or both at (612) 296–6157 or (800) 766–6000; TDD (612) 296–5484 or (800) 657–3929.

Museums. The Judy Garland Birthplace, 2227 U.S. Highway 169, about 1.5 miles south of Grand Rapids; (800) 664–JUDY. This was the first home the Gumm family ever owned. They lived there for seven years and moved from Grand Rapids when Judy was 4½. The house is restored to the year 1925 but does not contain family furnishings. Open daily May 1 through October 31 10:00 A.M. to 5:00 P.M. and by appointment only the rest of the year. Admission is $3.00 per person. Minnesota Museum of Mining, Highway

169 at the top of Main Street, Chisolm; (218) 254–5543 or (218) 254–5386. Literally tons of mining equipment are on display, from steam locomotives to early steam shovels and more modern electric shovels. Open daily during the summer 9:00 A.M. to 5:00 P.M. Admission: adults $3.00; seniors 65 and over $2.50; students $2.00; children under 5 free. The Virginia Area Historical Society's Heritage Museum, Ninth Avenue North in Olcott Park, Virginia; (218) 741–1136. Housed in the former residence for Virginia park superintendents, the exhibits cover logging, economic changes in the Virginia area, and life in a log cabin. Open May through September, Tuesday through Saturday 11:00 A.M. to 4:00 P.M.; October through April, Thursday through Saturday 11:00 A.M. to 4:00 P.M. Donations are suggested.

Winter Alternatives

Cross-country Skiing. Trails are open daily at the Forest History Center (218–327–4482) on Golf Course Road southwest of Grand Rapids. McCarthy Beach State Park (218–254–2411) has 9 miles of trails near Hibbing.

Downhill Skiing. Giants Ridge, State Highway 135 north to Biwabik from Virginia, about 20 miles northeast of Virginia (218–865–4143 or 800–688–7669; www.giantsridge.com), offers thirty-eight runs, a halfpipe, and a snowboard park. Giants Ridge has become one of the best ski resorts in the Midwest and is known for impeccable grooming of its trails and a great snowmaking system.

Snowmobiling. More than 2,000 miles of groomed trails run from Grand Rapids through the Iron Range to Ely and International Falls via the Taconite and Arrowhead Trails. Call (800) 777–8497 or (212) 749–8161.

Special Events

January to February. Polar Bear Days, Chisolm; (218) 254–3600 or (800) 422–0806. Annual International Snowmobile Hall of Fame, Grand Rapids; (218) 326–6619 or (800) 472–6366. Snowboard, downhill, and children's cross-country ski races, Giants Ridge, Biwabik; (218) 865–4143 or (800) 688–7669.

March. Sport and Travel Show, Civic Center, Grand Rapids; (218) 326–6619 or (800) 472–6366.

June. Land of the Loon Arts and Crafts Festival, Virginia; (218) 749–5555. Crafts, ethnic foods, live entertainment, a parade, a street dance, and children's games.

International Polka Fest, Ironworld Discovery Center, Chisolm; (800) 372–6437.

Judy Garland Festival, Grand Rapids; (800) 472–6366. A film festival and a chance to meet some of the original Munchkins.

July. Annual Calumet Miner's Day, Hill Annex Mine State Park, Calumet; (218) 247–7215.

Annual Northern Minnesota Swap Meet & Car Show, Itasca County Fairgrounds, Grand Rapids; (800) 472–6366.

Annual Mississippi Melodie Showboat, Showboat Landing, Grand Rapids; (800) 722–7814. Includes a locally produced showboat production with singing and dancing.

Annual Woodcraft Festival, Forest History Center, Grand Rapids; (218) 327–4482.

Mines and Pines Jubilee, Hibbing; (218) 262–3895 or (800) 444–2246. Craft show with food booths.

August. Tall Timber Days Festival, downtown Grand Rapids; (800) 472–6366. Includes parades, a lumberjack show, children's activities, and a crafts show.

Itasca County Fair, Itasca County Fairgrounds, Grand Rapids; (800) 472–6366.

September. Annual Fall Art and Craft Festival, Bear Park, Hill City; (218) 697–2648. Craft booths, live entertainment, bake sales, and more.

Chisolm Fire Days Celebration, Chisolm; (218) 254–3600 or (800) 422–0806.

October. Hibbing World Class Rodeo, Hibbing; (218) 262–3895 or (800) 444–2246.

December. Winter Carnival, Giants Ridge, Biwabik; (218) 865–4143 or (800) 688–7669.

Other Recommended Restaurants and Lodgings

Grand Rapids

Eagle Nest Lodge, Chippewa National Forest; (218) 246–8701 or (800) 356–3775. Cozy knotty-pine-filled cabins have a sandy beach at your doorstep in the summer or 14 miles of groomed ski trails through the national forest in the winter. One- to three-bedroom cabins are available; some have fireplaces. A two-bedroom housekeeping cabin with a fireplace rents for $188 and up per night in the summer, with a three-day minimum. Rates are reduced in winter, and a two-day minimum stay is required. Located deep in the woods, about 20 miles north of Deer River, a total of about 35 miles from Grand Rapids.

Hong Kong Garden, 1300 East U.S. Highway 169; (218) 326–6510. Overlooking the Mississippi, Hong Kong Garden serves classic Chinese cuisine and American food. Open Monday through Saturday 11:00 A.M. to 9:00 P.M. Lunch runs $3.00 to $6.00; dinner $6.00 to $14.00.

Kenadian Acres Resort, HC1, Bigfork; (218) 245–1470 or (800) 542–1470; www.kenadian.com. This classic cozy resort rents only by the week during the peak summer season, for two-night minimums in the spring and fall, and by the night in the winter. Each cabin has a private bath, screened porch, and a complimentary fishing boat; some have fireplaces. A two-bedroom cabin with a fireplace runs about $580 a week in midsummer.

Pasties Plus, 22 Northwest Fourth Street; (218) 327–2230. The old-fashioned Cornish meat pie is served just about any way you want it; also curried beef rolls and chili, all for takeout. Pasties are $2.99 each or $32.00 a dozen. Open Monday through Saturday 10:00 A.M. to 7:00 P.M.

Quadna Hills Resort, 100 Quadna Road, Hill City; (218) 697–8444 or (800) 422–6649. Year-round lodging and dining on the 1,400-acre property that is a golf course in the summer and a ski resort in the winter. Accommodations range from lodge and motel rooms to multibedroom villas and town houses. A one-bedroom town house for two runs $120 a night from Thanksgiving to April 1 and Memorial Day through Labor Day, peak seasons are summer and winter, all rates are reduced midweek. A two-night minimum is required.

Iron Trail

Biwabik Lodge, State Highway 135 and County Road 4, Biwabik; (218) 865–4588 or (800) 383–3183;www.thebiwabiklodge.com. The lodge is close to Giants Ridge for skiing and golf and access to the snowmobile trail network. It offers a pool, sauna, spa, and lounge. Rooms run about $80 a night on summer weekends and include a contintental breakfast. Golf and ski packages are available.

McNair's Bed and Breakfast, 7694 County Road 5, Side Lake; (218) 254–5878. On Side Lake near Hibbing is a new house full of old character whose humble mining-cottage origins no longer show. The gourmet breakfast includes fresh fruit and a changing entree that could be anything from quiche to chocolate chip pancakes. All rooms have private baths. Rates range from $110 for a guest room to $150 for a suite with a kitchen. Open all year.

The Park Inn, 502 Chestnut Street, Virginia; (800) 777–4699 or (218) 749–1000; www.parkinnvirginia.com. This restored 1930s downtown hotel has modern amenities such as a hot tub, pool, and sauna in addition to Arizona's Restaurant and Lounge. The restaurant serves several specialties, from French dip sandwiches to fresh walleye, filet mignon, and prime rib ($7.00 to $20.00). Hotel rooms range from $79 for a standard room to $175 for a suite. Ski packages are available in conjunction with Giants Ridge.

For More Information

Chisolm Area Chamber, 10 Second Avenue Northwest, Chisolm, MN 55719; (218) 254–3600 or (800) 422–0806.

Grand Rapids Area Chamber of Commerce, 1 Northwest Third Street, Grand Rapids, MN 55744; (218) 326–6619 or (800) 472–6366; www. grandmn.com, or www.visitgrandrapids.com.

Hibbing Chamber of Commerce, 211 East Hibbing Street, P.O. Box 727, Hibbing, MN 55746; (218) 262–3895 or (800) 444–2246.

Iron Trail Convention and Visitors Bureau, 403 North First Street, Virginia, MN 55792; (218) 749–8161 or (800) 777–8497; www.irontrail.org.

Virginia Area Chamber of Commerce, 403 First Street North, P.O. Box 1072, Virginia, MN 55792; (218) 741–2717 or (218) 741–8825.

Bemidji

Minnesota Nice

2 Nights

Bemidji likes to be known as the "First City on the Mississippi." Settled originally by Native Americans, later by French Canadians, and then an influx of Scandinavians, Bemidji was once a logging capital of the country. Today it is one of the tourist capitals of the state.

Tourism arrived in Bemidji more than one hundred years ago—as it did in most northern communities—about the same time as the train tracks. By then stories and legends of the great forests and thousands of lakes had circulated all over the country, drawing people from hundreds of miles away to hunt, fish, and vacation in the North Woods. So it's no surprise that when logging died out, tourism did not, and today visitors continue to come here.

- ☐ Forests
- ☐ Bike Trails
- ☐ Powwows
- ☐ Arts

Included in the enticing stories of the North Woods were the tall tales of the giant lumberjack, Paul Bunyan, and his companion, Babe the Blue Ox, which is why every old logging-community-turned-resort lays claim to Paul's birthplace. Bemidji is no exception. In fact, Bemidji insists on first rights because its statues of Paul and Babe, two of the most photographed figures in the state, were dedicated in 1937, making them the oldest ones in the area. (Even Brainerd's followed by a couple of years.)

The legends may be myth, but Bemidji truly is the first city on the Mississippi River, and the pride in that honor shows, from its beautifully redone lakefront to citywide restorations of homes and buildings. So now when the sun shines on Lake Bemidji, the entire town sparkles.

Although it's only 50 miles from Park Rapids and about 70 miles from Grand Rapids, two other prominent resort communities, Bemidji stands out as a cultural oasis in the heart of the wilderness. Boasting the oldest summer stock theater in the state, a state university, nationally known language camps, and a well-established arts council, Bemidji offers recreational, entertainment, and educational opportunities as diverse as its heritage.

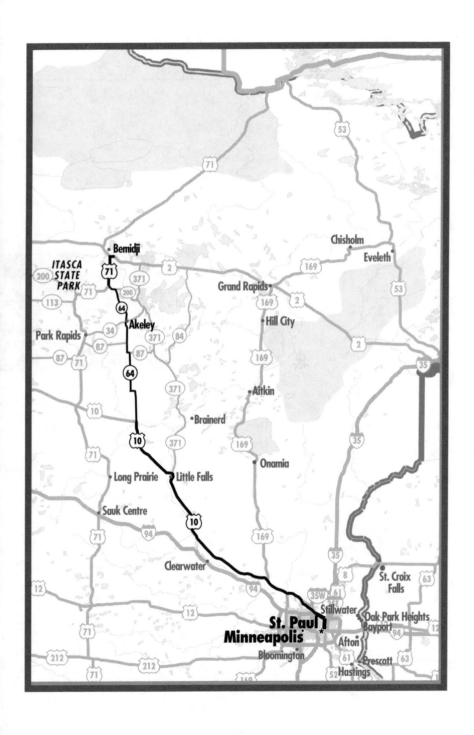

Day 1 / Morning

It's a hefty drive to this hearty region: a good four hours. Get an early start and plan on eating lunch in Akeley, about three hours north of the Twin Cities. The best route, being both scenic and the most direct, is to follow U.S. Highway 10 northwest out of the Twin Cities to Motley and then pick up State Highway 64, which will take you straight north to Akeley.

LUNCH: Winner's Restaurant, at the junction of State Highways 64 and 34 in Akeley (you can't miss it), is a great place to stop for lunch. It serves down-home meat-and-potatoes kind of fare. "Breakfast is best" here, so hope to arrive before noon and select from the grand breakfast buffet (about $5.00). You can't go wrong, however, with lunch or dinner either, especially if you order the chicken, ribs, or steak dinners ($7.00 and up). Open daily 7:00 A.M. to 4:00 P.M., until 7:00 P.M. on Tuesday and Thursday and until 8:00 P.M. on Friday and Saturday. Call (218) 652–2525.

Afternoon

Continue out of Akeley north on State Highway 64, through **Kabekona State Forest** to State Highway 200 and the town of Kabekona, and then west to U.S. Highway 71. Follow Highway 71 north to the southern edge of Bemidji, where it turns into State Highway 197 and goes north to the lake. Take a left on Bemidji Avenue (County Road 21) and follow it a few blocks along the lakeshore to the **Tourist Information Center.** Paul and Babe will be standing right there to welcome you.

The recently redone pavilion is a great place to get your bearings and pick up brochures and a city map. (Be sure to get a copy of *Historic Sites in Bemidji Area*). It is also the new home to the **Fireplace of the States.** The fireplace started out as the whim of a local resort owner in the 1930s, but the result was a collaborative national, almost philanthropic, venture. Each stone has a special origin, whether it came from Franklin D. Roosevelt's home in Hyde Park, New York, or Yellowstone National Park. It involved county directors, state governors, and even some residents at the St. Cloud Reformatory in its making.

DINNER: Enjoy the lakefront, take some pictures of Paul and Babe, and then head across the street to **Union Station First City Brewery and Grill,** the corner anchor of the mall **Union Square.** If it's a little too early, you can browse in the adjacent shops.

Union Station has been a restaurant for more than twenty years—it

Paul Bunyan and Babe the Blue Ox

was one of the first buildings in town to be rehabbed for a new use—and it's been a brewery since March 1997. It has an extensive menu with an array of Mexican and Italian favorites, but the Maplewood Grill specialties should not be overlooked. Your choice of meat or fish, from a seven-ounce sirloin steak ($12) to a salmon fillet ($14), will be perfectly grilled over sugar-maple embers and then smothered in your choice of béarnaise, bordelaise, garlic butter, onion marmalade, or numerous other mouthwatering sauces. If you have room, go for the homemade Bailey's chocolate chip cheesecake ($3.25). Open daily 11:00 A.M. to 11:00 P.M. in summer, with reduced hours between Labor Day and Memorial Day. Call (218) 751–9261.

LODGING: Beltrami Shores Bed and Breakfast, located 10 miles northeast of Bemidji, is a three-bedroom lodge that sits on the shore of Lake Beltrami. Each of the North Woods–style bedrooms has a cedar-log bed, vaulted ceiling, and furniture with knotty pine accents. The lodge also features a great room with fireplace, a second-floor sitting room and library, a three-season porch and herbarium, walk-out decks on two levels, a gift shop, and a cedar-log swing overlooking a hummingbird garden and the lake. Weekend breakfasts are hearty affairs inspired by the North Woods, while a continental breakfast is served on weekdays. Rates start at $75 per night with a two-night minimum stay. Call (218) 586–2518 or (888) 746–7373 or visit www.beltramishores.com.

Day 2 / Morning

BREAKFAST: Beltrami Shores Bed and Breakfast.

LUNCH: Stop at the **Coachman Cafe,** 509 Beltrami, and pick up a few sandwiches to go. The Coachman specializes in breakfast and lunch, offering breads, such as oatmeal and yogurt, and its own cookies and bars. Hearty eat-in lunches include pork chops and meat loaf served family-style, and every sandwich imaginable is available, from cold meats to chicken and tuna salads. For about $5.50 you can get a tuna sandwich, chips, coleslaw, cookie, and a beverage! Call (218) 751–0436.

Afternoon

Armed with your sandwiches, head to **Lake Bemidji State Park** for a picnic lunch. The park is on the north side of Lake Bemidji. Follow State Highway 197 north out of town as it turns into County Road 20, then watch for signs and follow County Road 21. Often overlooked because Itasca State Park is a big draw only 30 miles away, this park is another nice surprise. Enjoy your lunch and then walk the short boardwalk to the bog, where you can see native orchids growing along the way. There are also hiking and biking trails. For more information call the park at (218) 755–3843 or the Department of Natural Resources at (612) 296–6157 or (800) 766–6000; TDD (612) 296–5484 or (800) 657–3929.

Allow yourself time to return to your lodgings, rest, and freshen up for your evening out on the town.

DINNER: It's highly possible that **Tutto Bene Italian Ristorante** will single-handedly put Bemidji on the map as one of the finest places to dine in Minnesota. The decor, with sleek black tables, natural wood accents, gold tones sponged on the walls, antique mirrors, Venetian prints, and soft lighting, is sophisticated, yet the ambience is casual and friendly. The service is superb, and the food, including fresh handmade pastas and sauces made from scratch, is exquisite. The rotollo, sliced spirals of pasta filled with ham and ricotta cheese and delicately covered with Alfredo sauce, is an artistic presentation as delicious as it looks. Other choices include fresh greens and pasta salads, soups such as green olive or minestrone, garlic roast chicken, manicotti, sautéed shrimp, and several other classic Italian entrees. Music, from Italian opera to live classical, plays gently in the background; in the summer you can dine outside in the canopy-covered courtyard. Entrees range from about $8.00 to $18.00. Open daily from 11:00 A.M.; dinner service begins at 5:00 P.M. Call (218) 751–1100.

Evening

A perfect summer evening will be dinner at Tutto Bene followed by the 8:00 P.M. show at **The Paul Bunyan Playhouse** in the historic Chief Theatre, 314 Beltrami Avenue, the oldest continuously running summer stock theater in Minnesota. The plays, a repertoire of musicals and dramas, change weekly. The season runs June through August, Tuesday through Sunday, with additional holiday specials. Call (218) 751–7270 or (218) 751–0752; www.paulbunyanplayhouse.com.

LODGING: Beltrami Shores Bed and Breakfast.

Day 3 / Morning

BREAKFAST: Beltrami Shores Bed and Breakfast.

For a scenic drive and a finishing touch to this weekend, a tour of the permanent buildings at **Concordia Language Villages** is worth the out-of-your-way round-trip before you head home.

Follow State Highway 197 north through town (as if heading to Lake Bemidji State Park) to County Road 21/Bemidji Avenue, then go right on County Road 20. Continue about 6 miles and turn left just in front of the wooden sign that reads Concordia Language Camps.

The camps offer language immersion programs for all ages. There are four villages—French, German, Norwegian, and Finnish—composed of about ninety buildings that include a French château, a Norwegian church, and a Finnish log cabin that was built in Finland, dismantled, and reassembled here. Free guided tours are offered. It's best to call ahead, even if you just plan to drive through the grounds. The tours are fascinating and educational and include a chance to learn a few foreign words, depending on your guide. Call (218) 586–2214 or (800) 450–2214; www.cord.edu/dept/clr/.

There's More

Amusements. Putt 'N' Go, U.S. Highway 71 North (218–751–8286 or 218–751–7333), offers miniature golf, a waterslide, go-carts, and more. Open daily during the summer, 11:00 A.M. to 10:00 P.M.

Bemidji Bowl and Adventure Miniature Golf, 2317 Bemidji Avenue; (218) 751–2153. Indoor bowling and outdoor minigolf.

Art. The Bemidji State University Arts Center, Education Building, Sixteenth and Birchmont, Bemidji State University (218–755–2000 or 800–475–2001), has galleries that offer ongoing exhibits. The Bemidji Community Art Center, 426 Bemidji Avenue (218–444–7570), has changing exhibits and a gift shop.

Biking. It won't be long until the Paul Bunyan Bike Trail is paved from Bemidji to Hackensack, where it continues to Brainerd. The finished railroad-grade bike trail will be about 100 miles long. There are 5 miles of mountain bike trails in Lake Bemidji State Park (218–755–3844). Biking is also available in Itasca State Park (218–266–2114), about 30 miles south of Bemidji.

Bingo and Gaming. Northern Lights Casino, Cass Lake; (218) 335–7000 or (800) 252–PLAY. Twenty-four-hour gaming and hundreds of slot machines. Luxury lodging and dining are also available.

Camping. Some of the country's best camping is found in national forests. Chippewa National Forest (218–335–8600) has several primitive camp-sites. Camping is also available in Lake Bemidji State Park (218–755–3843) and Itasca State Park (218–266–2129). Call The Connection at (612) 922–9000 or (800) 246–CAMP for all state park camping reservations.

Golf. There are four golf courses in the area, and three of them offer eigh-teen holes: Bemidji Town and Country Club, on Birchmont Beach Road, about 5 miles north of Bemidji, (218) 751–9215; Greenwood Golf Course, Power Dam Road, about 8 miles east of Bemidji on County Road 12, (218) 751–3875; Castle Highlands, U.S. Highway 71, 10 miles northeast of Bemidji, (218) 586–2681; and Maple Ridge, about 4 miles south of Bemidji on Highway 71, east on North Plantagenet Road, (218) 751–8401.

Winter Alternatives

Cross-country Skiing. Lake Bemidji State Park (218–755–3843) offers 9 miles of trails. Itasca State Park (218–266–2100) offers 31 miles of trails. The Montebello Ski Trail (city of Bemidji) is lighted for nighttime skiing; (218) 751–0041.

Curling. Bemidji's Curling Club (218–751–1123; www.bemidjicurling.org) boasts of being the finest one in the nation.

Downhill Skiing. Buena Vista (218–243–2231; www.bvskiarea.org), about 12 miles north of Bemidji on County Road 15, offers fifteen runs and complete services, including rentals.

Snowmobiling. Bemidji offers access to more than 500 miles of trails via the North Country Trail System. Call (218) 751–9194.

Special Events

January through February. Bemidji Polar Daze includes a fishing tournament, a Taste of Northern Minnesota, and Paul Bunyan Dogsled Races.

February. Annual Logging Days, Buena Vista; (218) 243–2231. Demonstrations and old-time storytelling.

Annual Jazzfest, Bemidji State University; (218) 755–3935.

March through April. Maple-tree tapping to syrup making, Lake Bemidji State Park; (218) 755–3843.

Native American powwows are held throughout the spring and summer months; (218) 751–3541 or (800) 458–2223.

June. The Mid-Summer Fest. Food, activities, and a dance around the maypole.

July. Annual Jaycees Water Carnival.

Art in the Park, Library Park, Bemidji waterfront. Entertainment, ethnic foods, and nearly one hundred artists.

Annual Paul Bunyan Vintage Car Show, fairgrounds.

September. Ji-jabaa-ditiwebishkigeny (Cass Lake Bemidji Bike Tour); (218) 335–9897.

Annual North Country Arts and Crafts Workshop, Concordia Language Villages; (218) 586–2884.

November. The Night We Light draws the whole town to the lakefront the day after Thanksgiving to see the town instantly lit up for the holidays.

December. The Santa Lucia Festival, a celebration of Bemidji's Scandinavian heritage, includes a Crown of Candles parade.

NOTE: For more information on these special events in Bemidji, call the Bemidji Chamber of Commerce and Visitors and Convention Bureau at (218) 751–3541 or (800) 458–2223.

Other Recommended Restaurants and Lodgings

Best Western Bemidji, 2420 Paul Bunyan Drive; (218) 751–0390. An indoor pool, spa, and free breakfast bar serving muffins, bagels, cereals, juice, tea, and coffee are among the amenities offered. A standard double-occupancy room is about $70 per night (reduced rates in winter).

Finn'n Feather Resort, Lake Andrusia; (218) 335–6598 or (800) 776–3466; www.finn-n-feather.com. A great place for families to vacation together, amenities include use of watercraft, a hot tub, recreational facilities, and organized activities for children. Rentals run Saturday to Friday during the midsummer season with two-night minimum stays during the off-seasons of May 1 through June 14 and August 30 through the first week of October. A two-bedroom cabin for four rents for about $1,040 to $1,280 a week in midsummer.

Kohl's Resort, 15707 Big Turtle Drive Northeast, about 10 miles north of Bemidji on County Road 22; (218) 243–2131 or (800) 336–4384; www.kohlsresort.com. Located in the Buena Vista State Forest near the Buena Vista Ski Resort, Kohl's offers superb accommodations all year long. There are condos, cabins, and cottages to choose from, with amenities such as fireplaces and whirlpools. The resort also has an indoor swimming pool. During midsummer a deluxe two-bedroom cabin for four with a whirlpool, fireplace, and air-conditioning rents for $1,040 a week, Saturday to Saturday.

For More Information

Bemidji Chamber of Commerce and Visitors and Convention Bureau, 300 Bemidji Avenue, Bemidji, MN 56601; (218) 751–3541 or (800) 458–2223; www.bemidji.org or www.visitbemidji.com.

Lanesboro

Bicycles and Buggies

2 Nights

Less than a decade ago, very little was happening in this southeastern corner of Minnesota. Lanesboro was a sleepy little town with an inn and a B&B, both visionary endeavors, and nearby Harmony was known for its Amish community. It was a splendid drive, but rarely a destination. Thanks, in part, to the Root River Trail, renovation has run rampant in the past few years: The storefronts are full of antiques and gifts, and Lanesboro is bustling.

Nestled in the Root River Valley, about midway on the bike trail, Lanesboro is now home to numerous restaurants, lodgings, a winery, and a nationally recognized theater company. Today it is worth the drive just for dinner and a play.

- ☐ B&Bs
- ☐ Biking
- ☐ Antiques
- ☐ Amish Tours

Day 1 / Morning

Lanesboro is about a three-hour drive from the Twin Cities following U.S. Highway 52 south past Cannon Falls and Rochester. Cannon Falls is home to **Midwest of Cannon Falls,** importers of charming Christmas ornaments and novelty and home decorations. Its outlet store is open to the public and is a good place to buy gifts or stock up for yourself. Follow the exit to Cannon Falls, go right at the stoplight, and drive about 1 mile to Cannon Mall, just south of downtown on Fourth Street. Open Monday through Saturday 9:00 A.M. to 5:00 P.M., and Sunday seasonally. Call (507) 263–4150.

LUNCH: Your best bet for a quick lunch, and to avoid touring downtown Rochester on your trip south, is the **Stone Mill Coffee House and Eatery,** 432 West Mill Street in Cannon Falls (follow the Cannon Falls exit). This darling cafe has an ice-cream-parlor atmosphere and serves terrific homemade soups, grilled sandwiches, salads (about $5.00 each), and gourmet coffees. Outdoor seating overlooks the Cannon River. Open

Monday through Saturday 6:30 A.M. to 5:00 P.M., Thursday until 7:00 P.M., and Sunday 8:30 A.M. to 7:00 P.M. Also, the Store Mill Marketplace, a collection of nine assorted shops, opened in 2001. Call (507) 263–2580.

Afternoon

Rochester, of course, is internationally famous for the Mayo Clinic and was home to numerous Mayo generations. **Mayowood,** the original summer home of Dr. Charles H. Mayo, built in 1910, is on the National Register of Historic Places and definitely worth the stop. Looking like a cross between the Biltmore Mansion and an arts-and-crafts bungalow, the home was lived in by a Mayo family as recently as 1965 and is affectionately referred to as a " '60s house," as tour guides explain the heavy use of green in the decorating. The home changed a lot over the years as it was handed down, but it's hard to keep track of who did what when; every generation of Mayos had at least one Charles. The Mayos traveled all over the world, and the furnishings reflect this. They were also visited by several prominent people. A highlight of the tour is the guest book in which Helen Keller's signature is on display; she visited frequently. Mayowood is on the southwest side of Rochester, which makes it easy to visit en route to Lanesboro, but it's tricky to find. From U.S. Highway 52, exit on County Road 8. Wind on County Road 8 to Meadowood Road. Take a right on Meadowood, continue on the road to the far side of the huge stone and white-wood barn, go right, and follow the signs. Tour times vary throughout the year. Summer weekend times are 11:00 A.M., 1:00, 2:00, and 3:00 P.M. on Saturday; 1:00, 2:00, and 3:00 P.M. on Sunday. Arrive at least fifteen minutes early to purchase your tickets. Admission: adults $10.00; children 15 or under $5.00. Call (507) 282–9447.

Continue south on U.S. Highway 52 to County Road 16, just beyond Preston, where you turn east to Lanesboro. The few miles on this road into town offer some of the best scenery in the state as you cut through rocky bluffs and quickly descend into the Root River Valley. There are sudden hairpin curves, and for a little while you'll feel like you're driving in the mountains. Your ears may even pop!

Turn left on Parkway, continue into town, and enjoy the rest of the afternoon wandering the streets of Lanesboro.

You will notice the extra-wide shoulders on the stretch of U.S. Highway 52 in this area all the way to the Iowa border and the sign that reads AMISH BYWAY. There are many Amish farms in the vicinity, and

Biking on the Root River Trail

their black horse-drawn carriages, traveling on the shoulders, frequent this road. The carriages are fun to spot, but you need to be especially careful driving and sharing the road with them. The Amish are a private people, but it is okay to stop at the farms that advertise items for sale such as honey or furniture. You may even get a little tour of a workshop. Otherwise, stick to the commercial tours that have special arrangements with certain Amish families.

DINNER: It's hard to believe that such a little town has so much to choose from for dinner, and it will be difficult to decide, but the **Old Village Hall Restaurant and Pub,** 111 Coffee Street, is an excellent choice. The restored Village Hall has an elegant interior and offers fine dining, but it often caters to bikers, so attire is casual. Mouthwatering doesn't begin to describe the spaghetti and chicken penne primavera ($15) flavored with roasted garlic, sun-dried tomatoes, basil sauce, and imported Romano cheese. Entrees such as lamb chops, salmon, and roast duck are also available ($18 to $21). Cash and checks only. Call for reservations. Open for dinner nightly, May 1 through October 31; Friday, Saturday, and Sunday only, November 1 through April 30. Lunch is served on Saturday and Sunday all year. Call (507) 467–2962.

LODGING: Mrs. B's Historic Lanesboro Inn and Restaurant, 101 Parkway at the edge of downtown. This is country lodging at its best, and charm abounds. Homemade cookies, brownies, and lemonade sit on the buffet in the tiny but very welcoming lobby. The rooms are cozy, sunny, and inviting, with the amenities of home such as a private bath and air-conditioning. Some rooms even have fireplaces. Weekend rates for two are $94 to $104 per night and include a full breakfast. Smoke free. Call (507) 467–2154 or (800) 657–4710.

Day 2 / Morning

BREAKFAST: Breakfast at Mrs. B's is an all-you-can-eat affair served downstairs between 8:00 and 9:00 A.M. It includes oatmeal, buttermilk pancakes, a fruit cup, cottage bacon, coffee, and juice. It's a great way to start your day!

Even if you put yourself at the opposite end of the spectrum from "sports enthusiast," take a spin on the **Root River Trail,** one of the most popular bike trails in the state because of its scenery. The trail is paved and follows the abandoned railroad bed, so it's virtually flat. You can go west to

Fountain, or east to Rushford; eventually you will be able to bike it all the way to Houston. There are currently 41.3 finished miles of trail that takes you along the Root River, through the bluff country, and across several railroad bridges. If you didn't bring your own bike, there are three sports rental places in downtown Lanesboro.

LUNCH: Going east on the bike trail is a good choice, especially if you time your ride to be in Whalan when you start to get hungry. The trail goes past the **Aroma Pie Shop,** about 4.5 miles outside of Lanesboro. (Yes, you can drive there, too.) The Aroma is the only eating place in Whalan, so be prepared for standing room only on a busy weekend; you can always take your food outside and eat on the grass if you like. Generally seating is available on the porch or inside, including stools at the antique bar. The Aroma serves soups, sandwiches, and cinnamon rolls, but it's famous for its homemade pies. Choose from raspberry, caramel apple, chocolate addicts fudge, banana cream, and others (around $2.50 a slice). Open May 1 through November 1, Spring hours are Thursday through Sunday 9:00 A.M. to 7:00 P.M. Summer hours run from late May to early September and are 8:00 A.M. to 7:00 P.M. seven days a week. Fall hours are Friday through Sunday, 8:00 A.M. to 7:00 P.M. Call (507) 467–2623.

Afternoon

Bike back to Lanesboro; you will probably want to rest and freshen up for your gourmet dinner.

DINNER: Dinner at Mrs. B's is an event that starts at 7:00 P.M.; it is also about three hours in delectable duration. The preselected menu changes daily, but usually costs about $30 per person. This is a creatively hearty meal, and just hearing your menu will be intoxicating. Plan to be surprised, but count on something delicious, possibly starting with a Caesar salad and one of Mrs. B's famous homemade breads, progressing to roast turkey breast with sweet onion chutney and sautéed vegetables, and topping it off with a piece of chocolate almond torte with rum crème anglaise. You do not have to be a guest of the inn to stop for dinner, but reservations are required. Served Wednesday through Sunday only. Call (800) 657–4710 or (507) 467–2154.

LODGING: Mrs B's.

Amish buggy

Day 3 / Morning

BREAKFAST: Mrs. B's.

The perfect way to round out your excursion to southeastern Minnesota is with a tour of the Amish community. Backtrack to U.S. Highway 52 and head south for a few miles to Harmony. **Michel's Amish Tours** is located at 45 Main Avenue North. A private guide will join you in your car as you wind through the countryside to see the Amish community up close. Many of the Amish families have quilts, furniture, and other crafts for sale at their farms. Car tours run $30 per vehicle and last from two to two and a half hours. Tours are offered Monday through Saturday 9:00 A.M. to 3:00 P.M. No tours are offered on Sunday. Call (507) 886–5392 or (800) 752–6474 for reservations.

LUNCH: For a great country lunch, head to **The Old Barn Resort,** 4 miles south of Preston on County Road 17. The resort offers a sixty-bed hostel for groups, a campground, a nine-hole golf course, and a restaurant outfitted with handmade Amish furnishings. This is a lot of good food. You can order anything from a hamburger to a fine steak ($2.00 to $12.00), although the hot beef or pork sandwich seems most appropriate out on the farm (about $3.00). Save room for homemade pumpkin or apple pie (about $2.50 a slice). Open Sunday through Thursday noon to 8:00 P.M., Friday and Saturday noon to 10:00 P.M. There's a fish fry on Friday, 5:00 to 10:00 P.M. Call (507) 467–2512 or visit www.barnresort.com.

There's More

Avian Acres, Route 2, Box 5, Lanesboro, MN 55949; (507) 467–2996 or (800) 967–BIRD. Bird-watching is considered one of America's favorite pastimes, second only to gardening. Avian Acres, about 1.5 miles southwest of Lanesboro, on a gravel road, offers a petting zoo that includes deer, lambs, ferrets, and ducklings and active feeders that draw hundreds of species of birds for watching. Open daily all year, 9:00 A.M. to 7:00 P.M.

Bike and Canoe Rentals. Bikes are available for rent at Capron Hardware Store (800–726–5030), Little River General Store (507–467–2943 or 800–944–2943; www.lrgeneralstore.com), and Root River Outfitters (507–467–3400), on Parkway in Lanesboro. Trail Station Sports, 2145 North Fourth Street, Cannon Falls (507–263–5055 or 888–835–BIKE), offers bike and in-line skate rentals for the Cannon Valley Trail that runs from Cannon Falls to Red Wing. (A $2.00 pass is required to bike the trail.)

Camping. Hidden Valley Campground, Route 1, Box 56, Preston, MN 55965 (507–765–2467), offers full hookups, fishing, and canoe trips; off Highways 16 and 52. Sylvan Park, downtown Lanesboro (507–467–3722 or 800–944–2670), is a lovely site right on the Root River, with tent sites ($10) and sites with electricity and water ($20). Sylvan Park is the city park.

Forestville/Mystery Cave State Park in Forestville, off State Highway 16 near Preston, is a restored historic fur-trade center and village with costumed "residents." A natural cave is also in the park and offers one- and two-hour-long tours. The shorter tour is wheelchair accessible. Dress warmly. Open Memorial Day through Labor Day, Monday through

Thursday 8:00 A.M. to 4:00 P.M., Friday 8:00 A.M. to 10:00 P.M., Saturday 9:00 A.M. to 9:00 P.M., Sunday 9:00 A.M. to 6:00 P.M.; weekends only in September and October. A daily vehicle permit is required unless you have an annual pass. Call the park (507–352–5111), the cave (507–937–3251), the village (507–765–2785), or the Department of Natural Resources (612–296–6157 or 888–MINN–DNR).

Golf. Cannon Golf Club, 1 mile north of Cannon Falls just off U.S. Highway 52 and County Road 88 (507–263–3126), offers eighteen holes, a pro shop, and a clubhouse. The Lanesboro Golf Club, Parkway Avenue South, Lanesboro (507–467–3742), has a nine-hole course on the bluff overlooking town. The Old Barn Resort, 4 miles south of Preston on County Road 17 (507–467–2512 or 800–552–2512), offers a driving range and a nine-hole course.

Live Theater. The nationally recognized Commonweal Theatre Company is located in Lanesboro, twice ranked as one of the 100 best small art towns in America by John Villani. The company's professional productions include everything from Neil Simon to William Shakespeare; the season runs from mid-February through December. Curtain times are Tuesday through Saturday at 8:00 P.M., Sunday at 3:00 P.M., and a Fourth of July performance at 5:00 P.M. Tickets: adults $15.00; children and students $7.00. Call (507) 467–2525 or (800) 657–7025; www.commonwealtheatre.org.

Niagara Cave, (507) 886–6606 or (800) 837–6606; www.niagaracave.com. Hidden within the bluffs and full of stalactites, stalagmites, and fossils, the cave offers an unusual way to spend your day. About 4.5 miles southeast of Harmony on State Highway 139. Open daily May through September 9:30 A.M. to 5:30 P.M.; weekends only in April and October 10:00 A.M. to 4:30 P.M.

Winter Alternatives

Cross-country Skiing. The Root River Trail converts to cross-country ski use when the snow falls and offers 45 miles of groomed trail.

Special Events

January. The Cannon Valley Classic Sled Dog Race draws teams from all over the country, Cannon Falls.

February. Norske Vinter Fest, Lanesboro.

June. Art in the Park, Lanesboro.

July. Fillmore County Fair, Preston.

August. Buffalo Bill Days, Lanesboro. Includes a parade, flea market, music, food, and carnival.

September. Fall Foliage Festival, Harmony.

October. Oktoberfest, Lanesboro. Twelve hours of German food and polka music.

December. Norwegian Lutefisk Dinner and Craft Shop, Preston.

For more information on special events in Cannon Falls, call the Cannon Falls Area Chamber of Commerce at (507) 263–2289; in Lanesboro, call the Lanesboro Visitor's Center at (507) 467–2696 or (800) 944–2670; in Harmony, call (507) 886–2469 or (800) 247–MINN.

Other Recommended Restaurants and Lodgings

Cannon Falls

Country Quiet Inn Bed and Breakfast, 37295 112th Way; (800) 258–1843 or (651) 258–4406.

Quill and Quilt Bed and Breakfast, 615 Hoffman Street West; (507) 263–5507 or (800) 488–3849; www.quillandquilt.com.

Lanesboro

Das Wurst Haus, 117 Parkway Avenue North; (507) 467–2902. Here's the place to go for the finest in homemade brats, sauerkraut, sausages (95 percent lean), breads, mustards, and baked beans (that the chef spent nine years perfecting). Order homemade root beer (or Schell's Bier) to wash it all down. To top it off, everything comes with free live polka music on the side. From $1.50 for a serving of baked beans to $5.00 for the Reuben.

Open daily April 1 through October 31.

Green Gables Inn, 303 Sheridan Street, State Highway 16; (507) 467–2936 or (800) 818–GABLES. A new and very charming country motel, this is perfect for those who aren't impressed by antiques and Victoriana. Summer weekends have a two-night minimum. A standard room on the weekend runs $74 per night and includes a continental breakfast. Wheelchair accessible.

Historic Scanlan House Bed and Breakfast, 708 Parkway; (507) 467–2158 or (800) 944–2158; www.scanlanhouse.com. This is a full-service Victorian experience. You will be so well taken care of here, you may not want to go home. Plan to allow at least an hour for the extraordinary five-course breakfast. Additional amenities—with additional prices—include roses, an I Love You teddy bear, wines, and deli trays. All rooms have private baths and range from $105 to $135 per night on the weekends in the summer. Bikes and cross-country skis are available for rent.

Nick's Ribs, 121 Parkway Avenue North; (507) 467–0101. Good food, good service, and owners with a good sense of humor are the hallmarks here. Barbecue is certainly their specialty—their sauce is available for sale—but salads and sandwiches are also offered. Prices range from $4.50 for a sandwich to $16.00 for the "Eat Like Nick" steak and ribs dinner. Open mid-February through mid-December, Wednesday through Thursday 11:30 A.M. to 9:00 P.M., Friday and Saturday until 10:00 P.M., Sunday and holidays noon to 8:00 P.M. Call for winter hours.

River Trail Picnic Basket, 100 Parkway Avenue North; (507) 467–3556. This is the place to go for a respite from canoeing, biking, or just shopping. Order some espresso and a couple of scones, and take them along on a walk in the park. Open all year to accommodate sightseers, bicyclists, canoeists, and skiers.

The Trail Inn Cafe, 111 Parkway Avenue South; (507) 467–2200. This is definitely the place to stop if you're traveling with children; homemade pizza (medium cheese is $8.00), a huge variety of sandwiches (starting at $1.50), hamburgers (starting at $1.95), and a kids' menu are available. Open Tuesday through Saturday 11:00 A.M. to 8:00 P.M., until 7:00 P.M. on Sunday.

The Victorian House, 709 Parkway South; (507) 467–3457. The one-time executive chef for the Hilton and Royal Caribbean Cruise Line now serves his fine French cuisine in a romantic and elegant Victorian setting.

The menu changes every six to eight weeks, and the five-course dinner has a fixed price of about $28. Opens Tuesday through Saturday at 5:30 P.M.; closing hours vary. Reservations a must.

For More Information

Cannon Falls Area Chamber of Commerce, 103 North Fourth Street, Cannon Falls, MN 55009; (507) 263–2289; www.cannonfalls.org.

Harmony Tourism, Box 141B, Harmony, MN 55939; (507) 886–2469 or (800) 247–MINN; www.harmony.mn.us.

Historic Bluff Country Convention and Visitors Bureau, 45 Center Street, Harmony, MN 55939; (507) 886–2230 or (800) 428–2030; www.bluff country.com.

Lanesboro Visitor's Center, 100 Milwaukee Road, Lanesboro, MN 55949; (507) 467–2696 or (800) 944–2670; www.lanesboro.com.

Rochester Convention and Visitors Bureau, 150 South Broadway, Rochester, MN 55904; (507) 288–4331 or (800) 634–8277; www.rochestercvb.org.

The Minnesota River Valley to Pipestone

The Edge of the West

2 Nights

The route to Pipestone takes you through the lush Minnesota River Valley into rolling farmland and out to the plains to the edge of the West. If you've spent most of your life in the Twin Cities or vacationing in the North Woods, surrounded by lakes, this will be one of those trips in which the land "doesn't feel like Minnesota." It sure feels like America though! In fact, as you wind your way through cornfields, especially in the early fall, you may find yourself humming "America the Beautiful" (and maybe wanting to change the lyrics to "amber waves of corn tassels"). This is the heartland: simple towns, friendly people, and seemingly endless country roads and prairie land.

- ☐ American Indian Crafts
- ☐ History
- ☐ State Parks
- ☐ Festivals

Pipestone, named for the soft red rock used by American Indians to make ceremonial pipes and fetishes, was once at the edge of the Wild West, which accounts for its late establishment as a city. The first building went up in 1874, and the train arrived so soon afterward that Pipestone flourished quickly. Four railroad lines served the city and turned Pipestone into a major railroad and business center. By 1879 Pipestone had become the county seat. The sudden affluence is still visible in the massive stone buildings, all of which are on the National Register of Historic Places, constructed with Sioux quartzite quarried nearby.

For centuries American Indians have regarded the pipestone quarries as sacred ground. And it was stories from this area that inspired Henry Wadsworth Longfellow, in part, to write *The Song of Hiawatha*. The appeal continues today, drawing thousands of people to the Pipestone National Monument and the welcoming town of Pipestone.

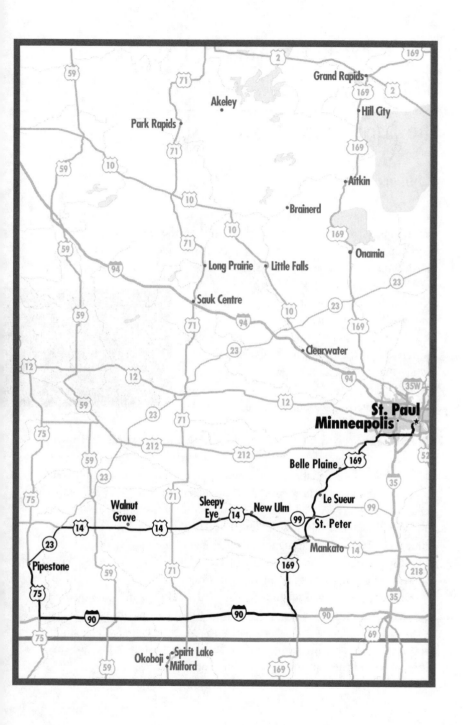

Day 1 / Morning

Pipestone is a three-and-a-half- to four-hour drive southwest of the Twin Cities. Get an early start, not because of the drive, but because this is one of those rare opportunities to have breakfast at **Emma Krumbee's,** a restaurant, bakery, and apple orchard in Belle Plaine. Follow U.S. Highway 169 south. Belle Plaine is less than an hour into your trip, and Emma Krumbee's sits right on the highway. You can't miss it, or any of the billboards that precede it, for that matter. Emma's country-fried breaded pork tenderloin steak (about $6.00) is a farm-style favorite, but you shouldn't pass up the cinnamon-caramel-apple French toast or the apple buttermilk pancakes (both under $5.00) because apples are what make this restaurant so famous. If you're in a hurry, or not that hungry, one of the world's best apple flips (about $1.50) will make you glad you stopped. Open daily 6:00 A.M. to 11:00 P.M. Call (952) 873–4334 or visit www.emmakrumbees.com.

As you near Le Sueur, the highway takes you deep into the Minnesota River Valley—or as baby boomers may recall, "the Valley of the Jolly, Ho-Ho-Ho, Green Giant"—and your surroundings suddenly become thick green woods. Le Sueur is also the first Minnesota home of Dr. W. W. Mayo, who, with his sons, founded the famous Mayo Clinic in Rochester. The little white Gothic **W. W. Mayo House,** 118 North Main Street, is open to the public Memorial Day through Labor Day, Tuesday through Sunday and holidays 1:00 to 4:30 P.M., and on the weekends just preceding and following the main summer season. Admission: adults $3.00; seniors 65 and over $2.00; children 6 to 16, $1.00. Call (507) 665–3250 or (888) PAST–FUN.

St. Peter, too, sits right on the Minnesota River. This "safe and friendly" town, as its residents call it, is home to Gustavus Adolphus College and the Treaty Site History Center.

At the south end of St. Peter, follow State Highway 99 west to U.S. Highway 14 all the way to New Ulm.

LUNCH: New Ulm, famous for its Oktoberfest, looks like a German festival, and you will be compelled to stop. From U.S. Highway 14, turn left on Center Street; the unmistakable, looming red-brick-with-white-trim Brown County Museum will be on the corner on your left. If possible, park in the center-of-the-street area in front of the museum on Center Street.

Walk down Center to Minnesota Street and turn left. **Veigel's Kaiserhoff,** 221 North Minnesota Street, will be just a couple of blocks up on your left. This is the place to stop for German food. You can get a

Brown County Museum, New Ulm

hamburger (about $6.00) or one of several *Deutsche Spezialitaten,* such as Wiener schnitzel (up to $12), but the Kaiserhoff is famous for its barbecue ribs ($11 to $14) or, at least, its barbecue sauce on just about anything. Don't skip the potato salad! Open Sunday through Thursday 11:00 A.M. to 9:00 P.M., Friday and Saturday 11:00 A.M. to 9:30 P.M. Call (507) 359–2071.

You will want to time your brief stay in town to hear and see the **Glockenspiel,** about 1.5 blocks farther up Minnesota Street. The characters in this musical German clock "perform" at noon, 3:00 P.M., and 5:00 P.M. Head there after lunch, or backtrack around the corner to the **Brown County Museum.** The museum has exhibits on the region, on the historic Sioux Uprising, and on Wanda Gag, the local children's book writer and illustrator of *Millions of Cats* fame. Open Monday through Friday 10:00 A.M. to 5:00 P.M., Saturday and Sunday 1:00 to 5:00 P.M. Admission is $2.00 per adult; students and children are free. Call (507) 354–2016.

Afternoon

Continue west on U.S. Highway 14. This stretch of road, from Mankato all the way to De Smet, South Dakota, is known as the **Laura Ingalls Memorial Highway.** You will soon approach the town of Sleepy Eye, with several historic buildings and homes, and about 40 miles farther on, Walnut Grove. Although a very little town, Walnut Grove played a big part in the life of Laura Ingalls Wilder and has spent years developing **The Laura Ingalls Wilder Museum,** 1 block in from the highway. Recent acquisitions include the mantel and Pa's powderhorn and gun from the *Little House on the Prairie* television series and the actual home of the Ingallses' neighbors, the Nelsons. Open Memorial Day through September, Monday through Saturday 10:00 A.M. to 5:00 P.M., Sunday noon to 5:00 P.M.; October to Memorial Day, Monday through Saturday 10:00 A.M. to 3:00 P.M., Sunday noon to 3:00 P.M. Admission: adults $3.00; children 5 to 12, $1.00. Call (507) 859–2358 or (800) 528–7280; www .walnutgrove.org.

About 1.5 miles out of town is the Ingallses' original dugout site along **Plum Creek.** Nothing is left but a depression in the ground, but if you are traveling with *Little House* fans, the visit will be appreciated. The site is on private property and is closed fall through spring. A donation of $3.00 per car is suggested.

The rest of the drive to Pipestone is uneventful, but it is interesting to watch the terrain change as you travel farther west. From rolling farmland to plains to hills and rocky outcroppings, the land changes suddenly, then changes back again. Stay on U.S. Highway 14 west to State Highway 23 south. Highway 23 merges with U.S. Highway 75 and takes you into Pipestone on the east side of town. Take a right on East Main Street to get to the **Historic District.**

DINNER AND LODGING: The Historic Calumet Inn, 104 West Main Street, along with the other large stone buildings downtown, suddenly appears on the plains like an outcropping of rock sculpture. Famous for its historic accommodations, the inn has an equally reputable restaurant. The extensive menu includes seafood, steaks, and pastas. Barbecue ribs are a specialty ($9.95), and the seafood fettuccine ($9.95) is excellent.

So many things happened so fast in Pipestone, it's no surprise that when the original Calumet Hotel burned to the ground in 1886, the new one was built and opened within two years, allowing the "new" Calumet a long history of its own. Constructed with Sioux quartzite, visible throughout the building, the three-story Historic Calumet Inn is, both architecturally and hospitably, one of the best places you'll ever stay. Rooms are either modern or antique in style. All have private baths, and some have whirlpool tubs. Cable television and a continental breakfast, served in the lounge, are included. An antique room for two is $75 per night. Parking is available on the street or in a lot behind the inn. Call (507) 825–5871 or (800) 535–7610; www.calumetinn.com.

Day 2 / Morning

BREAKFAST: Enjoy your self-service continental breakfast in the lounge, or order a full breakfast in the hotel's restaurant.

If you're getting an early start, head straight to the **Pipestone National Monument.** National parks and monuments typically open by 8:00 A.M. (long before the museums, antiques stores, and gift shops). Go north on Hiawatha to Reservation Avenue and take a left into the parking lot of the visitor center. You will pass the **Three Maidens,** six large granite boulders, and the Song of Hiawatha pageant grounds on your left. The Pipestone National Monument protects the sacred pipestone quarries. Only American Indians are allowed to quarry the stone, but visitors can take a self-guided walk through the park, past active quarries and the hidden Winnewissa Falls. The walking tour takes about forty-five minutes, depending on how closely you follow your map to find and identify all the landmarks. You'll be amazed to see how quickly the land changes from prairie to quarry to jutting rock on this brief walk.

The highlight of the monument is a chance to watch the American Indian craftsmen cut, carve, and polish the pipestone into ceremonial pipes and other articles, many of which are for sale in the gift shop. The visitor center, rest rooms, and most of the trail are wheelchair accessible. Open daily 8:00 A.M. to 5:00 P.M. with extended hours during the summer and the Song of Hiawatha Pageant weekends. Admission is $3.00 per person ($5.00 per family); 16 and under free. Call (507) 825–5464.

LUNCH: Instead of turning right on Hiawatha as you leave the monument, continue straight 1 block and go right on U.S. Highway 75. Follow the highway past East Main Street to **Lange's Cafe.** Lange's hasn't served as many generations as the Calumet, but it's just as solid a fixture in Pipestone. At Lange's everything is served twenty-four hours a day, including breakfast; everything is homemade, including the ice cream; and everything is reasonably priced. You can order a grilled cheese sandwich ($1.50), a taco salad (about $5.00), and every form of hamburger, chicken, or fish. Lange's has every appetite and preference covered. Call (507) 825–4488.

Afternoon

Head back to the Historic District and park in the lot behind the Calumet Inn. The entrance to the **Pipestone County Museum,** 113 South Hiawatha, is directly across the street. This is a great museum with exhibits on the region, American Indian history and culture, and life in nineteenth-century Pipestone. A highlight for children of all ages is a mechanical buffalo from the movie *Dances with Wolves,* helping depict Indian life on the plains. Open daily 10:00 A.M. to 5:00 P.M. and until 8:00 P.M. on pageant days. Admission: adults $3.00; children 12 and under free. Call (507) 825–2563.

Before you leave the museum, pick up the brochure *Pipestone: Past and Present* and take yourself on a walking tour of the Historic District. The stories behind the buildings are fascinating, and this will be a great way to explore the shops and the town at the same time.

DINNER AND LODGING: Historic Calumet Inn.

Day 3 / Morning

BREAKFAST: Historic Calumet Inn.

Stop by Lange's Cafe on your way out of town and order a nonperishable (if you forgot to bring your cooler) lunch to go. Include a few homemade cookies and some fruit, and you'll have a great picnic lunch to enjoy in **Blue Mounds State Park,** another one of those "best-kept secrets," about 20 miles southeast of Pipestone. Follow U.S. Highway 75 through Pipestone straight south to County Road 20 and go left to the entrance of the park. Signs will also direct you. This is an unusual arrangement in which the park and the interpretive center have separate entrances; the park has been added on to, bit by bit, for more than sixty years, and the idea to connect the two areas was abandoned in order to protect the virgin prairie. The entrance to the interpretive center is a couple of miles farther south on Highway 75 and then left on County Road 8.

Despite its Glacial Mound and the 90-foot cliff that attracts rock climbers, Blue Mounds State Park is best known as one of the largest prairie parks in Minnesota. It even has a buffalo herd grazing the grounds. The herd should be visible from the Mound Trail. Be careful if you hike that way, and don't provoke or tease the bison; they are in a contained pasture but can be unpredictable.

Enjoy your lunch and take advantage of the 13 miles of hiking trails or the swimming beach, but keep in mind that the best is yet to come.

Return to Highway 75 and continue south, and follow the signs down County Road 8 to the interpretive center. Yes, it is the Frank Lloyd Wright–looking house high up on the bluff. The building was once the home of author Frederick Manfred, whose studio was in the penthouse. The onetime home is attached to the cliff—as you will see in the center—by the raw quartzite–formed interior walls. It's the view you've come for, though. Look south and enjoy the prairie vista. Who would have thought that farmland could be so beautiful? For a panoramic view and access to the mysterious man-made line of rocks that lines up with the sunrise on the equinoxes, hike behind the visitor center to the outcropping of rock called **Eagle Rock.**

The park is open 8:00 A.M. to 10:00 P.M. A $4.00 vehicle permit is required for the day unless you have an annual pass. Call the park (507–283–4892), the interpretive center (507–283–4548), or the Department of Natural Resources (612–296–6157 or 800–766–6000; TDD 612–296–5484).

Instead of retracing your steps to Pipestone, you can follow U.S. Highway 75 a few miles south to connect with I–90, then head east to U.S. Highway 169 or I–35 and turn north to go home.

There's More

Camping. Blue Mounds State Park (507–283–1307) and Split Rock Creek State Park (summers only), 6 miles south of Pipestone off State Highway 23 (507–348–7908), offer standard state park facilities, including full hookups, flush toilets, and showers. Sites range from $12 to $15. A park permit is required for each. For reservations at either, call (866) 85PARKS; www.stayatmnparks.com.

Civil War Reenactments. The Thirteenth U.S. Infantry, Company D, holds reenactments in Pipestone during mid-August of every even year. Call (507) 825–2563.

Family Aquatic Center, 510 Sixth Street Southeast, Pipestone; (507) 825–SWIM. The pool features a 126-foot waterslide, water play, and lap lanes. Volleyball courts and concessions are also available. Admission: adults

$4.26, children 5 and up, $3.20, seniors and observers $2.13; 4 and under $1.60.

Hermann Monument, Center and Monument Streets, New Ulm (507–359–8344), is a 102-foot monument to the ancient soldier Hermann, who defended Germany and defeated the Romans nearly 2,000 years ago. Open daily Memorial Day through Labor Day 10:00 A.M. to 4:00 P.M. Admission to the park is free. One dollar per person is charged to climb to the top of the monument—more than worth it for the spectacular view.

Live Music and Theater. The Pipestone Performing Arts Center, 104 East Main Street; (507) 825–2020 or (877) 722–2787; www.pipestone.mn.us. Superb entertainment in a nostalgic setting. Whether you're watching the Calumet Players in a drama or singing along with the Inkspots, the evening is well worth it. Ticket prices depend on the artist/performance. Check with the Historic Calumet Inn for lodging/theater specials.

Morgan Creek Vineyards and Winery. Take U.S. Highway 169 to State Highway 68 toward New Ulm. Before New Ulm, follow County Road 47 to County Road 101 South; the vineyard is the first farm on the left. Tours and tastings from May to December, Monday through Saturday 11:00 A.M. to 9:00 P.M., Sunday noon to 6:00 P.M. Call (507) 947–3547.

Winter Alternatives

Snowmobiling. There are 100 miles of groomed snowmobile trails near Pipestone, including 7 miles in Blue Mounds State Park. Call Hiawatha Sno Blazers; (507) 825–3906.

Special Events

April. Minnesota Festival of Music, New Ulm; (507) 354–7305. Celebration of Minnesota musicians featuring bluegrass, country, and more. Admission is charged.

June. The Watertower Festival, Pipestone; (507) 825–3316. Features an arts, crafts, and antiques show, a street dance, and other entertainment.

July. Heritage Fest, New Ulm; (507) 354–8850; www.heritagefest.org. A parade, ethnic food, European musicians, children's activities, and more. Admission charged.

The Laura Ingalls Wilder Pageant, "Fragments of a Dream," Walnut Grove; (507) 859–2174. Admission is charged.

July through August. Song of Hiawatha Pageant, Hiawatha Club, Box 1B, Pipestone, MN 56164; (507) 825–4126 or (507) 825–3316. The internationally recognized pageant, with its cast of 200, has been bringing Indian legend to life for more than fifty years. Song of Hiawatha pageant grounds are near Pipestone National Monument. Admission: $8.00 per person; children 7 and under free.

August. Buttered Corn Day, Allison Park, Sleepy Eye; (507) 794–4731 or (800) 290–0588. Children's rides, music, and all the free buttered corn you can eat.

Founder's Day Festival, Pipestone; (800) 336–6125. A pedal tractor pull for kids, bed racing, international foods, American Indian dancing and pipe making, sack races, a barbershop quartet, and a hoedown.

August through September. Emma Krumbee's Annual Apple Jubilee, Belle Plaine; (952) 873–3006. Apple picking, hayrides, pony rides, games, and crafts. Admission charged.

September through October. Annual Great Scarecrow Festival, Emma Krumbee's, Belle Plaine; (952) 873–3006. Includes pumpkin picking, games, and a scarecrow contest. Admission charged.

October. Oktoberfest, New Ulm; (507) 354–4217 or (507) 359–2941. Includes musical entertainment, ethnic food, and a crafts show. Admission charged.

November through December. Annual Festival of Trees, Calumet Inn, Pipestone; (507) 825–5871 or (800) 535–7610. A display and contest of beautifully decorated Christmas trees; donations go to charity. Activities include Christmas caroling and horse-drawn wagon rides.

Other Recommended Restaurants and Lodgings

New Ulm

Deutsche Strasse Bed and Breakfast, 404 South German Street; (507) 354–2005; www.deutschestrasse.com. A B&B is a rare find in New Ulm, and this 1893 Victorian is within walking distance from downtown. A room for two with a private bath and a full breakfast—served on the porch—runs $89 a night in summer.

Holiday Inn New Ulm, 2101 South Broadway; (507) 359–2941 or (800) HOLIDAY. Amenities include a pool, whirlpool, sauna, exercise room, game room, restaurant, and lounge. A poolside room for two is about $90 to $105.

Pipestone

The Arrow Motel, 600 Eighth Avenue Northeast; (507) 825–3331. The Arrow is a clean, classic by-the-roadside motel. Accommodations include cable television (including HBO), an outdoor pool, and a continental breakfast. Double occupancy, April through October, is $38.

Gannon's Restaurant and Lounge, the junction of Highways 23, 30, and 75; (507) 825–3114. The restaurant is famous for its Sunday brunch and its Buff Burger, a hamburger with everything on it (about $5.00). Gannon's also features homemade soups and pies and offers fine dining choices, from barbecue ribs to a nineteen-ounce T-bone steak (about $10.00). Open daily 6:00 A.M. to 1:00 A.M.

St. Peter

The Country Pub, State Highway 22 South; (507) 931–5888. Rumor has it that this once may have been a speakeasy. Although nothing documents that bit of gossip, every rumor you've heard about the good food is true. This is fine dining in a casual atmosphere out in the country overlooking a private creek.

Ruttles Grill & Bar, 605 South Minnesota; (507) 931–6464. Ruttles offers 1950s decor, complete with a checkerboard floor and a classic-car theme on its menu. It serves "America's Foods in a Celebration of the Open Road." Menu items include buffalo burgers, Texas chili burgers, and Hollywood cobb sandwiches, all under $6.00. The highlight is the top-it-yourself Boppers: hamburgers and an extensive condiment bar. Open Sunday through Thursday 11:00 A.M. to 11:00 P.M., Friday and Saturday 11:00 A.M. to 1:00 A.M.

Sleepy Eye

W. W. Smith Inn, 101 Linden Street Southwest; (507) 794–5661 or (800) 799–5661. The wealth of banker William Watkins Smith is evident throughout this magnificent home, built at the turn of the twentieth century and now on the National Register of Historic Places. The extraordinary curved veranda offers just a hint of the grandeur inside. The interior rooms are ornately trimmed in both cherry and oak and adorned with original Steuben glass and Tiffany lamps. There are five rooms available. Three have private baths, and one is the carriage house suite, set in the gardens, with a private whirlpool. A full breakfast, served in the formal dining room, is likely to be quiche, French toast, or old-fashioned biscuits and gravy. A stay here will make you feel like royalty. Rates range from $75 to $125, depending on the room and length of stay.

For More Information

New Ulm Area Chamber of Commerce/Visitors Information Center, 1 North Minnesota Street, New Ulm, MN 56073; (507) 354–4217 or (888) 463–9856; www.newulm.com.

Pipestone Chamber of Commerce/Visitors Information Center, U.S. Highway 75 and State Highway 23, Pipestone, MN 56164; (507) 825–3316 or (800) 336–6125; www.pipestonestar.com.

St. Peter Area Chamber of Commerce, Tourism and Visitors Bureau, 101 South Front Street, St. Peter, MN 56082; (507) 931–3400 or (800) 473–3404; www.st-peter.mn.us.

Sleepy Eye Area Chamber of Commerce and Convention and Visitor's Bureau, 108 West Main Street, Sleepy Eye, MN 56085; (507) 794–4731 or (800) 290–0588; www.sleepyeyenews.com.

The North Shore: From Duluth to Grand Marais

North-By-Northeast

3 Nights

Utter the words "the North Shore" in a roomful of people, and the "aah"s will move through the crowd like ripples on water. Some people will recall the burnt-orange hues of fall foliage, others the views from the tops of mountains while skiing or hiking, and for others, well, it's memories of the hot tub after skiing or hiking all day.

Technically the North Shore is the 646-mile stretch along the western and northern shores of Lake Superior from Duluth to Sault Ste. Marie, Ontario, Canada. It consists of one road (State Highway 61, changing to Provincial Highway 17 in Thunder Bay, Ontario), numerous little towns that are sometimes no bigger

☐ Hiking

☐ Wildlife

☐ Woods

☐ Lake Superior

than a grocery store, tremendous lodgings, lots of woods, state and provincial parks, and, of course, endless views of Lake Superior.

It's easy to turn a visit to the North Shore into a weeklong vacation, but three nights will give you a good taste of the scenic North Woods, whether it's solitude, family time, recreation, or romance that you're seeking. Keep in mind, too, that no matter how remote the North Shore may seem, it's popular both winter and summer, and you *will* need reservations, even to camp.

Day 1 / Morning

Pack a picnic lunch before you head out, and plan to enjoy it on the grounds of **Split Rock State Park.** Pick up I–35 and follow it north to Duluth, then follow State Highway 61 north out of Duluth, about forty-five minutes, to Split Rock State Park near Two Harbors. The whole drive should take three and a half to four hours.

LUNCH: Split Rock State Park is one of the finest state parks in

Minnesota and is a beautiful spot for lunch. A $4.00 permit is required to enter the park, unless you have a valid annual pass. During lighthouse hours proceed directly to the lighthouse and purchase tickets for the tours, which will include a vehicle permit for the rest of the park. Parking and picnicking areas are available at the base of the lighthouse. The park is open daily 8:00 A.M. to 10:00 P.M.; the lighthouse is open daily mid-May through mid-October 9:00 A.M. to 5:00 P.M. Lighthouse tour prices: adults $8.00; seniors 65 and over, $7.00; children $6.00. The maximum family rate is $12.00. Call the park at (218) 226–6377 or the historic site at (218) 226–6372.

Afternoon

The lighthouse tour includes the lighthouse, the restored keeper's quarters, the fog signal building, and admission to the museum. Between the lighthouse and the keeper's quarters is access to the trail that leads below the cliff, the vantage point from which the famous pictures of the Split Rock Lighthouse are shot. Don't forget your camera!

After you leave Split Rock, continue north to Lutsen, about forty-five minutes from the park. Lutsen is an incorporated township, but to tourists, it's a village of ski resorts with some of the best accommodations in the state. Unlike many other Minnesota resort areas that have summer-season-only activities and often close for the winter, Lutsen is a winter retreat that has made clever use of its natural resources for the summer.

DINNER AND LODGING: Lutsen Resort, on the shore of Lake Superior, will be just what you hoped for: a honey-colored rustic lodge with a huge fieldstone fireplace, a cozy room, and good food. It's a great place to curl up and read a book, watch the snow fall outside, or retreat to after a full day of activity. The dining room provides fine dining in a casual atmosphere from 5:30 to 9:00 P.M. Lutsen Resort is famous for its cuisine, with good reason. Entrees range in price from $11 to $25, and it will be very hard to decide between the grilled Atlantic salmon with squash and a cream sauce; the shrimp linguine tossed with olive oil, garlic, and artichoke hearts; or the oven-roasted chicken with wild rice, just to mention a few. A room for two with a lakeside view, midsummer, is $145 per night. Facilities also include an indoor pool, a golf course, jogging paths, and tennis courts. Townhomes and log cabins are other lodging options. Call (218) 663–7212 or (800) 258–8736; www.lutsenresort.com.

Day 2 / Morning

BREAKFAST: Enjoy your breakfast in the dining room between 7:30 and 11:30 A.M. With the golden glow of the pine logs, it will seem as if the morning sun is shining inside the lodge; it's a splendid way to start your day on the North Shore. Choose from Ingie's buttermilk pancakes, Lutsen pecan cakes, Lutsen's famous raisin rye French toast, or even a breakfast burrito (all between $4.00 and $6.50).

Eat heartily and then head to **Lutsen Mountains** for a surprisingly fun summer day on the slopes. Your best bet is to buy an all-day activity pass for $27 (children 6 and under ride free with a paid adult), and keep in mind that some of the resorts offer packages with their accommodations. The all-day pass will allow you unlimited rides on the gondola, which takes you to **Moose Mountain** for biking and hiking, and unlimited rides up the chairlift to **Eagle Mountain** and down the alpine slide, a half-mile contoured slide down the mountainside. It takes about ten minutes to reach the summit by chairlift and about two minutes to come down. The gondola, used to transfer skiers in the winter, transfers bikers— and their bikes—up to the trails and back during summer. The miles and miles of trail range from beginner to advanced and are well marked, just like the ski hills. If you didn't bring your own equipment, a variety of bikes and helmets is available for rent. A front-suspension bicycle runs about $36 per day. Hiking is also an option. Open 10:00 A.M. to 6:00 P.M., weather permitting.

LUNCH: Take a breather and stop for lunch at the **Mountain Top Deli** on the top of Moose Mountain. If you've been spending the morning on the alpine slide, you'll have to switch over to the gondola to ride up to the top. The deli has a small variety of sandwiches, such as chicken salad, ham, and turkey (about $5.00), and soup and chili (about $2.45 and $2.95 a bowl, respectively).

Afternoon

Resume your afternoon on the mountain. If you've been sliding all morning, maybe it's time to go for a walk. The mountains have trails that range from 0.5 mile of easy walking to 6 miles of moderate terrain to 3 miles of a strenuous uphill climb.

DINNER: Stop at **Papa Charlie's,** at the base of the mountains in the parking lot. Constructed of knotty pine inside and out, Papa Charlie's is

Split Rock Lighthouse, Split Rock State Park

the perfect place to relax. The extensive menu ranges from sandwiches such as pepper-jack chicken (about $6.00) to filet mignon (about $18.00), with homemade soups, pastas, and pizzas in between. Veranda seating overlooks the Poplar River, Moose Mountain, and the gondola. There is also a full bar, dance floor, and a stage that hosts musical groups such as Lamont Cranston, The Jayhawks, and Mango Jam. Sit back and enjoy your evening. Call (218) 663–7800 or (218) 663–7281; www.lutsen.com/papacharlies.

LODGING: Lutsen Resort.

Day 3 / Morning

BREAKFAST: Skip the idea of a hearty breakfast and head north to Grand Marais to the little red building on the corner of Wisconsin Street, home of the **World's Best Donuts.** For more than twenty years this family business was known as The Donut Shop, but with so much return business and comments such as "these are the world's best doughnuts," the owners felt compelled to change the name a few years ago. The walls are filled with snapshots and testimonials from locals, summer regulars, and people just passing through. If you buy one of their mugs, you have to have your picture taken where you use it—whether it's Duluth, England, or your own kitchen table, and mail your photo back to the shop. The specialty is the Skizzle, a close relative of the elephant ear, but soft and often served warm. Open late May through September 7:00 A.M. to 1:00 P.M. on weekdays, until 4:00 P.M. on weekends. Call (218) 387–1345.

Grand Marais is the last town before the Canadian border, and also the start of the **Gunflint Trail.** Get your doughnuts and eat them in the car as you drive the trail, once an old logging route and now a scenic passage that offers access to camping and the Boundary Waters Canoe Area Wilderness. The Gunflint Trail offers one of the best opportunities to see moose and other wildlife along the North Shore.

LUNCH: Return to Grand Marais for lunch at the **Angry Trout,** State Highway 61, between Fourth and Fifth Avenues West, an exceptionally popular restaurant described by some aficionados as Lucia's meets the North Shore—avant-garde and rustic at the same time. The Angry Trout is in the heart of town, right on the edge of Lake Superior overlooking the harbor. The simple yet sleek wood-and-glass interior has the look of an art gallery. It's no surprise that the works of local artists, from carvings to pottery to watercolors, are displayed on a rotating basis. Even the chairs were locally made. The masterpiece, of course, is the view of Lake Superior through walls of glass, and the food is not only good, but very interesting. The Angry Trout specializes in fish and is well known for smoked foods and homemade potato chips. The menu includes salads (the wild rice salad is excellent), and prices range from $6.75 to $19.00. Open daily for lunch and dinner 11:00 A.M. to 7:30 P.M., May through mid-October. Call (218) 387–1265.

Afternoon

Wander the streets of Grand Marais and, if weather permits, walk out to the lighthouse. Then continue your trip north, about 15 miles, to one of the best-kept secrets of the North Shore.

DINNER AND LODGING: The **Naniboujou Lodge and Restaurant** was built in the 1920s as an exclusive men's club, with Jack Dempsey and Babe Ruth among its first members. The club idea failed during the Depression, and the lodge was used and abandoned by several different groups over the years. Now, beautifully restored right down to the brightly painted Cree wall decorations and rare light fixtures, the lodge offers excellent food and superb accommodations just a stone's throw from Lake Superior. Dinner is served in the old Great Hall, where many of the furnishings, including the chandelier (suspended from the 25-foot ceiling) and the largest fieldstone fireplace in the state, are original. The organic menu, with homemade breads and locally grown salad greens, has an Italian flair. The French onion soup with salad and French bread is a meal in itself ($8.00), but if you're hungrier than that, try the fabulous linguine a la carbonare with chicken, asparagus, mushrooms, and sun-dried tomatoes in a garlic cream sauce (about $15.00). Open every day mid-May through mid-October, weekends only the rest of the year, with special packages from late December through mid-March. A cozy room for two with a fireplace runs $95 per night. Call (218) 387–2688 or www.naniboujou.com.

Day 4 / Morning

BREAKFAST: Start your morning with another incredible Naniboujou meal: blueberry flapjacks, orange-pear waffles, or French toast (about $5.00).

After breakfast cross the road to the woods for a hike to the mysterious **Devil's Kettle,** a waterfall about 1 mile into the woods. When the water is rushing, there are actually two falls: one whose route is visible, and one whose outlet has yet to be discovered (or so the story goes, despite the number of Ping-Pong balls and other objects used to try to track the stream).

Hike back to the lodge and enjoy just sitting in one of the colorful Adirondack chairs looking out at the lake, collecting lake-washed rocks in unique shapes and sizes, or skipping the flat ones as far as you can; you'll feel like you have all the time in the world.

LUNCH: Enjoy another meal at the lodge before you head home. This time, try the Naniboujou chicken salad with fruit or the trapper's flatbread—grilled French bread topped with a basil pesto sauce and herbed cheese—both about $7.00.

There's More

Camping. Grand Marais Recreation Area RV Park and Campground

(State Highway 61 before you get into town; 218–387–1712 or 800–998–0959) has full hookups, bathhouses, a marina, and playground. Primitive camping is available throughout the Superior National Forest: Isabella Ranger Station (218–323–7722) or Kawishiwi (Ely) Ranger Station (218–365–7600). Call (800) 280–CAMP for reservations. The state parks of Split Rock (218–226–6377), Tetagouche (218–226–6365), and Gooseberry Falls (218–834–3855) have excellent camping. Call (866)85PARKS for reservations; www.stayatmnparks.com.

Canoeing. Daytime and evening guided canoe trips are offered by the Gunflint Canoe Company, Grand Marais, departing from the Coast Guard station. Brunch or lunch is included during the day trip. Open mid-June through August. Rates for a morning trip with brunch: adults $30; children 12 and under $20. Call Cascade Lodge for reservations; (218) 387–1112. Many other outfitters offer equipment rentals and guided tours. Call (218) 387–2524 or (888) 922–5000 for more information.

Golf. Superior National Golf Course, State Highway 61, Lutsen; (218) 663–7195. They say Superior National is so beautiful, "it's hard to keep your eye on the ball." The course offers eighteen holes, great views, and glimpses of wildlife. Many resorts offer golf packages. The Gunflint Hills Golf Course and Driving Range (218–387–9988) offers nine holes and is located 4 miles up the Gunflint Trail from Grand Marais.

Grand Marais Playhouse, Broadway and County Road 7; (218) 387–1036. More than twenty-five years old, this theater presents regional and local talent, comedy to drama, from early June through mid-October. Performances are presented in the Arrowhead Center for the Arts.

Kayaking. Superior Coastal Sports (on the shore between the East Bay Hotel and Best Western Hotel) offers sales, rentals, and guided tours. Tours start at $40 per person. Open late May through late September. Call (218) 387–2360 or (800) 720–2809; www.superiorcoastal.com.

Superior Hiking Trail. Superior Hiking Trail Association; (218) 834–4436. Boundary Country Trekking; (800) 388–4487 or (218) 388–4487; www.shta.org. The Superior Hiking Trail is about 200 miles of path winding up and down through the wilderness from Two Harbors to the Canadian border. Camping is available along the route for the hard-core hiker, but several of the resorts and lodges participate in "Lodge to Lodge Hiking."

Winter Alternatives

Skiing and Snow-tubing. Lutsen Mountains, State Highway 61, Lutsen; (218) 663–7281;www.lutsen.com. Celebrating more than fifty years of winter fun with seventy-two runs, Lutsen has elevations of more than 1,000 feet above sea level, chalets, a gondola, a lighted tubing run, and luxury accommodations.

Snowmobiling. The 154-mile State Trail is accessible from many smaller trails in the area; some are accessible from resorts. Call the Minnesota Department of Natural Resources; (218) 834–6600, (218) 834–4005, or (800) 554–2116.

Special Events

August. Juried art exhibit, Grand Marais Art Colony; (218) 387–2524 or (888) 922–5000.

Other Recommended Restaurants and Lodgings

Grand Marais

The Cascade Lodge, State Highway 61 in the woods of Cascade River State Park; (218) 387–1112 or (800) 322–9543; www.cascadelodgemn.com. Dating from the 1930s, complete with a fieldstone fireplace, the lodge rents rooms and cabins and houses a family-style restaurant. Open all year. Rooms range from $77 to $146 a night; cabins range between $91 and $220 a night during peak season.

The Gunflint Motel, 101 West Fifth; (218) 387–1454. Located at the start of the Gunflint Trail on the edge of town, this is an older motel with small-town charm and deluxe rooms. Rates run $59 to $89, depending on the unit; some have kitchenettes. Open all year, with reduced rates in the winter.

Sven and Ole's Pizza, 9 West Wisconsin Street; (218) 387–1713. *The* pizza place in Grand Marais; also home to the Pickled Herring Lounge. Summer hours: 11:00 A.M. to 10:00 P.M. every day. Winter hours: 11:00 A.M. to 9:00 P.M. Sunday through Thursday, 11:00 A.M. to 10:00 P.M. Friday and Saturday.

Lutsen / Tofte

Bluefin Bay, State Highway 61, Tofte; (218) 663–7296 or (800) BLUEFIN; www.bluefinbay.com. Motel suites, townhomes, and condominiums with a variety of rates depending on the season are offered. A standard guest room with a lake view runs about $159 on a weekend night in the summer; a townhome, with a whirlpool, fireplace, and view of the lake, runs about $299. The restaurant serves breakfast, lunch, and dinner with fine dining choices. Dinner entrees run $18 to $32.

Eagle Ridge, Lutsen Mountains; (218) 663–7284 or (800) 360–7666; www.lutsen.com/eagleridge. Eagle Ridge has a variety of accommodations, from studio units to three-bedroom suites. Some have whirlpool tubs. Rates can almost double from midweek in the summer to a weekend in the winter. A studio for two, with a whirlpool, on a peak weekend in the summer is $129 per night. Keep in mind that there is a two-night minimum on weekends and a three-night minimum on holidays. Smoke and pet free.

For More Information

Grand Marais Chamber of Commerce, 15 North Broadway, Grand Marais, MN 55604; (218) 387–2524 or (888) 922–5000; www.grandmarais.com.

Lutsen–Tofte Tourism Association, State Highway 61, Box 2248, Tofte, MN 55615; (218) 663–7804 or (888) 61–NORTH; www.mn-northshore.com.

Minnesota Department of Natural Resources, East State Highway 61, Grand Marais, MN 55604; wildlife (218) 387–3034; fisheries (218) 387–3057.

USDA Forest Service, Gunflint District, West State Highway 61, Grand Marais, MN 55604; (218) 387–1750.

Ely: A Boundary Waters Primer

Wilderness Headquarters

3 Nights

Saying you're taking a trip to the Boundary Waters is a little like saying you're taking a trip to South America. It sounds exotic and familiar at the same time, but it will promptly elicit the question "Which part?" from the more experienced traveler who has been there before. More than two million acres of water and woods make up the region known, on the American side, as the Boundary Waters Canoe Area Wilderness (the BWCAW) and, on the Canadian side, as Quetico Provincial Park, and there are currently eighty-six official points of entry, state-side alone.

☐ Wolves

☐ Fishing

☐ Dogsleds

☐ Cabins

Despite the official names, the area has always been the Boundary Waters, but for more than twenty years, it has been actively preserved as wilderness. If you plan to enter the *true* BWCAW, you should make reservations as early as February to get the location you prefer. About 200,000 visitors trek into the BWCAW each year, so entries and campsites have daily quotas and are monitored closely. Everyone needs a permit to enter; permits for overnight campers now have user fees. Permits are available at many locations and from ranger stations and "outfitters" (the well-informed, experienced canoe-travel planners who provide everything from advice to sleeping bags, including food and cooking equipment).

First-timers should definitely work with an outfitter, but they don't necessarily need guides; after all, permit purchasers are required to watch an educational video on the BWCAW. Most agree that entry points six and seventy-seven are good for beginners. (When planning, remember that ease is measured by number of portages, and portages are gauged by rods: One rod equals one canoe length.) In fact, entry seventy-seven, which takes you past the Hegman Pictographs, considered one of the finest

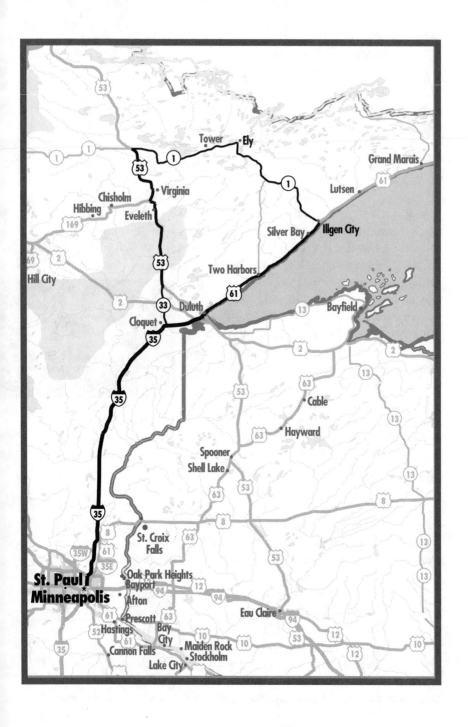

examples of original Native American inscriptions, is a good day trip. Probably the best approach for beginners is to stay at one of the resorts in the area that has access to the BWCAW, and get acquainted with the region slowly.

Staying at one of the many resorts around Ely may be enough of a wilderness experience for some visitors. Ely sits in the corridor of roads and other man-made structures in the heart of the BWCAW. Keep in mind that it is difficult to reserve a cabin or resort lodgings for less than a week in the prime season (mid-June through mid-August), but it's worth the call. If the motels and hotels only have weekend availability but aren't the wilderness environment you were hoping for, wait until fall. Ely is spectacular when the leaves start to change, and many of the resorts that stay open will allow shorter stays. No matter when you go, or how few days you may have, Ely is worth the trip.

Day 1 / *Morning*

Ely is about 260 miles north of the Twin Cities, and the route is not a straight shot. One way is to follow I–35 north to Cloquet, then State Highway 33 north to U.S. Highway 53 north, through the Iron Range towns of Eveleth and Virginia. You can also drive up the North Shore from Duluth and cut west at Illgen City. Whatever you do, you'll find yourself on State Highway 1, a back road, winding through the wilderness to get there. It is easily a four-hour drive, but it will offer you glimpses of eagles, bears, moose, and deer. Highway 1 turns into State Highway 169 and then becomes Sheridan Street as it takes you through downtown Ely, a town of about 4,000.

LUNCH: By now you're hungry. Head straight down Sheridan Street to **Sir G's Italian Restaurant,** 520 East Sheridan Street, a simple cafe serving hearty portions of classic homemade Italian food, including pizza, lasagna, and manicotti, all reasonably priced. Open 3:00 to 9:00 P.M. Call (218) 365-3688.

Afternoon

Take some time to wander through the town, and be sure to venture off the main street. You'll find gift shops and antiques stores scattered throughout Ely. Then, before checking in for the night, stop at the information center for area information and discount coupons for attractions.

(The center is at the intersection of State Highways 169 and 1.) Be sure to pick up a map for the **Echo Trail.**

DINNER AND LODGING: Silver Rapids Lodge Resort is north on State Highway 169, southeast on County Roads 58 and 16, about 5 miles out of town. It sits right on the road, but once beyond the office you'd never know it. A getaway spot since 1919, Silver Rapids offers camping, charming cabins, and several housekeeping motel units that have a rustic feel, overlook the lake, and are available on a nightly basis.

Knowing how hungry people get out in the wilderness, Silver Rapids Lodge serves just the kind of meal you'd expect: barbecue rib dinners with homemade sauce, walleye served three different ways, fish buffets on Friday nights, and prime-rib specials on Saturdays. Desserts include old-fashioned favorites such as bread pudding (it's wonderful), apple crisp, and chocolate cake. Dinners range from $10 to $20. The restaurant is open to the public, too, 11:00 A.M. to 9:00 P.M. daily.

Other Silver Rapids Lodge facilities include a fish house (for cleaning the catch), a game room, a laundry room, a "spa" with a hot tub and sauna, and a lounge. Rates vary, depending on the size of the room or cabin, season, and length of stay. A cabin for four in midsummer runs 870 to $1,250 for a week. The Lakeside Suites (motel rooms) run from $60 a night in the off-season to $126 midsummer. Open year-round. Call (218) 365–4877 or (800) 950–9425; www.silverrapidslodge.com.

Day 2 / Morning

BREAKFAST: There's no need to start driving again so soon after arrival. Stay put at Silver Rapids Lodge and enjoy orange juice, coffee, and one (or more) of the scrumptious homemade cinnamon rolls or muffins (about $3.50).

The **Dorothy Molter Museum,** State Highway 169 North, is just down the road from the resort and worth a visit. Dorothy Molter, affectionately known as the "Root Beer Lady," was the last person to live in the BWCAW. She was known for her hospitality (she ran the Isle of Pines Resort from 1948 to 1975) and for the thousands of bottles of homemade root beer she served to travelers. With support from friends, she defied the Wilderness Act of 1975 that banned residency in the BWCAW and was granted lifetime tenancy. She remained in the wilderness until her death in 1986. The museum consists of two of her cabins—moved log by log to Ely—full of her treasures, including the broken paddles left by canoeists that became her "picket" fence. Open Monday through Saturday 10:00 A.M. to 5:30 P.M. and Sunday noon to 5:30 P.M., weekends only during May and September. Admission: adults $4.00; children 6 to 16, $2.00; children 5 and under free. Family fee $5.00 maximum.

If you plan to tour the International Wolf Center, the Dorothy Molter Museum, and the Ely-Winton History Museum, buy a "master" ticket at any of the sites for $8.00 per adult. The discount is not offered for children.

LUNCH: A couple of blocks into town, on your right, will be the **Minglewood Cafe,** 528 Sheridan Avenue. The menu changes daily, offering a variety of ethnic foods in the course of the week. Mondays and Thursdays are Oriental, Wednesdays are Greek, Fridays are Mexican, and Saturday and Sunday offer a delectable surprise: chef's choice. Homemade soups and desserts are also available. Most items run about $6.00 to $7.00. Open Monday through Saturday 6:00 A.M. to 8:00 P.M., Sunday 6:00 A.M. to 2:30 P.M. Call (218) 365–3398.

Afternoon

Silver Rapids Lodge has boats for rent, and, supposedly, some of the best fishing is right in the channel. Life jackets are provided, and the fee for gas is based on use. Wear a lot of clothing, both for the dropping temperatures at night and to provide protection against the mosquitoes. If you go for the fish and don't catch anything, you might be disappointed, but if you go for the scenery and the chance to see deer—even mink— along the water's edge, you'll remember it forever.

DINNER: Silver Rapids Lodge.

Day 3 / Morning

BREAKFAST: Britton's Cafe, 5 East Chapman Street, for stuffed hash browns, cooked with ham and cheese (about $5.00). This friendly little cafe, with booths and an old-fashioned counter with stools, also serves omelettes and French toast for breakfast and hamburgers, fish and chicken fillet sandwiches, and other choices (including two daily specials) for lunch and dinner ($5.00 to $6.00). Britton's also has a huge selection of baked goods, including homemade pies. The arts and crafts on display are the works of local artists and are for sale. Open Monday through Saturday 5:00

Snow-covered cabin, Ely

A.M. to 7:00 P.M., until 2:00 P.M. on Sunday. Phone (218) 365–3195.

Before you leave, have Britton's pack you a picnic lunch and then take a drive down the **Echo Trail,** a 52-mile-long scenic route that leads to many points of interest and many points of access to the BWCAW. You don't have to drive all of it; in fact, the Ely guide takes you only as far as Mile 21, and only 10 miles are paved. (The rest of the trail is part of the USDA Forest Service, Cook, Minnesota.) The trail was changed into a road by the efforts of the Civilian Conservation Corps in the 1930s. Drive it slowly, bring your fishing rod, and take time to hike some of the trails. You will see wildflowers, berries, portages, old CCC camps, lakes, and animals. Then pick a spot for your lunch.

LUNCH: Your picnic basket.

Afternoon

Return to the Silver Rapids Lodge and enjoy the rest of your day; maybe try some more fishing or work up an appetite with a canoe ride.

DINNER: The Chocolate Moose, on the corner of Central and Main, has an atmosphere you'd expect to find in the North Woods, but food you thought you could only find in the city. The giant moose trophy and the wildlife prints are rustic accents to this almost elegant log cabin. The motto here is "casual dining, serious food." Dinner entrees include salt-rubbed, sesame-crusted salmon with cucumber salsa; buffalo strip steak with sun-dried tomato and rosemary butter; and chipotle chicken with corn bread stuffing. There is also an incredible wine list and a variety of beers, from microbrews to imports. Entrees range in price from $11 to $23. (Try the huevos rancheros or the smoked salmon with leeks for breakfast!) Open 7:00 A.M. to 9:00 P.M., until 10:00 P.M. on Friday and Saturday. Call (218) 365–6343.

Day 4 / Morning

BREAKFAST: Silver Rapids Lodge.

Before you head home, spend a couple of hours at **The International Wolf Center,** just east of town on State Highway 169. Exhibits include a fascinating history of the role the wolf has played in the life of mankind, from Roman times through the present. It explores the relationship between wolves and humans and even gives insight to the mind of your pet dog. A children's room has hands-on exhibits with pelts to touch and a chance to make a wolf mask. Kids can also make an origami wolf to string with others and symbolically join the effort to protect the still-threatened species. Of course, the highlight of your visit will be a chance to see the center's resident wolf pack, born into captivity about seven years ago. "Snacks" of dry dog food are tossed into the wolves' area, near the viewing windows, to lure the three females and one male from their den a few times a day. You can count on at least one of the wolves making an appearance. The center is open daily May through October 9:00 A.M. to 5:30 P.M. It is open Saturday and Sunday only from November through April, with reduced hours. Admission: adults $7.00; children 6 to 12, $3.25; seniors over 60, $6.00. Call (218) 365–4695 or (800) ELY–WOLF; www.wolf.org.

There's More

Ely

Arts. The Northern Lakes Arts Association, 30 South First Avenue East, Ely; (218) 365–5070. The association presents a summer full of music, theater, and dance. Admission depends on the program.

Golf. Ely Golf Course, 901 South Central Avenue; (218) 365–5932. Nine holes are surrounded by woods.

Hiking. Trails are as abundant as wildlife in the wilderness. Stop at the visitor center, 1600 East Sheridan Street, for trail maps, but if you are pressed for time and want a chance to hike in the wilderness, try the Trezona Trail, across from the International Wolf Center. It isn't completely secluded, but it is pretty, manageable (following an abandoned railroad bed), and short.

History. The Ely-Winton History Museum, located in the Vermillion Community College Complex, 1900 East Camp, has exhibits that include photographs, maps, and artifacts from the Ely area, with information from the time of the voyageurs through the development of ore mining to the present. There is also an impressive exhibit on the Will Steger and Paul Schurke Arctic expedition. Located just east of Ely on State Highway 169, the center is open daily 10:00 A.M. to 5:00 P.M. Memorial Day through Labor Day. Admission: adults $2.00; children 6 to 15, $1.00. Call (218) 365–3226.

Outfitters. There are several competent outfitters in the Ely area. Call the

Ely Chamber of Commerce (218–365–6123 or 800–777–7281) for names and full-color brochures.

Tower

Casino. Fortune Bay Resort and Casino, about 27 miles outside of Ely on County Road 77; (218) 753–6400 or (800) 992–7529. It is owned and operated by the Bois Forte Band of Chippewa.

Winter Alternatives

Cross-country Skiing. The Ely area abounds in cross-country ski trails. Some are groomed, some require fees, some are designated "classic" or "skate" only, and some, such as the Hegman and North Arm Trails, utilize BWCAW portages. Be sure to use caution on the lakes. Call (218) 365–6123 or (800) 777–7281 for maps.

Dogsledding. Wintergreen Lodge, Ringrock Road off County Roads 58 and 16, offers everything from training and lodge-to-lodge tours for beginning dogsledders to international treks through the snow for more experienced and adventuresome mushers. All equipment provided. Hosted by Paul Schurke, the modern-day Arctic explorer. Call (218) 365–6602 or (800) 584–9425.

Downhill Skiing. Giants Ridge, State Highway 135, Biwabik; (800) 688–7669 or (218) 865–4143. About 40 miles southwest from Ely, the resort has more than forty runs, rentals, a chalet, and lodging.

Ely is home to the 170-mile-long Taconite Trail (which heads west) and the 86-mile-long Tomahawk Trail (which heads east) that provide access to more than 1,000 miles of snowmobile trails in the region. Call (218) 365–6123 or (800) 777–7281.

Special Events

February. The Voyageur Winter Festival, Ely. Held during the month's first two weeks, it includes a powwow, snow sculpting, dogsled and reindeer sleigh rides, ski races, and more.

July. The annual Blueberry Arts Festival, Whiteside Park, Ely. An original art exhibit, handicrafts, ethnic foods and music, pancake breakfasts, and activities for children are included.

August. Loony Day, Ely; (218) 365–3141. Sidewalk sales and a loon-calling contest.

Embarrass Region Fair, Timber Hall, Embarrass. Mud run, crafts, and other events.

September. The Harvest Moon Festival, Ely; (218) 365–6123 or (800) 777–7281. Arts-and-crafts exhibits, ethnic foods, chainsaw carving, music, and more.

Other Recommended Restaurants and Lodgings

The Ely Steak House, 216 East Sheridan, Ely; (218) 365–7412. A classic steak house, it has an extensive menu, from appetizers (such as pickled herring, about $4.50) to sandwiches (such as the prime-rib crisper, about $7.00) and fine steaks (such as the twenty-two-ounce porterhouse, about $26.00). A children's menu is also available. Open daily 11:00 A.M. to 10:00 P.M.; the bar is open until 1:00 A.M.

Northern Grounds Cafe, 117 North Central, Ely; (218) 365–2460. Coffee and coffee drinks of all kinds, breakfast, lunch, and desserts.

Pine Point Lodge and North Country Canoe Outfitters, east of Ely a few miles from the intersection of State Highway 169 and County Roads 16 and 58; (218) 365–5581 or (800) 552–5581. Experts in service and advice, they offer one of the most complete brochures and outfitting packages for planning a BWCAW trip in the whole area. The rustic, clean cabins run between $675 and $1,025 a week, depending on cabin size and season. The resort is open from the first week in May to the last week in September and rents by the week only, except for the first two and last two weeks of the season.

Timber Trail Lodge and Outfitters, 5 miles down County Road 16 on Farm Lake, about 1.5 miles east of Ely on State Highway 169; (218) 365–4879 or (800) 777–7348; www.timbertrail.com. A full-service fishing resort. Depending on the cabin, weekly rates run from $835 to $1,600 during the peak season.

Timber Wolf Lodge, about 10 miles south of Ely on County Road 21, Superior National Forest; (218) 827–3512 or (800) 777–8457; www.timberwolflodge.com. Cabins here are nicely spaced in the woods and have full kitchens and private docks. They rent by the week in the summer and for a two-night minimum in the winter. A one-bedroom cabin with a fire-place on the lakeshore runs $675 to $800 a week.

The Trezona House Bed and Breakfast, 315 East Washington Street, Ely; (218) 365–4809. In this century-old mine superintendent's house, the four rooms are furnished according to themes: the Cabin, on the rustic side; the Miner, with twin beds and mine artifacts; the Hunter, with wildlife prints; and the Angler, with rods and reels. Rates run $85 to $110 a night and include breakfast, which features the "internationally acclaimed omelette," stuffed and covered with a potato sauce, an old Scottish recipe. Shared baths. Open all year.

For More Information

BWCAW Reservations, P.O. Box 450, Cumberland, MD 21501; (800) 745–3399; fax (301) 722–9808.

Ely Chamber of Commerce, 1600 East Sheridan Street, Ely, MN 55731; (218) 365–6123 or (800) 777–7281; www.ely.org.

Minnesota Department of Natural Resources, 1429 Grant McMahan Boulevard, Ely, MN 55731; (218) 834–6600.

USDA Forest Service: Isabella, State Highway 1, Isabella, MN 55607; (218) 323–7722. Kawishiwi, winter, 118 South Fourth Avenue East, Ely, MN 55731; (218) 365–7600; summer, International Wolf Center, State Highway 169, Ely, MN 55731; (218) 365–7681.

Stillwater

Where Past Meets Present

1 Night

Less than forty-five minutes from the Twin Cities, and with numerous residents who commute to work in Minneapolis or St. Paul, Stillwater is often considered part of the Twin Cities. For anyone living within the first-ring suburbs, however, Stillwater is a destination. And it's one of the best.

☐ Antiques

☐ Shops

☐ Victorian Homes

☐ Great Food

Known as the "Jewel of the St. Croix," scenic Stillwater also calls itself the "Birthplace of Minnesota," with a fairly complicated story behind the nickname. As part of Wisconsin Territory, booming Stillwater had once been expected to be the new Chicago. But in 1848, when Wisconsin gained statehood and its state boundaries were drawn, the tract of land between the St. Croix and Mississippi Rivers, where Stillwater lies, was excluded. The Territorial Convention that petitioned Congress to establish Minnesota Territory was held in Stillwater, and Stillwater then became part of Minnesota Territory.

From historic birthplace of the state to modern-day cradle of cultural and culinary arts, and with old architecture and thriving gift and antiques shops, Stillwater continues to grow and attract visitors—and settlers—as a prosperous river town.

Day 1 / Morning

The most scenic approach to Stillwater is from the south on State Highway 95. Follow I–94 east through St. Paul to the right-hand exit for Highway 95, then go left (north) through Bayport. Soon you will catch glimpses of the glistening St. Croix River. On a busy weekend, especially during the fall color change, the traffic slows long before you hit the edge of Stillwater. Don't panic about parking: Follow Main Street through town and park in one of the large public lots across the street from **Mill Antiques.** It will take all day to shop this antiques mecca, and the Mill is a good place to start. **Mulberry Point, Chelsea Rose Antiques,**

Country Charm Antiques, and the **Midtown Antiques Mall** are just a few more of the easily fifteen antiques shops in town. Other popular stores include **Kmitsch Girls,** a doll shop; **St. Croix Antiquarian Booksellers; Seasons Tique,** a Christmas store; and **J. P. Laskin,** filled with traditional North American goods.

LUNCH: The Dock, 425 East Nelson, has a great riverbank location. The nautical decor and lots of windows provide a perfect backdrop to great salads and unusual flavor combinations such as sautéed tomatoes and pea pods tossed with pasta and chicken. Try the wild rice soup! Outdoor seating is available. Lunch prices range from $7.00 to $14.00; dinner from $8.00 to $24.00. Open Monday through Thursday 11:00 A.M. to 10:00 P.M., Friday and Saturday until 11:00 P.M. Call (651) 430–3770.

Afternoon

Stop at **Tremblay's,** 308 South Main, or **Barbara Ann's,** 317 South Main, for some homemade fudge or other treats, finish shopping Main Street, and when you get back to Mill Antiques, walk a little farther north to **The Warden's House Museum,** 602 North Main Street. The house was built in 1853 and was home until 1914 to twelve wardens for the Minnesota Territorial State Prison. The building also houses the Washington County Historical Society. The museum has a military room with Civil War artifacts, a lumber room dedicated to the logging industry, and a prison room featuring photographs and artifacts of the Younger brothers, who spent twenty-five years in the Stillwater prison for their participation in an attempted bank robbery in Northfield, Minnesota. Allow about an hour. Open Thursday through Sunday 1:00 to 5:00 P.M. Admission: adults $3.00; children 6 to 16, $1.00. Call (651) 439–5956, or visit www.wchsmn.org.

DINNER: Queen Victoria's Restaurant, 101 Water Street South; (651) 439–6000. With white linens and lovely tableware, opulent Queen Victoria's serves anything but standard fare. The creole crab cakes ($6.95), the grilled chops and loin of lamb ($24.95), and pecan duckling ($23.95) are exotic favorites, but the menu also offers steaks, lobster, and pastas. The restaurant is located in the hotel that will provide your accommodations.

LODGING: The Lumber Baron's Hotel, 1 block off Main Street at 101 Water Street South, is the restored Lumber Exchange Building that was converted into a luxury hotel with a bar, restaurant, and complete banquet facilities. With its original elaborate tin ceilings and majestic interior pillars, the new Victorian decor looks splendidly natural. There are thirty-six rooms; each has a hand-carved mahogany queen-size bed, a gas fireplace, and a double whirlpool bath. Many of the rooms overlook the St. Croix River. Ten of the baths have original vault floors (many wealthy lumber barons exchanged money here), adding to the charm of the building's history. Weekend rates for two, including breakfast in Queen Victoria's, run between $139 and $199, with reduced rates Sunday through Thursday. Open all year. Call (651) 439–6000; www.lumberbarons.net.

Day 2 / Morning

BREAKFAST: Take your breakfast on the veranda, if weather permits, or downstairs in the breakfast room of Queen Victoria's. Breakfast choices may vary, but expect something such as an English malted waffle (about $5.00); the Baron's breakfast (about $7.00), which includes eggs, hash browns, and choice of meat; or a continental breakfast with homemade pastries (about $4.00).

Take a stroll along the river's edge, watch the boats, and relax. From the Lumber Baron's Hotel you're within a couple of blocks of Lowell Park, which has benches and picnic tables. Stop at **Brine's Bar and Restaurant,** 219 South Main Street; (651) 439–7556. Established in 1958, it is a Stillwater landmark. The extensive menu has something for everyone, and it's an especially good place to get a bowl of chili, a hot sandwich, or a hamburger. The bar is downstairs; the family restaurant is upstairs. Prices hover between $3.00 and $5.00, except for the more expensive dinner specials. Today, however, you'll want to order a bag lunch to go—a choice of just about any kind of sandwich, chips, a pickle, coleslaw, and a Brine's cookie (about $5.50)—and head to Pioneer Park for lunch.

LUNCH: Pioneer Park, high on the hills of Stillwater, has a wonderful view of the river. To get to the park, follow Myrtle Street 2 blocks up the hill to Second Street. Go right, the equivalent of about 5 blocks, to Laurel Street (which goes to the left), and you will be at the entrance to the park.

Afternoon

If you have time, take an afternoon tour on the **Stillwater Trolley,** 400 Nelson Street. Narrated tours last forty-five minutes and take you past the prison and sawmills and then up into the hills to see some of the lumber-

Main Street shopping, Stillwater

baron mansions. It's a great way to spend a leisurely afternoon before you head home. Open mid-May to November 1, running every hour from 10:00 A.M. to 5:00 P.M. Fare: adults $9.00; seniors $8.50; children 14 or under $6.00. Call (651) 430–0352; www.stillwatertrolley.com.

There's More

Biking. Park-and-ride takes on a new meaning if you park your car near Lake Phalen in St. Paul and bike 17 miles of the Gateway Trail to Stillwater. Pick up Gateway Trail (also known as Willard Munger Trail) at the north end of Lake Phalen in Phalen Regional Park, Arcade Street and

U.S. Highway 61. Follow the trail 15.3 miles east to Pine Point Park on County Road 55. Stillwater proper is a couple of miles southeast of the park. Call (651) 430–1938.

Camping. William O'Brien State Park and Afton State Park have camp-sites. A vehicle permit is required. Call William O'Brien, (651) 433–0500; Afton, (651) 436–5391; for reservations, (612) 922–9000 or (800) 246–CAMP.

River Cruises. Two-hour-long lunch and dinner cruises depart from the waterfront just south of the Dock Cafe, on an old-fashioned paddle wheeler on the St. Croix River. Fare: adults $16.50 to $30.00; children 5 to 12, $14.00 to $25.00. Call Andiamo Enterprises, (651) 430–1236; www.andiamo-ent.com.

Train Rides. The *Minnesota Zephyr,* 601 North Main; (651) 430–3000 or (800) 992–6100. This famous dining train travels for a little more than three hours through the St. Croix River valley and includes a perfor-mance of the Zephyr Cabaret. Open all year.

Washington County Historic Courthouse, 101 West Pine Street; (651) 430–6233. Visit Minnesota's oldest standing courthouse, listed on the National Register of Historic Places. This is also an excellent source of his-toric information about Stillwater.

Winter Alternatives

Cross-country Skiing. There are 18 miles of trails in Afton State Park (651–436–5391) and 11 miles of trails in William O'Brien State Park (651–433–0500). There are also 10 miles of groomed trails along the Gateway Trail between St. Paul and Stillwater. The Gateway trailhead is in Pine Point Park, a couple of miles west of Stillwater (651–430–1938).

Downhill Skiing. Afton Alps, Afton; (651) 436–5245; www.aftonalps.com. Forty-one runs, snow-tubing, four chalets, rentals, and lessons.

Special Events

Contact the City of Stillwater Chamber of Commerce (651–439–4001; www.stllwtr.com/chamber) for more information on the following events:

February. Brine's Annual Bocce Tournament.

March. St. Croix River Annual Eagle Watch.

April. Washington County Antique Show and Sale.

May. Victorian Tea and Open House at the Wardens House Museum.

Mother's Day Victorian Homes Tour and Tea.

June. Washington County Antique Show and Sale.

Stillwater Art Crawl.

Taste of Stillwater.

ID Club Annual Hot Air Balloon Rally.

July. Music on the Waterfront Concert Series begins.

St. Croix Garden Tour.

Lumberjack Days.

Washington County Fair.

August. Teddy Bear Tea at the Warden's House Museum.

St. Croix Valley Kennel Club Dog Show and Obedience Trial.

September. Rivertown Restoration Annual Home Tour.

Wild Rice Festival at St. Mary's Church.

Stillwater Bike Classic Bike Tour.

October. Fall Colors Fine Art and Jazz Festival at Lowell Park.

International Antiquarian Book Fair.

November. Victorian Christmas at the Historic Courthouse.

December. Victorian Holiday Celebration.

Victorian Bed-and-Breakfast Inn Tour and Tea.

Stillwater *Nutcracker.*

Other Recommended Restaurants and Lodgings

Best Western Stillwater Inn, 1750 West Frontage Road off State Highway 36; (651) 430–1300 or (800) 647–4039. The inn has a unique Scandinavian decor and offers its guests a pool, spa, and continental breakfast. About $72 per night for two.

The Brunswick Inn, 114 East Chestnut Street; (651) 430–8111; www.brunswickinnstillwater.com. The Brunswick has an unassuming exterior that looks modest against its Victorian neighbors, but the service, accommodations, charm, and especially the food are not. The inn is filled with antiques, all rooms have fireplaces and whirlpools (ranging in price from $135 to $165), and a gourmet breakfast is delivered to your door in the morning.

The James A. Mulvey Residence Inn, 622 West Churchill Street; (651) 430–8008 or (800) 820–8008; www.jamesmulveyinn.com. This is a majestic bed-and-breakfast in an 1878 Italianate home and carriage house. Each room has a private bath with a double whirlpool tub; two rooms have balconies. A four-course breakfast is offered. The menu changes constantly, but it features foods such as homemade scones, chocolate-dipped strawberries, and eggs Benedict. Bicycles are available for guest use. Open all year. Rates run from $99 to $199, depending on the day and the season.

The Lowell Inn, 102 North Second Street; (651) 439–1100. Dubbed the "Mount Vernon of the West," the inn offers twenty-one rooms and three restaurants. Its menu includes numerous seafood selections such as king salmon béarnaise ($26.95) and rock lobster tail ($39.95) and many beef and poultry items. Weekend packages for two, including breakfast each morning and dinner, start at $209.

Savories, 108 North Main Street; (651) 430–0702. This European bistro and cafe, with its charmingly elegant atmosphere, features gourmet food from scratch, including hearth breads and salad dressings, and numerous organic and vegetarian selections. Lunches are less than $10; dinner entrees range from $14 to $20. Open Monday through Friday 10:30 A.M. to 9:00 P.M., Saturday and Sunday 8:00 A.M. (for breakfast) to 9:00 P.M.

The Supreme Bean, 402 North Main Street; (651) 439–4314. This great little cafe is wedged between antiques stores and offers a pleasant reprieve from the hard work of antiques hunting. You can design your own vegetarian sandwich for about $4.50 or simply sip espresso while you regenerate for more shopping. Open 7:00 A.M. to 7:00 P.M. Monday through Saturday, until 6:00 P.M. on Sunday.

The William Sauntry Mansion, 626 North Fourth Street; (651) 430–2653 or (800) 828–2653; www.sauntrymansion.com. The mansion clearly housed one of the wealthiest families in Stillwater. Today it's one of the finest bed-and-breakfast inns in the state. The furnishings and decor are breathtaking, the dining table dates from the original family, and, if asked, the current owner will be happy to play the harpsichord for you. Breakfast delights include homemade breads and rolls, baked quiches, an apple pancake dish, and fruit soups. All rooms have a private bath (two of them are separate, but just down the hall); weekend rates run from $139 to $199 per night. Open all year.

For More Information

Greater Stillwater Chamber of Commerce, P.O. Box 516, Stillwater, MN 55082; (651) 439–4001; www.ilovestillwater.com.

Park Rapids

Forest Gateway

2 Nights

A hundred years ago most of the people drawn to the woods around Park Rapids were loggers and farmers. Those industries continue, but today most of the people who come to this area are supporting the business of tourism. And it's thriving. There are more than 300 lakes in the vicinity, abounding in walleye, muskie, bass, and numerous fish stories.

Park Rapids boasts hundreds of resorts, good shopping, a neighboring town known as the "restaurant capital of the world," homemade chocolates, a main street movie theater, the oldest paved railroad bed/bike trail in the state, and easy access to Itasca State Park.

☐ Fishing
☐ Dining
☐ Biking
☐ Shopping

There is plenty here to fill a weekend, but keep in mind that this is a resort community, and most resorts typically rent week to week. To stay in a resort on the weekend, you'll probably have to visit in the off-seasons of May and mid-August through September. You can still have a great midsummer weekend, though, by choosing one of the B&Bs, hotels, or motels.

Day 1 / Morning

Get an early start so you can make the three-and-a-half-hour drive and be in Park Rapids for lunch. Follow I–94 west to Sauk Centre and exit into town following U.S. Highway 71 north, down Main Street, and out of town. Highway 71 will take you through Wadena and all the way to Park Rapids. A left on State Highway 34 will take you into downtown.

LUNCH: You'll be charmed by the **MinneSODA Fountain,** 205 South Main Avenue. Originally known as Schmider's, this place has been a soda fountain since 1922. With the checkerboard floor, the Coca-Cola memorabilia adorning the walls, great sandwiches, and menu items that make numerous Minnesota puns (like The Mega Malt: The Malt of America, $2.85), you can't help but enjoy yourself. The prices are great,

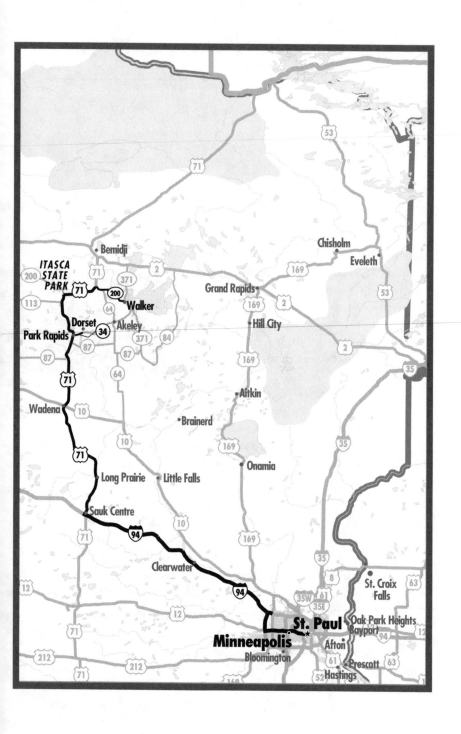

too. The most expensive sandwich is the Main Street Special, loaded with deli meats and cheeses for $5.95. Veggie options are also available. Summer hours: Monday through Saturday 10:00 A.M. to 10:30 P.M., Sunday noon to 5:00 P.M. Winter hours: Monday through Thursday 10:00 A.M. to 5:30 P.M., Friday and Saturday 10:00 A.M. to 10:00 P.M. Call (218) 732–3240.

Afternoon

As long as you're in town, you might as well get the local shopping out of the way. Downtown Park Rapids has a variety of good stores. **Aunt Belle's Confectionery,** 110 South Main, will be impossible to pass (even if you did just knock off a turtle sundae with hot fudge and caramel sauce at the MinneSODA). Aunt Belle's is an old-fashioned candy store with everything from caramels to turtles, but it specializes in real homemade fudge and hand-dipped chocolates. Mail order is also available. Call (218) 732–7019.

As you wander downtown, look for **The Trading Post,** 204 South Main, for good souvenirs; **Amish Oak,** 403 South Main, for Amish crafts and furniture; and **Ament's Bakery,** 203 South Main, where you might want to pick up some cookies for a snack later on.

DINNER: You've probably noticed the crowd bustling in and out of **Schwarzwald Inn,** the German restaurant on the corner of First Street and Main Avenue. This is the place to eat, especially if you like German food. Of course, the specialties are the bratwurst dinner ($5.15) and Wiener schnitzel ($7.95), but there are also chicken-fried steak, roast pork, and broasted chicken dinners (all between $5.50 and $7.50). The best part may be the choice of homemade noodles or real mashed potatoes and the homemade German bread. Open all year Monday through Friday 7:00 A.M. to 7:00 P.M., Saturday and Sunday 7:00 A.M. to 2:00 P.M. Call (218) 732–8828.

LODGING: On the north end of town, on the edge of the Fish Hook River, nestles **Gramma's Riverview Cabins,** 900 North Park Avenue, a handful of pale gray cottages with red shutters. It's not the usual lace and Victoriana; after all, this is the North Woods. Instead, its charm-filled log cottages with log interiors and nostalgic details make you feel at home— more like at your gramma's. Each cottage has cable television and a spacious private bath. It's 7 blocks from the Heartland trailhead and footsteps from the river. A fishing boat, paddleboat, and canoe are at your disposal.

Five units are open May through October; two winterized units are available all year. There is a three-night minimum on summer weekends. Double occupancy ranges from $70 to $100 per night. Call (218) 732–0987 or (888) 732–0987; http://customer.unitelc.com/grammasbb/.

Day 2 / Morning

BREAKFAST: Since each cozy cabin has a kitchen, you can make your own (gourmet or basic, your choice!) or grab some goodies from Ament's Bakery.

Treat yourself to a morning canoe ride on the Fish Hook River and then head to **Summerhill Farm** for some specialty shopping. Follow U.S. Highway 71 north about 7 miles to this collection of blue-gray buildings that look like seaport cottages. The five different shops, including the Stable and Carriage House, are full of unique gifts and shopping fun. Open mid-May through mid-September, Monday through Saturday 10:00 A.M. to 6:00 P.M., Sunday noon to 4:00 P.M. (The restaurant closes at 4:00 P.M.) Call (218) 732–3865.

LUNCH: Linger on **The Sun Porch** at Summerhill Farm for a light lunch. Choose from specialty sandwiches, quiches, and salads and save room for ice cream. The restaurant is reasonably priced, and lunch in the country will make you feel like you have all the time in the world.

Afternoon

The best way to spend the afternoon, and work up an appetite for dinner, is to go for a bike ride on the **Heartland Trail.** Head back to Park Rapids, but instead of returning to Gramma's, park your car in Heartland Park. To get to the park, take a right on Mill Street (north) and follow it to the park. You can rent a bike at Guerney's (about a block west of Mill Street, across the bridge on Beach Road) and pedal east.

You probably won't make it any farther than **Dorset.** Not because you'll be tired—Dorset is only 4 miles away—but because Dorset is one of the most pleasant surprises in the North Woods. It is the self-proclaimed "restaurant capital of the world" and boasts more restaurants per capita than any other city. With twenty-two residents and at least four places to stop and eat, it's probably true.

Dorset is a "we" town. If the store clerk says, "We open mid-May and close mid-October," that means the whole town (or most of it). The entire town also collaborates on an annual single-issue newspaper, the *Dorset Daily Bugle,* that pokes fun at itself and the Twin Cities, the source of most of its clientele. One edition commented on Dorset's skyline, the population boom, and things like domed stadiums, not to mention the famous fork and meatball in the Dorset Sculpture Garden.

For some reason, it seems that whenever restaurant owners have a good sense of humor, they tend to create good food, and Dorset is a prime example. So it won't hurt to be in town early for dinner. Dorset is no secret to resort-goers in this area; on weekends there can easily be a two-hour wait. So depending on when you arrive, put your name on the list at **Compañeros, La Pasta,** the **Dorset House,** or the **Dorset Cafe** (the only restaurant open all year), and then browse **The Antique Shop, Sister Wolf Books,** or **Woodstock North** for gifts, watch art in action at **Stained Glass Creations,** consider a boat at **Bob's Business,** or have an old-time photo taken at **Professor Nils,** and you will have done the town.

DINNER: The atmosphere at **Compañeros Restaurant** is just plain fun. The walls are bedecked with souvenirs, and salsa music plays in the background. The extensive menu features everything you could hope for in Mexican fare, from burritos to quesadillas, but the chimichanga wins the prize. It's filled with beef, refried beans, cheese, and tomatoes and then deep-fried and topped with Compañeros' own sauce and a dollop of sour cream. Olé! Combination dinners and specialties range in price from $6.00 to $10.00. Daiquiris and a large selection of Mexican beers are available. Open mid-May through mid-October, Monday through Thursday noon to 9:00 P.M., Friday and Saturday noon to 9:30 P.M., and Sunday noon to 8:30 P.M. Call (218) 732–7624.

On a pleasant summer evening, you may choose to wander the town with an ice-cream cone, bike a little farther on the Heartland Trail, or return to Gramma's for an evening boat ride.

LODGING: Gramma's Riverview Cabins.

Day 3 / Morning

BREAKFAST: Same as Day 2.

Park Rapids is considered the southern gateway to **Itasca State Park.** Although it's 20 miles north, it's worth the drive to Minnesota's oldest state park and a chance to step across the Mississippi River at its headwaters. Just follow U.S. Highway 71 north, all the way to the park. A $4.00 vehicle permit is required to enter the park unless you have an annual pass.

Drive to the headwaters, tiptoe across the river, drive the Wilderness Road, peruse the museum, and maybe even take a walking tour of the historic log buildings. This visit will probably whet your appetite for a longer one (see Minnesota Escape Thirteen), but if you're unsure of your return trip, at least stay in Itasca State Park long enough for lunch.

LUNCH: The Historic Douglas Lodge (218–266–2122) is a rustic lodge with a great dining room. The menu runs from a roast beef dinner (about $10) to Itasca walleye, a lodge specialty (about $16). The menu also includes several vegetarian entrees ($5.00 to $11.00). Wines, made in McGregor from hand-picked fruits and berries by Minnesota Grown, are available by the bottle.

There's More

Amusements. Evergreen Park, 10 miles north of Park Rapids on U.S. Highway 71; (218) 732–9609. The park has water wars, miniature golf, bumper boats, and batting cages. Open daily 10:30 A.M. to 6:00 P.M. from mid-June through September 1 (and weekends just before and after). Admission charged. Kartland, 1 mile east of Park Rapids on State Highway 34; (218) 732–9064. Go-carts, trail rides, a golf range, and petting zoo are offered. Wheelchair accessible. Seasonal; open 11:00 A.M. to 8:00 P.M.

Camping. Itasca State Park (218–266–2129) and Chippewa National Forest (218–335–8600).

Golf. Evergreen Lodge, 5 miles north on County Road 4, has nine holes and rentals; (218) 732–4766. Headwaters Country Club, 2 miles north on County Road 1, has eighteen holes, rentals, a pro shop, a driving range, putting greens, snacks, and beverages; (218) 732–4832. Eagle View, 8.5 miles north on U.S. Highway 71, has eighteen holes and rentals; (218) 732–7102. Brookside, on Two Inlets Lake, has nine holes, a club, and pull-cart rentals; (218) 732–4093.

Horseback Riding. BK Ranch, located about 15 miles north of Nevis on County Road 2; (218) 652–3540.

Winter Alternatives

Cross-country Skiing. Soaring Eagle, 8.5 miles north of Park Rapids on U.S. Highway 71, a groomed state trail, requires a pass. Call (800) 247–0054 for maps.

Snowmobiling. Hundreds of miles of trails go through Two Inlets and Paul Bunyan State Forests and Itasca State Park. Call (800) 247–0054 for maps.

Special Events

June. Paul Bunyan Days, Akeley; (218) 652–3230 or (800) 356–3915.

July. Annual Headwaters Rodeo; (800) JOKELA–1. Mid-Minnesota Annual Craft Fair. Annual Blueberry Festival, Lake George; (218) 266–3353.

August. Hubbard County Fair, Park Rapids. Taste of Dorset, Dorset.

September to October. Fall colors peak late September to early October.

Other Recommended Restaurants and Lodgings

AmericInn, State Highway 34 East; (218) 732–1234 or (800) 634–3444. Amenities include a pool and spa, complimentary continental breakfast, and a charmingly furnished lobby. A standard room for two on a weekend runs about $78.

Rapid River Logging Camp, Rapid River Logging, County Road 18, about 6 miles northeast of Park Rapids; (218) 732–3444. The camp serves breakfast, lunch, and dinner family-style at long logging tables. Logging demonstrations are given on Tuesday and Friday. Open Memorial Day weekend through Labor Day, 7:30 A.M. to 9:00 P.M. Reasonably priced.

The Red Bridge Inn, 118 North Washington; (218) 732–0481 or (800) 897–0366. This B&B offers a luxurious visit to the North Woods. All rooms have private baths (whirlpools are available); a country breakfast is included. Rooms range from $85 to $100 per night.

Wamboldt's, County Road 7; (218) 732–3012. North of Dorset and on Upper Bottle Lake, this is one of the area's original resorts. Today it is still a favorite family vacation spot. The rustic cabins have modern housekeeping amenities; rates include the use of a fishing boat. Cabins rent by the week; a one-bedroom cabin for two runs about $345.

For More Information

Park Rapids Chamber of Commerce, P.O. Box 249, U.S. Highway 71 South, Park Rapids, MN 56470; (218) 732–4111 or (800) 247–0054; www.parkrapids.com.

Itasca State Park

Little House in the Big Woods

2 Nights

It was Minnesotan Charles Lindbergh who said, in a speech from the steps of his boyhood home in Little Falls in 1973, "Parks symbolize the greatest advance our civilization has made." Minnesota has more than 200,000 acres of rivers, lakes, and woodlands preserved within sixty-eight state parks. Each one is unique, with a spectacular-natural-resource of a reason for being a state park, and each one is worth the visit.

☐ Woods

☐ Log Cabins

☐ Mississippi Headwaters

Lake Itasca (Itasca is a combination of two Latin words, *verITAS CAput,* meaning "true head") received its state park status on April 20, 1891, narrowly winning its place by one legislative vote at the height of the power of the lumber industry, when the area was worth a literal fortune in timber to the lumber barons. Today Itasca State Park is the oldest state park in one of the oldest state park systems in the country and includes a 2,000-acre virgin forest, the Itasca Wilderness Sanctuary, that stands as a natural monument to the North Woods.

Just about everyone knows that Itasca State Park is the location of the headwaters of the Mississippi. You may not know, however, that you don't have to camp to enjoy an overnight stay at the park. For as long as the park is old, guests have been staying in its rustic lodge and nearby cabins. The lodge has a full-service restaurant with a wonderful menu catering to those hearty North Woods appetites. It's no wonder reservations are made a year in advance: This is clearly a favorite getaway for many travelers.

Day 1 / Morning

Itasca State Park is about 225 miles northwest of the Twin Cities. Follow I–94 east to Sauk Centre and pick up U.S. Highway 71, going north. Follow Highway 71 through Wadena to Park Rapids.

LUNCH: Stop at the **MinneSODA Fountain,** 205 South Main

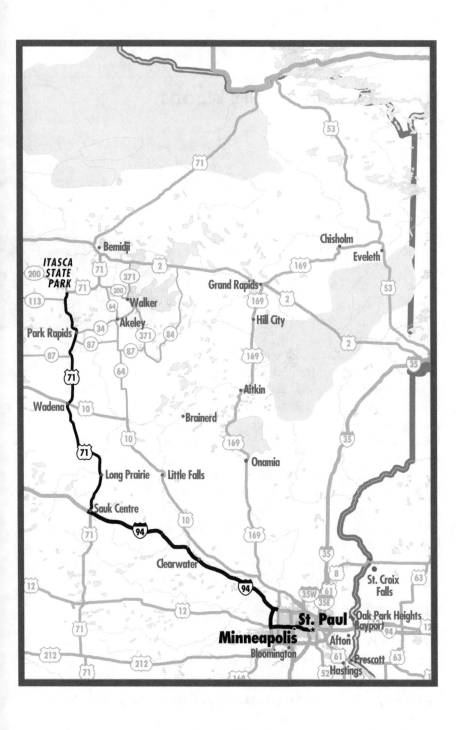

Avenue, Park Rapids, for a quick sandwich and a milk shake if you can't hold out until you get to the park. Call (218) 732–3240.

Afternoon

Continue north on U.S. Highway 71 to the east entrance of **Itasca State Park,** buy your permit, and continue to the **Historic Douglas Lodge** to register and unpack. Douglas Lodge is directly to your left after you pass the entrance gate. With a log-beamed ceiling and a fieldstone fireplace, the lodge is so majestically rustic, you'll feel as if you are staying with the Cartwrights on the Ponderosa.

DINNER: The menu at Douglas Lodge includes everything from a roast beef dinner (about $10) to Itasca walleye, a lodge specialty (about $16). The menu also includes several vegetarian entrees ($5.00 to $11.00). Wines, made in McGregor from hand-picked fruits and berries by Minnesota Grown, are available by the bottle.

LODGING: Douglas Lodge has guest rooms upstairs, with private or shared baths, for about $57 per night and $86 per night for a suite that will sleep up to four. There are several other cabins and lodgings on the grounds that date from the Civilian Conservation Corps and Veteran Conservation Corps projects of the 1930s. All are built of logs and have that rustic-woodsy feel. Some have fireplaces, and all, except the primitive Lake Ozawindib Cabin, have modern bathrooms. Staying in any of these will be luxury "camping." The one-bedroom cabins, with bathroom and fireplace for one or two people, run about $86 to $94 per night. Larger cabins are available. Both cabin numbers eight and eleven, outside Douglas Lodge, have a fireplace and will make you feel like you're in your own Little House in the Big Woods. Call (218) 266–2122.

Day 2 / Morning

BREAKFAST: Douglas Lodge. Enjoy a hearty North Woods breakfast and choose from omelettes ($3.25), pancakes, French toast ($3.95), or something simple, such as fruit and cereal ($1.60).

If you didn't bring your bike, head down to **Itasca Sports Rental,** on the west side of Park Drive, about 4 miles from the East Contact Station, and rent one for the day. It's the best way to enjoy the park. (A single-speed bike runs about $15 a day; you can arrange to pick it up the night before.) Follow the paved trail that leads to the headwaters of the

The headwaters of the Mississippi

Mississippi. It's a little more than 5 miles long. If you pick up the trail at Itasca Sports Rental, you're practically there. Pop your bike in the rack near the parking lot and tour the interpretive center, then follow the path behind the buildings over the little bridge and through the woods to what millions make the trek to see: the trickling headwaters of the Mississippi.

Only here can you step across "Old Man River," so slip off your shoes and let the water run over your feet as the "mite of the Mississippi" heads north (yes, north) to Lake Bemidji before it picks up steam and turns south. With shoes in hand, you can follow the stream around the bend to the little bridge; you'll recognize it as the one you crossed. Be careful going up the stone steps; they're pretty slippery.

LUNCH: If not lunch, then at least a snack. Backtrack to the **Brower Inn,** about 4.25 miles from the East Contact Station, for a sandwich or a light salad. It is open daily during the summer from 11:00 A.M. to 6:00 P.M.

Afternoon

Get back on the trail, go past the headwaters, and follow the **Wilderness Trail.** This 10-mile "trail" is a road that tours the north, west, and south sides of the park and is shared with motorized vehicles. The traffic travels slowly, but use caution. Your tour will take you past the oldest red and oldest white pines (about 300 years old) in the state. Stop and hike the short trails. If you feel up to it, climb the **Aiton Heights Fire Tower** for an aerial view of the park.

DINNER AND LODGING: Douglas Lodge.

Day 3 / Morning

BREAKFAST: Douglas Lodge.

Take time to enjoy the other historic buildings in the park. Pick up a *Historic Buildings Tour Guide* at the lodge or park entrance. **The Forest Inn** is considered one of the best works of the Civilian Conservation Corps and now houses a wonderful souvenir shop where you can select anything from an *Itasca Guide Book* to Douglas Lodge china. Arrange your walking tour in a loop to end at Douglas Lodge. There you can enjoy the lobby, peruse the books in the library, and sit in the original restored wicker furniture before, of course, grabbing some lunch prior to heading home.

There's More

Bike and Boat Rentals. Itasca Sports Rental offers bikes, boats, canoes, kayaks, paddleboats, and pontoon boats; in season (218) 266–2150, off-season (218) 657–2420; www.itascasports.com. The firm also features a well-stocked "vacation needs" store that includes everything from bait to sunscreen.

Boat Tours. Board the *Chester Charles* for a one-and-a-half-hour tour of Lake Itasca and follow the same route as the original explorers. You're likely to see both loons and bald eagles and are guaranteed great photo opportunities. Open late May to the end of the park season, with varied departure times. Fares: $8.00 per person; children 3 and under free. Call (218) 732–5318.

Camping. Itasca State Park (218–266–2100) has two campgrounds with 245 campsites, including 11 backpack or hike-in sites. About one hundred of the sites offer electricity. The hike-in sites are very primitive. Register at the Campground Registration Station, 2.5 miles north of the East Contact Station. Camping reservations are made by calling (866) 857–2757 or at www.stayatmnparks.com.

Museum. Follow the Itasca story. The museum is near the Brower Inn and the beach at the north end of the park.

Winter Alternatives

Itasca State Park. Thirty-one miles of cross-country skiing and snowmobiling, a warming house, and winter camping. A ski pass is required to ski on all trails in the state park system. Ski passes are $1.00 daily or $5.00 annually per person.

Special Events

June. The first Sunday in June is the Annual Minnesota State Park Open House. No vehicle permit required.

The Annual Ozawindib Walk. A fund-raiser that includes a 5K and 10K walk and a fun run. It follows the Ozawindib Trail deep into Itasca State Park. Registration fee; register at the Forest Inn.

July. Annual Butterfly Count and Hike. Learn to spot and record butterflies and their activities.

August. The Annual Snowsnake Games, Forest Inn. Make and use your own snowsnake. Prizes awarded.

September. The Annual Headwaters Bike Ride. Tours 100 miles of country roads between Lake Itasca and Park Rapids. Call the Park Rapids Chamber of Commerce; (218) 732–4111 or (800) 247–0054.

Other Recommended State Park Lodgings

Itasca State Park, Mississippi Headwaters Hostel, operated by Hostelling International, offers bargain accommodations for individuals and large groups. A kitchen is available. Write Mississippi Headwaters Hostel, HC05 Box 5A, Lake Itasca, MN 56460; (218) 266–3415.

St. Croix State Park, State Highway 48, Hinckley, MN 55037; (320)

384–6615. Guest house and camper cabins.

Tettagouche State Park, 5702 State Highway 61 East, Silver Bay, MN 55614; (218) 226–6365. On the North Shore, the park has beautiful newly restored camper cabins, hike-in only. The camper cabins are open year-round; in the winter it's snowshoe or ski-in only.

Wild River State Park, 39755 Park Trail, Center City, MN 55012; (651) 583–2125. Wild River State Park, near Center City, has camper cabins open year-round.

For More Information

All reservations for camping and lodging in the Minnesota State Park system are handled by calling toll-free (866) 857–2757 or at www.stayatmnparks.com. For wheelchair accessibility information on all parks, call (651) 296–6157 or (800) 766–6000.

Itasca State Park, U.S. Highway 71, Lake Itasca, MN 56460–9701; summer (218) 266–2114; winter (218) 266–2100.

Minnesota Department of Natural Resources, 500 Lafayette Road, St. Paul, MN 55155–4040; (651) 296–6157 or (800) 766–6000; TDD (612) 296–5484 or (800) 657–3929; www.dnr.state.mn.us.

Minnesota Office of Tourism, 100 Metro Square, 121 Seventh Place East, St. Paul, MN 55101–2112; (651) 296–5029 or (800) 657–3700.

MINNESOTA–WISCONSIN
ESCAPES

The Great River Road: To Winona and La Crosse

Highways and Byways

2 Nights

Sometimes there's nothing better than meandering. And if you like river towns, bluff country, antiques, and watching the sky for bald eagles, then there's nothing better than meandering the Great River Road.

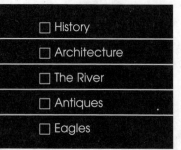

□ History

□ Architecture

□ The River

□ Antiques

□ Eagles

Of course, the Great River is the Mighty Mississippi, and the designated road is part of a national program, begun in 1938, designed to follow the Mississippi and its tributaries and provide tourists with access to recreation and sightseeing throughout the river valleys from Ontario, Canada, all the way to the Gulf of Mexico. Each of the ten states that flank the Mississippi has its own Riverway Commission offering information on local sights and recreation. In both Minnesota and Wisconsin, the Great River Road actually has two parts. In Minnesota there is a 430-mile-long national route that hugs the river and a 755-mile-long state route that wanders the countryside a little more. In Wisconsin the Great River Road follows the St. Croix River from St. Croix Falls to Prescott and the Mississippi River from Prescott to Dickeyville in the southwestern corner of the state.

The land changes as the Great River Road traverses a huge chunk of North America, but the opportunities remain vast. The route takes you through great scenery, whether it's forests or meadows, into wildlife refuges, up and over river bluffs, and near many lakes, equally luring the hiker, biker, boater, photographer, and sightseer.

Sometimes, too, the Mississippi takes you back in time as it ambles through historic river towns. Winona, Minnesota, and La Crosse, Wisconsin, are two such towns. Both are thriving college towns; both offer bluff vistas, historic sites, and river recreation; and together they make a wonderful weekend escape.

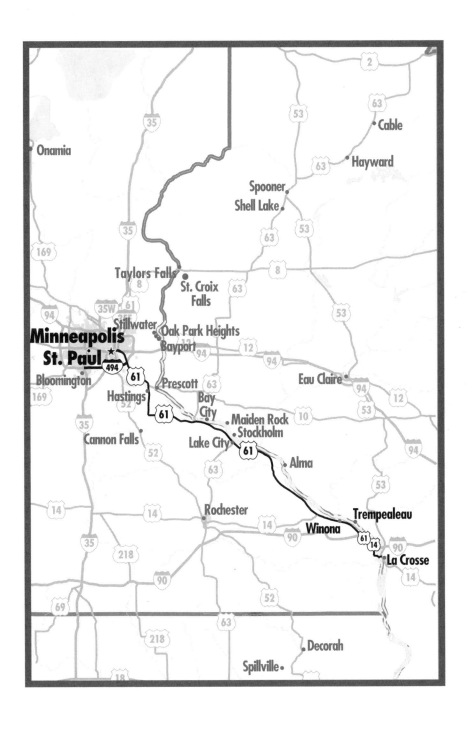

Day 1 / *Morning*

Follow I–494 to U.S. Highway 61 southeast of St. Paul, the Great River Road, and head south. The highway jogs away from the Mississippi River after Hastings but jogs back at Red Wing and then follows it closely all the way to Winona. At a distance of 120 miles, Winona is only about a two-hour drive from the Twin Cities, but you'll be hard-pressed to make the trip in that amount of time, especially if you like making spontaneous stops in little towns at gift shops and street-side antiques stores. You could spend hours browsing the shops in Red Wing alone.

If you drive straight through, you'll have time to overshoot Winona by about 5 miles and visit the **Bunnel House,** U.S. Highway 16/14, in the teeny town of Homer. (The dark brown house sits on a bluff to your right and is easy to miss, so watch for the signs.) Built in the 1850s, this steamboat Gothic-style house belonged to Willard Bunnel and his family, some of the first permanent settlers in the area. The museum offers insight to early pioneer life and also has a wonderful gift shop. Open Wednesday through Saturday 10:00 A.M. to 5:00 P.M. and Sunday 1:00 to 5:00 P.M., Memorial Day through Labor Day, and by appointment. Admission: adults $3.00; students 6 or older $1.00. Call (507) 452–7575.

Backtrack to U.S. Highway 61, go north back to Winona, and take a right on Huff Street. Huff Street takes you across Lake Winona to downtown, but first it passes the **Winona Visitor's Bureau** on the edge of town. Be sure to pick up a copy of *Winona's Glorious Glass,* a tour guide to the stained-glass windows in Winona, and a street map. The center is seasonal, open daily from April through October. Call (507) 452–2278.

LUNCH: Unless you've meandered so much that it's actually dinnertime, you must be hungry for lunch. Continue down Huff Street to Second Street, go right on Second Street to Center Street, and follow Center Street to the river's edge and the **Jefferson Pub & Grill,** 58 Center Street. This is a sports bar with great food and an extensive menu offering traditional favorites, from beer-batter onion rings ($3.00 for a half basket) to juicy Lucy hamburgers (about $6.50), and many dinner entrees, from pastas to walleye fillets (about $10.00). The Cajun chicken salad with honey mustard dressing (about $6.50) is top-notch! Open daily 11:00 A.M. to 1:00 A.M. Call (507) 452–2718.

Afternoon

You are in the heart of the historical district that abounds with antiques stores and gift shops. Browse them as you move block to block on a historic walking tour of the "island city," home to the largest collection of commercial Victorian architecture in this part of the Mississippi River Valley.

Steeped in the industries of flour milling and logging, and boasting both river and rail transportation systems, Winona was once a leading commerce center, frequently referred to as a "Gateway to the West." By the late 1800s it is said that Winona had more millionaires per capita than any other city in the country. Whether this is true or not, incredible wealth is still evident in the town's magnificent architecture. Even more intriguing than the number of Victorian mansions and tremendous churches and commercial buildings are the stained-glass windows adorning them. Winona may very well have more stained glass per capita, too.

From the Jefferson Pub & Grill you are within easy walking distance of four prime examples of stained-glass windows and their architectural hosts. Create your own tour by walking about 3 blocks southwest to the **Winona County Historical Society Armory Museum,** 160 Johnson Street, which has windows depicting the history of Winona. The museum is also one of the largest historical society museums in Minnesota and is worth visiting. Open Monday through Friday 10:00 A.M. to 5:00 P.M., Saturday and Sunday noon to 4:00 P.M. Admission: adults $3.00; students 7 or older $1.00. Call (507) 454–2723.

Continue west on Johnson to the **Winona County Courthouse,** at Third Street, which has nearly one hundred stained-glass windows. Although most are in private offices, at least twenty are visible to visitors. From Johnson go 1 block east to Main Street to the **Winona National Bank and Savings,** 204 Main Street. The windows in the bank, designed by George Maher, were made by Tiffany Studios in 1916 and include a skylight. Don't just step inside, though; the window in the entry needs to be viewed from the second-floor balcony. From the Winona National Bank, turn and head northeast, about 4 blocks, to **The Merchants National Bank,** 102 East Third Street. The Merchants Bank is one of the best examples of prairie-style architecture in the country. Typical of prairie style, straight lines and geometric shapes play a strong role in the design. In this building the geometric stained-glass panels, spanning more than

1,500 feet, are a major part of the structure. Again, don't just peek inside. Go up to the second-floor balcony for the full effect. If you're up to walking another 5 blocks or so, make the worthwhile trip east to the **J. R. Watkins Company Administration Building,** 150 Liberty Street. This building, also designed by Maher, is considered one of his masterpieces. The window over the main entrance depicts Sugar Loaf Mountain, Winona's famous bluff. The J. R. Watkins building also offers tours by appointment. Call (507) 457–3300.

The **J. R. Watkins Heritage Museum,** Liberty and Third Streets, has exhibits on the company's more-than-century-long business. Open Monday through Friday 10:00 A.M. to 4:00 P.M., Saturday 10:00 A.M. to 2:00 P.M. Free. Call (507) 457–6095.

The art of making stained-glass windows has been going on in Winona for more than a century. Today there are seven glass studios in the area. All are family businesses, and most have been handed down through numerous generations. If you're interested in seeing some artists at work, call **Conway Studios** (507–452–9209) or **Cathedral Crafts** (507–454–4079). The studios will give tours (groups only, $3.00 per person), but despite how large and costly a church window can be, these facilities are small and shouldn't be "dropped in on."

Allow time to visit **Latsch Island** and the **Boathouse Community** as you head to dinner. Take a right on Winona Street and follow it as it turns into State Highway 43 to cross the river and follow the signs to the island. After much ado, these floating houses have managed to earn their right to stay, although the island still isn't zoned for such residences. It's fun just to see the variety in design and the novelty of this "neighborhood."

DINNER: Retrace your route to State Highway 43, cross the river to the Wisconsin side, turn right onto State Highway 35, and head south about 4 miles to the **Hillside Fish House.** Set in the cliffs overlooking the Trempealeau Wildlife Refuge, this old railroad hotel still looks like a Wild West saloon. The atmosphere is uniquely casual, with its tall wooden booths for seating and fishing nets hanging from the ceiling, and the seafood is excellent. The shrimp, whether it's bacon-wrapped or the peel-and-eat kind (about $12 a pound), is a must. Walleye ($10), salmon ($11), and even frog legs ($11, any way you want them) are offered. If you don't like seafood, you can always order the chicken breast ($9.00 for two) or the New York strip steak ($12.00). The restaurant is small and fills up fast, though outdoor seating is available. Be sure to get a reservation to avoid a two-hour wait on weekends. Open Monday through Thursday 4:30 to 9:30 P.M., Friday and Saturday until 10:00 P.M. Call (608) 687–6141.

LODGING: Return to Winona on State Highway 43, which turns into Winona Street; take a right on Broadway, where just about every home appears to have B&B potential; and tuck in for a cozy night at **Windom Park Bed and Breakfast,** 369 Broadway. This bed-and-breakfast inn is unlike most: The style is colonial revival with hints of the arts-and-crafts movement, including a prairie-style billiard room. It is also a family home turned B&B, in which the furnishings and mementos have family meaning. Its warm decor will instantly make you feel like a friend of the family, but with three full floors, the house is big enough to get lost in. You might decide to do just that: hide out in your room, or curl up with a book in the billiard room. The rooms have private baths and range in price from $99 to $175 per night for two. Call (507) 457–9515; www.windompark.com.

Day 2 / Morning

BREAKFAST: A large continental breakfast is served in your room at Windom Park. You don't even have to get dressed!

No trip to Winona is complete without a visit to the bluffs. **Sugar Loaf Mountain,** the 585-foot-tall rock-topped bluff looming over town near the junction of Highways 14/61 and 43, is the most famous but is not accessible by tourists. For the best view—in fact, about a 60-mile panoramic vista—head to **Garvin Heights Park,** which is two or three bluffs upriver from Sugar Loaf Mountain. Follow Huff Street across Lake Winona, past the visitor's bureau, across U.S. Highway 61, and take a left on Lake Boulevard. Follow the signs that read SCENIC OVERLOOK. The road will take you to a parking lot; the overlook is on a paved path just 0.5 block farther. Don't forget your camera, but rest assured that if you never carry one, the scene will leave an indelible image in your memory.

The Mississippi River Valley is known for its bird-watching, but it's possible to travel the region, even tackle the bluffs, and not get a chance to spot a noteworthy bird. If you've been unlucky so far, make sure you drive through the **Trempealeau Wildlife Refuge** on your way to La Crosse. Retrace your route to last night's restaurant, following Winona Street across the river to Wisconsin. Take State Highway 35 south about 5 miles to the entrance to the refuge, on your right, and follow the several-mile-long circle drive. This 706-acre sanctuary is a haven to hawks, cuckoos, owls, geese, ospreys, and sandhill cranes. You might even see a bald eagle, especially in the morning or late afternoon. You are also welcome to pick the nuts and berries along the trail as a snack if you get hungry.

As you leave the refuge, turn right on State Highway 35 and continue south on the Wisconsin side of the river. The road will zigzag through little towns, including **Trempealeau.** Most of the original town of Trempealeau was destroyed in a fire in 1888. Six surviving buildings were moved to a new location and became the "new" downtown; they are now on the National Register of Historic Places. This is a little town with remarkably good restaurants and an old hotel.

LUNCH: Stop at the **Historic Trempealeau Hotel,** 150 Main Street, for a memorable lunch. The hotel overlooks the river, offering a great backdrop to an even better meal. This restaurant caters to vegetarians and is known for its walnut burger (about $6.00) made fresh on the premises, with ground walnuts, eggs, cheese, and spices, but its steaks, seafood, pastas, and fajitas (about $10.00) are also very good. If you're looking for something lighter, order a bowl of homemade broccoli-mushroom chowder (about $3.00) and dip into it with a homemade potato roll. Open Sunday through Thursday 11:00 A.M. to 5:00 P.M., Friday and Saturday until 10:00 P.M. Open Thursday through Sunday only, November 1 through March 31, 11:00 A.M. to 5:00 P.M. Call (608) 534–6898.

Afternoon

After lunch continue south to La Crosse, about a half hour beyond Trempealeau. Keep in mind that State Highway 35 turns into West Street and runs north and south through the center of La Crosse.

With more than 50,000 residents, La Crosse is about twice as big as Winona, and far more industrial, but it has the same river-town flavor and abundance of interesting architecture as its smaller Minnesota counterpart. It's not as easy to get around as Winona because of its size, but several large landmarks will help you keep your bearings: the **Cass Bridge,** the immense blue bridge that carries U.S. Highway 14/61 across the river and enters about the middle of the city; the Giant Six Pack (yes, it is really full of beer), trademark of the **City Brewery,** 1111 South Third Street, several blocks south of the bridge; and the river, which will always be to the west.

Follow West Street to State Street, go right toward the river, and drive into **Riverside Park.** Riverside Park is where the visitors bureau is located (stop in and get brochures and a copy of the *La Crosse Commercial*

La Crosse Riverwalk /Island Girl

Historic District Walking Tour), but it is also where the **La Crosse Queen** docks. The *La Crosse Queen,* a true paddle wheeler, is a replica of the boats that commanded the river at the turn of the twentieth century. During the main summer season, mid-June to September, the boat departs daily at 11:00 A.M. and 1:30 and 3:30 P.M. for sightseeing tours. The trip takes you upriver to **Lock and Dam #7,** under one of the few surviving railroad swing bridges, and the guide gives an entertaining account of history in the area and points out various wildlife and landmarks along the way, such as the island that Buffalo Bill Cody once owned, known today as **Pettibone Park.** Cruising the river is a pleasant way to spend the afternoon and seems a most appropriate way to tour a river town. Fares: adults $11.45; seniors over 60, $10.95; children 2 to 11, $5.95. It's best to call ahead; (608) 784–2893.

DINNER: Leave your car where it is and walk east through the park to **The Freighthouse Restaurant,** 107 Vine Street. The building, visible from the park, is the restored Milwaukee Road Freighthouse, a National

Historic Site. The atmosphere is rustic elegance, and the food is excellent. Children are more than welcome, but this also is a great place for dinner for two. The Freighthouse specializes in steaks and seafood (fresh fish is flown in every day) and its famous prime rib ($17 to $20), but vegetarian meals are also done well. Be sure to leave room for dessert! Homemade winners include grasshopper pie, carrot cake, and cheesecake. There is a full bar and live entertainment on the weekends. Open Monday through Thursday 5:30 to 10:00 P.M., Friday and Saturday 5:00 to 10:30 P.M., and Sunday 5:00 to 9:30 P.M. Call (608) 784–6211; www.freighthouserestaurant.com.

LODGING: After dinner head north of La Crosse to the small town of Onalaska and the **Lumber Baron Inn Bed and Breakfast,** 421 Second Avenue North, the 1888 dream home of prominent lumberman C. H. Nichols. The house sits on a beautiful bluff overlooking Lake Onalaska, which is part of the Mississippi River. Two favorite activities of inn guests are eagle watching and enjoying spectacular sunsets over the lake. Rates for double occupancy in one of the five rooms run from $79 to $119 per night. Call (608) 781–8938; www.wbba.org.

Day 3 / Morning

BREAKFAST: Lumber Baron Inn.

With good reason, Mark Twain called La Crosse a "choice town" in his book *Life on the Mississippi.* Not only do three rivers converge here, but the area is also surrounded by natural springs; this abundance of water brought numerous entrepreneurial opportunities. Job seekers started breweries, dealt lumber, and capitalized on river trade. In 1896 the town was booming.

Today, after more than one hundred years, the stately buildings Mark Twain admired are still standing, and La Crosse is promoting its **Downtown Historic District** with obvious pride.

The best way to enjoy this part of La Crosse is on foot, so now is the time to get out your walking-tour map, and don't worry about parking: Numerous lots and ramps are scattered throughout the district. You will probably want to concentrate your tour between Main and King Streets from the river to Sixth Avenue South in order to take in the **Pump House Regional Arts Center,** 119 King Street, and two relatively new and exceptional museums, **The Gertrude Salzer Gordon Children's Museum of La Crosse,** 207 Fifth Avenue South, and **The Museum of Modern Technology,** 149 Sixth Street South.

The Pump House, featuring visual and performing arts, is open Tuesday through Thursday noon to 5:00 P.M., Friday noon to 7:00 P.M., and Saturday and Sunday 10:00 A.M. to 3:00 P.M. Admission is free. Call (608) 785–1434; www.thepumphouse.com.

The Children's Museum has hands-on exhibits for children of all ages, including experiments with water, light, and medical wonders. Open Tuesday through Saturday 10:00 A.M. to 5:00 P.M., Sunday noon to 5:00 P.M., with extended Thursday hours through the summer. Admission is $3.50 per person. Call (608) 784–2652; www.childmuseum.org.

The Museum of Modern Technology is the newest addition to La Crosse's fine collection of museums. Exhibits cover everything from basic machines to space exploration and the atomic age and include national traveling exhibits from the Smithsonian Institution and a number of hands-on experiments in physics. An especially intriguing exhibit on American cycling history features bicycles from the mid-1800s to the 1950s, including a rare high-wheeler with the little wheel in the front instead of the back. Open Tuesday through Saturday 10:00 A.M. to 5:00 P.M., Sunday 1:00 to 5:00 P.M. Admission: adults $4.00; seniors and students $2.50; children 2 to 12, $2.00. Call (608) 785–2340.

LUNCH: If you haven't stopped at one of the restaurants in Historic Downtown, hop in your car and go east (away from the river) on State Street all the way to West Avenue to **Mr. D's Restaurant and Bakery,** a La Crosse landmark. This unassuming yet award-winning stop is on the corner of West Avenue and State Street. If you like ham-and-cheese sandwiches, order the duke's melt (about $5.00) for the world's best version of a classic. It includes grilled mushrooms, bell peppers, and sweet onions. The soups (about $3.00 a bowl) change daily and come with an original "puff bun," a muffinlike roll made with garlic, chives, and sour cream in the dough. Mr. D's, originally a doughnut shop, is still famous for doughnuts and fritters; you're bound to grab a couple for the road. Open Tuesday through Saturday 6:00 A.M. to 7:30 P.M. and Sunday 6:00 A.M. to 3:00 P.M. Call (608) 784–6737; www.mrdsrestaurant.com.

For a little different scenery from the route you followed south, take the Wisconsin Great River Road, State Highway 35, north through a variety of scenic river towns as you head home. You can cross back to Minnesota at Nelson, Wisconsin (to Wabasha, Minnesota) if you change your mind, or drive all the way to Bay City, Wisconsin (to Red Wing, Minnesota), or even wait until you're north of Hudson, Wisconsin, and cross back to Stillwater, Minnesota, to head into the Twin Cities.

There's More

Biking. There are 5.5 miles of paved bike trail around Lake Winona (507–452–2278 or 800–657–4972). The Great River State Trail covers 22.5 miles between La Crosse and Trempealeau, Wisconsin, traveling across bridges and through wetlands and wildlife refuges. Call the Wisconsin Department of Natural Resources; (608) 266–2621. Rental bikes are available at the Historic Trempealeau Hotel, 150 Main Street, Trempealeau; (608) 534–6898.

Camping. Prairie Island Campground, Winona (507–452–4501), near the Mississippi backwater area, 2 miles north of town on Prairie Island Road, has 200 sites, 80 of which offer electrical hookups. Grounds include showers and a deer park. Open April through November. Great River Bluffs State Park, Winona (the park, 507–643–6849; the DNR, 612–296–6157 or 800–766–6000), 16 miles south of Winona, has pull-through sites but no electrical hookups. A Minnesota permit is required. Perrot State Park (near Trempealeau; 608–534–6409) has hookups and is wheelchair accessible. A Wisconsin permit is required. Goose Island Park and Campground (5 miles south of La Crosse, on State Highway 35; 608–788–7018) offers more than 400 sites in a woodsy backwater area of the Mississippi River. Amenities include a store, playgrounds, and electrical and water hookups. Rates from $11 to $15 per night.

Canoe Rentals. Canoes are available at the Historic Trempealeau Hotel (150 Main Street, Trempealeau; 608–534–6898) for about a two-hour trip on the Mississippi backwaters. Goose Island Campground, La Crosse (608–788–7018), rents canoes for Mississippi backwater excursions.

Golf. Westfield Golf Course, 1460 West Fifth Street, Winona (507–452–6901), has nine holes, a pro shop, and refreshments. Cedar Valley Golf Course, 7 miles southeast on U.S. Highway 14/61, right on County Road 9, Winona (507–457–3241), has nine and eighteen holes, a driving range, pro shop, and restaurant.

Museums. The Polish Cultural Institute, 102 Liberty Street, Winona (507–454–3431), chronicles Polish history and preserves Polish culture. Open May through November, Monday through Friday 10:00 A.M. to 3:00 P.M., Saturday 1:00 to 3:00 P.M. Closed on Sunday. Donations suggested. The La Crosse County Historical Society/Hixon House, 429 Seventh Street, La Crosse (608–782–1980), was built in the 1860s by Gideon Hixon, a local but well-traveled lumber baron. Open daily, summer only. Admission: adults $4.00; seniors $3.00; children 12 and under $2.00; family rate $12.00.

Shopping. The historic districts of both towns offer the best shops and antiques stores. Don't miss the R. D. Cone Antiques Mall, 66 East Second Street, Winona, or Historic Pearl Street (the 200 block) and the Antique Center (110 South Third Street) in La Crosse.

Winter Alternatives

Cross-country Skiing. Saint Mary's University, 700 Terrace Heights, Winona (507–452–4430), offers 14.5 miles of groomed trails for all levels. Whitewater State Park, State Highway 74, Altura, Minnesota (507–932–3007), and Great River Bluffs State Park, Winona County Road 3, Winona (507–643–6849), each offer about 14 miles of groomed trails. A pass, available at each park office, is required. Call (800) 766–6000. There are 5 miles of trail in Goose Island Park, State Highway 35 just south of La Crosse, and 8 miles along the Great River Trail, near La Crosse; (800) 658–9424.

Downhill Skiing. The nearest slopes to Winona are at the Coffee Mill Ski Area, Wabasha, Minnesota (612–565–2777), about 30 miles north of town on U.S. Highway 61, which offers ten runs, a chalet, ski school, and rentals. Mt. La Crosse, Old Towne Road, La Crosse (800–426–3665), has eighteen slopes and runs for every level. Facilities include three chairlifts, ski instruction, and a chalet.

Ice-Skating. La Crosse has several outdoor skating rinks with warming houses. Call (608) 782–2366 or (800) 658–9424.

Snowmobiling. There are literally hundreds of miles of snowmobile trails crisscrossing the Mississippi River Valley in the Winona and La Crosse areas. For information in Winona call (507) 452–2272 or (800) 657–4972; in La Crosse call (608) 782–2366 or (800) 658–9424.

Special Events

March. Eagle Watch, departs from Quality Inn, Winona, Minnesota; (507)

452–2272 or (800) 657–4972. Includes a lecture the week before and a tour bus upriver to open water near Reads Landing. Admission: adults $8.00; children under 12, $4.00.

June. Sand Burr Days, La Crosse, Wisconsin; (608) 782–2366, (608) 782–4082, or (800) 658–9424.

Winona Arts and River Festival, downtown Winona.

July. Quilt Show, Winona; (507) 452–2272 or (800) 657–4972.

Steamboat Days, Winona; (507) 452–2272 or (800) 657–4972. Usually coincides with the Fourth of July and includes a carnival, parades, a beer garden, and fireworks.

Riverfest, Riverside Park, La Crosse; (608) 782–2366 or (800) 658–9424. Features magicians, music, food, contests, and fireworks.

Catfish Days, Trempealeau, Wisconsin; (608) 534–6780. Includes arts and crafts, a flea market, music, a parade, food, and more.

Art Fair on the Green, University of Wisconsin–La Crosse; (608) 782–2366, (608) 782–4082, or (800) 658–9424. Original art show and sale.

Jazz Festival, Lake Winona, Minnesota; (507) 452–2272 or (800) 657–4972. Free outdoor concert featuring regional musicians in the pavilion.

September. Victorian Fair, Levee Park, Winona; (507) 452–2272 or (800) 657–4972. Includes old-fashioned baseball games, home tours, The Victorian Promenade, sidewalk museums, food, and handicrafts.

Applefest, La Crescent, Minnesota; (507) 895–2800 or (800) 926–9480. Just across the river from La Crosse, the event includes live entertainment, carnival rides, food, a crafts-and-flea market, tours of orchards, and apple specialties.

September to October. Oktoberfest, La Crosse; (608) 782–2366 or (800) 658–9424. Parades, music, carnival, ball, craft show, and food.

November. Swan Watch, departs from the Best Western Riverport Inn and Suites, Winona; (507) 452–2272 or (800) 657–4972. Includes a lecture on Saturday evening and a bus tour the following Sunday upriver to Alma, Wisconsin, to a popular feeding area. Admission: adults $8.00; children under 12, $4.00.

Rotary Lights. Figurines and thousands of lights illuminate Riverside Park in La Crosse.

December. Victorian Christmas, Levee Park, Winona; (507) 452–2272 or (800) 657–4972. Includes Victorian home tours, lighting of the Julius C. Wilke Steamboat Museum, and caroling.

Other Recommended Restaurants and Lodgings

Winona, Minnesota

Best Western Riverport Inn and Suites, 900 Bruski Drive; (507) 452–0606 or (800) 595–0606. The inn has a restaurant and pub, suites, private whirlpools, and an indoor pool and spa. A standard double occupancy room is $89; rates are reduced after November 1. A good-size continental breakfast is included.

Carriage House Bed and Breakfast, 420 Main Street; (507) 452–8256; www.chbb.com. Housed in an authentic three-story carriage house, all four rooms have private baths; two of them have gas fireplaces. Rooms range upward from about $80. A continental breakfast is included. Smoke free. Open all year.

The Golden China, on U.S. Highway 14/61 as you approach town; (507) 454–4261. Hunan, spicy food, chow mein, and sweet-and-sour dishes are the specialties here. Open daily 11:30 A.M. to 9:00 P.M., Friday and Saturday until 10:00 P.M.

The Green Mill, located in the Holiday Inn, 1025 U.S. Highway 61; (507) 452–5400. Famous for deep-dish pizzas, pastas, and salads. Open daily 6:30 A.M. to 10:00 P.M., to 11:00 P.M. on Friday and Saturday.

Winona Steak House, 3480 Service Drive; (507) 452–3968. This is a renowned steak house that serves chicken and seafood as well as numerous cuts of beef. The average tab at the buffet runs $7.00 per person. It has a large salad bar and also offers a children's menu. Open Monday through Thursday 11:00 A.M. to 9:00 P.M., Friday and Saturday 11:00 A.M. to 10:00 P.M., Sunday 8:00 A.M. to 9:00 P.M.

La Crosse, Wisconsin

Courtyard by Marriott, 500 Front Street; (608) 782–1000 or (800) 321–2211. A pool, hot tub, exercise room, restaurant, and bar are offered.

Double occupancy room, Sunday through Thursday, $89; Friday and Saturday, $109.

Digger's Sting, 122 North Third; (608) 782–3796. Located in the downtown historic district, it is a modern-day landmark. Although a little dated with its movie-influenced decor, Digger's is still serving great barbecue ribs, prime rib, and halibut dinners ($10 to $20). Open Monday through Friday 11:00 A.M. to 10:00 P.M., Saturday 4:00 to 10:00 P.M.

Hotel Radisson La Crosse, 200 Harborview Plaza; (608) 784–6680 or (800) 333–3333. Overlooking the river and Riverside Park, its amenities include restaurants, entertainment, a pool, and spa. Double occupancy starts at $120 per night. Wheelchair accessible.

Rudy's, corner of Nineteenth and La Crosse; (608) 782–2200; www.rudysdrivein.com. An authentic diner reminiscent of the 1950s, it even has roller-skating carhops! Rudy's is a family-owned business and a surviving tradition featuring homemade root beer. The food is fast, fresh, reasonable (hamburgers are about $1.20), and lots of fun. Open daily March through October 10:00 A.M. to 10:00 P.M.

Trempealeau, Wisconsin

The Historic Trempealeau Hotel, 150 Main Street; (608) 534–6898; www.trempealeauhotel.com. The hotel has eight rooms overlooking the river, offering a complete getaway from it all: no phones or televisions. It has shared baths. The adjacent Doc West House, though, has luxury suites with whirlpools and fireplaces. Hotel rooms run about $35 a night; the luxury suites run $100 to $125. Smoke free. As the town's hub, the hotel offers local tours, has canoe and bike rentals, and presents outdoor concerts from May through September featuring artists such as Arlo Guthrie and the Nitty Gritty Dirt Band. Call (608) 534–6898 for concert information.

Sullivan's Supper Club, Sullivan Road; (608) 534–7775. A fixture on Sullivan Road for more than thirty years, Sullivan's provides great family dining and a lot of fun. It is well known for its St. Patrick's Day and New Year's Eve celebrations. Enjoy cocktails on the deck overlooking the Mississippi River, then move inside for a salad bar and dinner, from tenderloin tips to batterfried shrimp. Don't forget to browse the Irish gift shop. Entrees are $10 to $11; all batters, dressings, sauces, and most importantly the Irish stew, are made from scratch. Open daily, except Wednesday, 5:00 P.M. (Sunday noon) to 8:30 P.M.

For More Information

La Crosse Area Convention & Visitors Bureau, Riverside Park, 410 East Veterans Memorial Drive, La Crosse, WI 54601; (608) 782–2366 or (800) 658–9424; www.explorelacrosse.com.

Mississippi River Parkway Commission, Pioneer Building, 336 North Robert Street, St. Paul, MN 55101; (612) 459–2560.

Trempealeau Chamber of Commerce, Inc., P.O. Box 212, Trempealeau, WI 54661–0212; (608) 534–6780.

Winona Convention and Visitors Bureau, 67 Main Street, Winona, MN 55987; (507) 452–2272; during summer, (800) 657–4972 or (507) 452–2278; www.visitwinona.com.

Lake Pepin Loop

85-Mile Splendor

1 Night

Lake Pepin, the widest part of the Mississippi River (at Lake City, Minnesota, and Pepin, Wisconsin), is bounded by Kellogg, Minnesota, and Alma, Wisconsin, on the south, and Red Wing, Minnesota, and Bay City, Wisconsin, on the north. This 26-mile-long beautiful expanse of water, surrounded by river bluffs, has been likened to Lake of Lucerne,

□ Bluffs

□ Barges

□ Buoys

□ B&Bs

Switzerland. Pretend that the bluffs are the Alps, Minnesota and Wisconsin are the cantons, and the little river towns that dot the banks are hamlets—sounds like a fantastic stretch of the imagination, but after a drive on either state's shore, especially in the winter when the "Alps" are snow-covered, you'll fall for it, too.

Traveling the 85-mile Lake Pepin Loop, like the St. Croix National Scenic Riverway (Minnesota/Wisconsin Escape Three), is more of a route than an itinerary, and it's a route that allows for some serendipity along the way. The truth is, you could drive straight through and be in Wabasha, Minnesota, within a couple of hours of leaving home, and do the rest of the loop in equal time. But it's hard to be in Wabasha by nightfall if you explore every town in between, stop at the overlooks, take a hike in a state park, or enjoy a riverside meal. So to do Lake Pepin justice and enjoy it fully, you need at least a couple of days. Each town has its own identity, history, and claim to fame. In fact, just about every little town could be a getaway destination in itself. There are a few things that remain constant as you go: The river is always there, the scenery is spectacular, and your hosts will be glad to have you.

Day 1 / Morning

Follow I–494 east of St. Paul to U.S. Highway 61 south. (You'll notice the green sign, a ship's wheel, that tells you you are also on THE GREAT RIVER ROAD.) Highway 61 follows the Mississippi River on the Minnesota side,

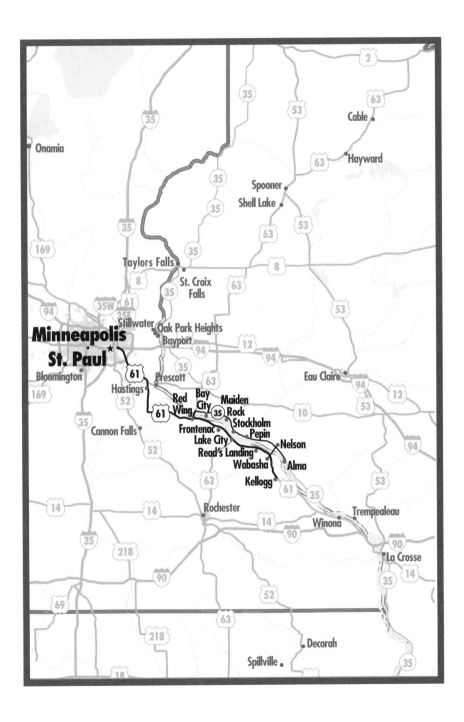

and State Highway 35 follows it on the Wisconsin side. Do keep in mind that, in this itinerary, there are only two places to cross the Mississippi: Wabasha, Minnesota, to Nelson, Wisconsin, and Bay City, Wisconsin, to Red Wing, Minnesota.

Less than an hour out of the Twin Cities is **Red Wing,** the first official town on the Lake Pepin Loop. Red Wing is most famous for Red Wing pottery, a desired collectible that includes the well-known sauerkraut crocks and water coolers (but not the colorful Fiesta Ware, a common assumption).

Before you get into town proper, you'll see a sign that reads POTTERY PLACE. Gift shops, restaurants, and antiques stores now occupy the thousands of square feet of the old Red Wing pottery plant. It's a must-stop for shoppers. To get there, turn left at the OLD WEST MAIN sign, a lighted intersection on U.S. Highway 61, and follow the old main street. Any interest in antiques will delay you for hours; there are numerous antiques stores along this stretch. You will also find the "modern" pottery plant and retail shop beneath the green-and-white highwaylike signs reading POTTERY SALESROOM. Here you can watch potters throw, decorate, and fire pieces for sale. A left at the stop sign and a quick right takes you into the parking lot of **Pottery Place.** The Pottery Salesroom is open seven days a week: Monday through Wednesday 8:00 A.M. to 6:00 P.M., Thursday through Saturday 8:00 A.M. to 7:00 P.M., and Sunday 9:00 A.M. to 6:00 P.M. Call (651) 388–3562 or (800) 228–0174; www.redwingpottery.com. Pottery Place is open Monday through Saturday 10:00 A.M. to 8:00 P.M. and Sunday 11:00 A.M. to 5:00 P.M. Call (651) 388–1428. Both complexes have reduced hours in the winter.

Continue down U.S. Highway 61 about 11 miles; the next river town is **Frontenac.** Frontenac consists of the original village of Old Frontenac, about a mile closer to the river, and Frontenac Station (or New Frontenac), near the highway and railroad tracks. The village, developed in the late 1800s, was an early vacation spot. Today, with most of its homes on the National Register of Historic Places, the entire village is a historic site. New Frontenac is best known for **Frontenac State Park** and **Mount Frontenac,** which offers skiing in the winter and golf in the summer.

Back on the highway, it's about 5 miles to **Lake City,** one of the finest stops on Lake Pepin. The lakeshore curves here, and the vista up and down the river is unsurpassed. The birthplace of waterskiing, invented by Ralph W. Samuelson in 1922, Lake City also boasts the largest small-boat marina on the Mississippi.

LUNCH: Depending on how much time you spent in Red Wing (and had to eat there) or whether you stopped for a hike in Frontenac State Park, it's lunchtime in Lake City. **Chickadee Cottage Tea Room and Restaurant,** U.S. Highway 61 at the north end of town, on the right as you approach from Frontenac, is the place to stop. A true cottage, the Chickadee offers indoor and porch seating. The cook is also a nutritionist; the food is healthy and homemade, and, unlike most home cooking, the servings are reasonably sized. The breads—biscuits, sourdough, and scones—are especially good. Whether you order a familiar spinach salad or turkey sandwich (each about $5.50) or something unusual such as pear and blue cheese crepes (an appetizer, about $4.50), you'll be pleased. Open mid-April through October 31, Monday through Thursday 7:30 A.M. to 3:00 P.M., Friday and Saturday 7:30 A.M. to 4:30 P.M., and Sunday 8:00 A.M. to 2:00 P.M. Tea is served at 2:30 P.M. Call (651) 345–5155 or visit www.chickadeecottagetearoom.com.

No matter when or where you ate lunch, if you're traveling this loop between mid-August and Thanksgiving, a stop at the **Pepin Heights Store** at the south end of town on U.S. Highway 61 is a given. Pepin Heights Orchards produces about 25 percent of the region's apples and specializes in scrumptious, crisp, and tart Haralson apples. Stop for a Pepin Heights apple dipped in Abdallah's caramel: What better combination could there be? Open seasonally 9:00 A.M. to 6:00 P.M. Call (651) 345–2305 or (800) 652–3779; www.pepinheights.com.

Afternoon

Before you depart Lake City, park near the marina and take a stroll on **Lakewalk,** a 2.5-mile-long parklike walkway along the shore, and bring your camera. The "photo ops" aren't the same as from the river overlooks, but the sailboats and hundreds of masts in the harbor make interesting subjects. Or you can sit on a park bench and just watch the barges go by.

Continue down the river, about 11 miles, to **Camp Lacupolis,** once a stopover point for settlers headed to Lake City and now a haven for anglers and snowmobilers, and then another 2 miles to **Read's Landing,** an early center for the Wisconsin lumber trade and transportation and now home to the **Wabasha County Historical Society's Museum,** U.S. Highway 61. The museum is housed in one of the oldest and largest brick school buildings ever built in Minnesota, which is surprising considering how little Read's Landing is today. Things were different once. In its heyday Read's Landing had as many as twenty-seven saloons! Displays include an extensive collection of vintage clothing and some Laura Ingalls Wilder items. Admission: adults $1.00; children 50 cents. Open mid-May through September 1:00 to 5:00 P.M. Call (651) 345–3987 or (651) 565–4251.

The next stop, within a couple of miles, is **Wabasha,** yet another river town with a milling, lumber, and railroad history, enjoying current fame for its starring role in the *Grumpy Old Men* movies. Wabasha has museums, full-service marinas, great shops, B&Bs, and the Anderson House (the oldest hotel in Minnesota) and will soon be home to the Great American Bald Eagle Interpretive Center, backed by the Audubon Society, in Beach Park.

This is a town where you can park on the street and walk wherever you want to go. Browse the shops along Main Street and then walk to dinner.

DINNER: For almost 150 years the **Anderson House,** 333 Main Street, along with four generations of family ownership, has been famous for its hospitality and food that follows the Pennsylvania Dutch tradition. All the food is homemade, the portions are hearty, and the setting is yesteryear. The dinner menu offers quite a range, from Pennsylvania Dutch beef rolls to scallops and shrimp in an herb sauce tossed with garlic linguine, with everything from steaks and walleye in between, but nothing beats Grandma Anderson's recipe for chicken and dumplings. Entrees range in price from $12 to $21; early-bird and weekend specials are also offered. Call (651) 565–4524 or (800) 535–5467; www.theandersonhouse.com.

LODGING: **Bridgewaters Bed and Breakfast,** 136 Bridge Avenue, is a beautifully restored old home with modern guests in mind. Despite its unassuming exterior, this is an ambling Victorian with gleaming hardwood floors and sunny rooms that are pleasantly decorated and filled with antiques. Shared and private baths are offered. The spacious Lafayette Bridge Room, about $145, includes a two-person whirlpool tub and a gas fireplace in the center of the room. Other rooms are available starting at about $79. Bridgewaters also has an antiques and gift store on the property. Open all year. Call (651) 565–4208 or visit www.bridgewaters bandb.com.

Day 2 / Morning

BREAKFAST: Bridgewaters will give you a good start to your day. Menus vary, but you can count on something such as a pecan waffle or a blintz soufflé with blueberry sauce, bacon or sausage, and apple crisp or poppyseed coffee cake. And, yes, it's all homemade.

At Wabasha you cross the bridge to Nelson, Wisconsin, to start the return of the Lake Pepin Loop. Don't cross over, though, before you visit **Kellogg,** Minnesota, just 5 miles farther south on U.S. Highway 61.

Kellogg is quiet, set back from the river and more farm town than river town. Turn on County Road 18 and follow the signs to **L.A.R.K. Toys** and the **Meadowlark Shops** complex, which includes an antique toy museum. What you don't want to miss is the **Lark Carousel,** a wonderful and whimsical hand-carved carousel that took at least ten years to make. There is only one horse on the carousel; the other animals include a dragon, swan, giraffe, and other creatures in delightful colors. The carousel costs only $1.00 to ride and runs every half hour. Open Monday through Friday 9:00 A.M. to 5:00 P.M., Saturday and Sunday 10:00 A.M. to 5:00 P.M. Call (507) 767–3387 or visit www.larktoys.com. Wheelchair accessible.

Turn around and head north 5 miles back to Wabasha, and take State Highway 25 east across the bridge to Nelson. Nelson, too, has shops and restaurants, but it is also adjacent to a stretch of virgin forest and Mississippi backwater called the **Tiffany Bottoms.** This area draws anglers and canoeists to the water and hang gliders to the bluffs.

Take a right at the end of the bridge and head south about 9 miles to **Alma.** Alma is one of the bigger little towns in the loop and has several shops and restaurants. It is also home to **Lock and Dam #4,** with a courtesy dock for water travelers just below the dam; **Buena Vista Park,** which offers one of the best views of the Mississippi River; **Rieck's Lake Park's Wildlife Observation Platform;** and two boat launching ramps, one at each end of town.

To continue the Wisconsin side of the loop, turn around and head north on State Highway 35. Return to Nelson and stop for lunch.

LUNCH: **Beth's Twin Bluff Cafe,** on State Highway 35, with its friendly looks-like-home atmosphere, offers the utmost in home cooking. Beth's has a standard menu with steaks, shrimp, and hamburgers but also offers breakfast, lunch, and dinner specials that change constantly. The roast beef dinner (about $5.25) is available Monday through Friday, but other noon specials can include corned beef and cabbage or hot pork sandwiches. Open daily all year 6:30 A.M. to 7:30 P.M., Friday and Saturday until 9:00 P.M. Wheelchair accessible. Call (715) 673–4040.

Laura Ingalls Wilder Wayside Park, Pepin, Wisconsin

Afternoon

Pepin, Wisconsin, namesake of the lake, is about 8 miles north of Nelson up State Highway 35. Pepin is the birthplace of Laura Ingalls Wilder, and the town pays tribute to her with the charming **Laura Ingalls Wilder Museum,** State Highway 35. In truth, there is very little here that belonged to Laura and her family—a couple of quilts and a letter, all from her later life—but it's a good museum depicting life in the mid-1800s and it's free; donations are suggested. About 7 miles out of town (turn right on County Road CC if you are heading north) is the reconstructed birthplace of Laura Ingalls Wilder. Due to vandalism, there is little to show what life was like for the Ingalls family (the collection has been moved to the museum), but it's a nice place to picnic and is worth the stop, especially if your group includes fans of the Little House books. Both the museum and the birthplace are open mid-May through mid-October. Again, donations are suggested.

The next town is **Stockholm.** Although it's one of the smallest towns on the loop, Stockholm has so many shops and galleries that some residents on the main street have been forced to put up signs that read PRIVATE HOME. This is a gem of a town. There are a few antiques stores, numerous gift shops, a couple of great places at which to eat, a little hotel, and the premier store, **Amish Country,** corner of Spring Street and State Highway 35, featuring Amish quilts and furnishings.

DINNER: Good Lovin', formerly the Star Cafe on State Highway 35 under the old Texaco sign, is an oasis of good food in this little town. The pale pine interior with stenciled floors looks like the background of a Carl Larsson illustration, the food is equally artistic, and the bar is charming. The chef uses fresh ingredients, including homegrown herbs, and the meats are smoked on the premises. The lunch menu includes a soup of the day, salads, and sandwiches (smoked ham, turkey, and vegetarian options, about $5.00 to $8.00). The dinner menu changes weekly, but chicken breast sautéed in cognac and tossed with avocado is a good example (entrees range from $15 to $20). Desserts include bread pudding with caramel sauce and chocolate torte with crème anglaise. Open daily late spring to early fall, 10:00 A.M. to 10:00 P.M. Call (715) 442–2023.

About 7 miles north of Stockholm is the next stop, **Maiden Rock.** Legend says Maiden Rock was named for the Indian maiden Winona, who leapt to her death from one of the bluffs to avoid marrying a man she did not love. The tragic story is easily forgotten in the beauty of this sunny, friendly river village enjoying its rebirth along the Great River Road. If you time your visit so that you spend a night at the **Harrisburg Bed and Breakfast** (see Maiden Rock, Wisconsin, Other Recommended Restaurants and Lodgings), you'll be privy to the most spectacular view of Lake Pepin and the surrounding bluffs, including the Maiden Rock Bluff.

Another 8 miles north is **Bay City,** the last town on the loop. There is little left of the original town, but Bay City plays a big part in developing and promoting the area for its residents and tourists. Bay City provides one last chance on this escape to wander the shores of the Mississippi before you cross the river back into Red Wing and head home.

There's More

Biking. Bike Minnesota's 20-mile-long Cannon Valley Trail from Red Wing to Cannon Falls. A bike pass is required. Call (507) 263–2289. Bike rentals are available at The Route, 401 Levee Street, Red Wing (651–388–1082; www.theroute.net) and at the Outdoor Store, 323 Main Street, Red Wing (651–388–5358).

Camping. Merrick State Park, Fountain City, Wisconsin; Frontenac State Park, 29223 County 28 Boulevard, Lake City, Minnesota (651–345–3855); and Hok–Si–La Municipal Park and Campground, about 2 miles north of Lake City (651–345–3855).

Concerts. "Meet Me Under the Bridge" concerts on Main Street, Wabasha, Minnesota, every Friday at 7:00 P.M. during July and August. Free.

Golf. Mount Frontenac Golf Course, U.S. Highway 61, about 9 miles south of Red Wing, Minnesota (651–388–5826, 651–345–3504, or 800–488–5826), offers eighteen holes with great views of Lake Pepin, a pro shop, and an on-course beverage service. Mississippi National Golf Links, 409 Golf Links Drive (651–388–1874), offers twenty-seven holes in a magnificent setting.

Live Theater. The Sheldon, Third and East Avenues, Red Wing (651–385–3667 or 800–899–5759; www.sheldontheatre.org), offers classical, country, and jazz music as well as family shows, plays, and old movies. Prices depend on the artist; old movies run about $5.00 per person. Lake Pepin Players, Inc., 417 Second Street, Pepin, Wisconsin (715–442–3109 or 877–823–3500; www.lakepepinplayers.com), specializes in comic productions and often includes nationally known actors and actresses. The season runs from late May through mid-October; performances are held Thursday through Sunday. Prices range from $5.00 to $17.00.

Museums. The Goodhue County Historical Museum, 1166 Oak Street, Red Wing (651–388–6024), is open Tuesday through Friday 10:00 A.M. to 5:00 P.M., Saturday and Sunday 1:00 to 5:00 P.M. Admission: adults, $5.00; seniors $3.00; children 16 and under are free. The Pepin Depot Museum, State Highway 35 in Laura Ingalls Wilder Park, Pepin, has displays of railroad memorabilia and logging history. Its restored ticket office includes a telegraph, train signals, and related items. Open daily mid-May through mid-October 8:00 A.M. to 5:00 P.M. Call (715) 672–5709 or (888) 672–5709.

Riverboats. The *Delta Queen, Mississippi Queen,* and the *American Queen* paddle wheelers frequently dock in Red Wing. Call (651) 385–5934 for schedules and more information.

Trolley Rides. Ride a restored converted San Francisco trolley around the streets of Red Wing. The trolley is closed in the winter. Call (612) 385–5934 or (800) 498–3444.

Winter Alternatives

Cross-country Skiing. Within Frontenac State Park, 29223 County 28 Boulevard, Lake City (651–436–5391), there are 6 miles of groomed cross-country ski trails. During the winter the Cannon Valley Bike Trail, 20 miles of trail between Cannon Falls and Red Wing, Minnesota (507–263–2289), converts to a cross-country ski trail. A state pass is required for skiing both trails.

Downhill Skiing. Mount Frontenac, near Old Frontenac on U.S. Highway 61 (651–388–5826 or 800–488–5826), has several runs, a chalet, and rentals. Welch Village, Welch, Minnesota (651–258–4567; www.welchvillage.com), about fifteen minutes west of Red Wing on County Road 7, has thirty-seven runs, chalets, a ski school, and rentals. Coffee Mill, just west of U.S. Highway 61 on State Highway 60 in Wabasha, Minnesota (651–565–2777; www.coffeemillski.com), boasts the "longest vertical drop south of Duluth" and offers ten runs with varying difficulty, a chalet, ski school, and rentals. Lift tickets: adults $25; children 6 to 14, $21. Rentals available.

Sliding. Frontenac State Park, Minnesota; (651) 345–3401.

Special Events

January. Winterfest, Lake City, Minnesota; (651) 345–4128 or (800) 369–4123. Includes skiing, golfing on the ice, an ice-fishing contest, snowmobile races, and fireworks over Lake Pepin.

February. Grumpy Old Men Festival, Wabasha, Minnesota; (651) 565–4158. Includes ice fishing and an ice-shack contest.

March to April. Bald eagle and tundra swan migration, Frontenac State Park, 29223 County 28 Boulevard, Lake City; (651) 345–3401.

May. The 85-mile Garage Sale; (715) 442–4003. Follows the Lake Pepin Loop and is participated in by area shops and residents.

Ethnic Days, River Bluffs History Center, Bay City, Wisconsin; (715) 442–4003.

June. Water Ski Days, Lake City; (651) 345–4128 or (800) 369–4123. Water-ski shows, crafts, music, parades, and more.

July. The Stockholm Art Fair, Stockholm, Wisconsin; (715) 442–3101. Features more than one hundred artists who set up in the park to show and sell their work.

Wabasha County Fair, Coffee Mill Ski Area, U.S. Highway 60, Wabasha. Includes 4-H exhibits and a carnival.

Riverboat Days, Wabasha; (651) 565–4158. Crafts, a lighted boat parade, and a water-ski show.

August. Nelson Days Festival, Nelson, Wisconsin; (715) 673–4804. A parade, tractor pull, street dance, and food.

September. Laura Ingalls Wilder Days, Pepin, Wisconsin; (715) 442–2461. A parade, crafts, food, and a Laura Ingalls Wilder look-alike contest.

Watermelon Fest, Kellogg, Minnesota; (507) 767–4953. Watermelon treats, a carnival, and a parade.

Mark Twain Days, Alma, Wisconsin; (608) 685–3330. A parade, sidewalk vendors, craft shows, and food vendors.

October. Johnny Appleseed Days, Lake City; (651) 345–4128 or (800) 369–4123. Art, crafts, and collector fairs; farmers' market; pancake breakfast; and an "unusual vegetable" contest. A free horse-and-wagon shuttle is available for transportation between some activities.

October to November. Tundra swans, migrating from Alaska and Canada, stop in Rieck's Park at the north end of Alma; (608) 685–3330.

Other Recommended Restaurants and Lodgings

Lake City, Minnesota

Victorian Bed & Breakfast, 620 South High Street; (651) 345–2167. This stick-style turn-of-the-twentieth-century mansion is furnished with antiques. The rooms have feather beds, private baths, and views of Lake

Pepin. Rates range from $75 to $95 for a room in the house to $140 for a room in the cottage that has a whirlpool and fireplace. All rates include a full breakfast.

Red Wing, Minnesota

The Candlelight Inn, 818 West Third Street; (651) 388–8034 or (800) 254–9194; www.candlelightinn-redwing.com. An award-winning bed-and-breakfast inn, this gracious Victorian offers five guest rooms, all with romantic fireplaces and private baths; some have whirlpools. Rates range from $129 to $199 and include a full gourmet breakfast. A minimum two-night stay is required on weekends.

The Rodeway Inn, at U.S. Highway 61 and Withers Harbor Drive; (651) 388–1502 or (800) 228–2000. A standard room starts at about $67; a deluxe room with a hot tub for two costs about $129; each includes a continental breakfast.

The St. James Hotel, 406 Main Street; (651) 388–2846 or (800) 252–1875; www.st-james-hotel.com. A Red Wing landmark for more than one hundred years, the beautifully restored hotel has sixty rooms (four with the original claw-foot tubs), restaurants, and numerous shops. Don't miss the original lobby that once faced the livery stable and was more conveniently located for river travelers than the current Main Street entrance. Weddings are frequently held on the grand staircase, and the restored library is a wonderful surprise. Room rates start at $110, but there are numerous packages, including the "Victorian Holiday" that offers a standard room, dinner for two at the Port of Red Wing, and breakfast in the Veranda Restaurant for about $240 a night.

Treasure Island Resort and Casino, about fifteen minutes north of Red Wing on County Road 18; (800) 222–7077 or (651) 388–6300. The resort includes a 250-room hotel, a marina, and four restaurants. A room for two starts at about $90. Midweek rates are lower.

Wabasha, Minnesota

The Anderson House, 333 Main Street; (800) 535–5467 or (651) 565–4524; www.theandersonhouse.com. In business since 1856, this is the oldest operating hotel in Minnesota. Except for some restoration, not much has changed. Most of the furniture and traditions date back to 1896, when the first of four consecutive generations acquired the hotel. You can have your shoes shined, order up a mustard plaster, or request a pet cat for the evening. There are twenty-four rooms; only three still share a bath. Rooms run $84 to $159 per night for double occupancy. Open all year.

Eagle's Nest Coffee House, 330 Second Street (just around the corner from the main drag); (651) 565–2077. Homemade muffins, bagels, soups, and sandwiches ($2.00 to $4.00) along with the usual lattes, cappuccinos, espressos, and twenty-one different flavors of coffee are served in a park-like setting. Open Sunday through Tuesday 7:00 A.M. to 5:00 P.M., Wednesday and Thursday until 7:00 P.M., and until 10:00 P.M. on Friday and Saturday, with live music most Saturday nights. Smoke free and wheel-chair accessible.

Great River Houseboats, 1009 East Main Street; (651) 565–3376; www.greatriverhouseboats.com. Here's where to go to rent a houseboat. The furnished boats (complete with kitchenette and bathroom) travel between 5 and 10 mph and offer a unique tour of the Mississippi River. Green and red buoys on the river mark the main channel (stay between them), and overnights can be spent at any of the numerous beaches along the way or at the marinas in the river towns. One of the most popular houseboats, a 30-foot catamaran-style that sleeps two to six people, rents for $495 (plus gas and pump-out fee) for three days and two nights.

Slippery's Tavern and Restaurant, 10 Church Street; (651) 565–4748. This is the bar mentioned in *Grumpy Old Men*. Sandwiches and hamburgers (about $4.50) are served from 11:00 A.M. to 10:00 P.M.; at 5:00 P.M. the full dinner menu is offered. Specials change daily; every Saturday is the prime-rib special with numerous accompaniments for about $14.

Alma, Wisconsin

The Alma Hotel, 201 Main Street North; (608) 685–3380. Great down-home cooking in a simple cafeteria setting. Reasonably priced. Open daily 6:00 A.M. to 8:00 P.M.

Currents, set in a restored brick building at 115 Main Street North; (608) 685–4880. This restaurant offers casual dining with an elegant, almost European, feel to its atmosphere, with lots of wood accents, eclectic decor, white tablecloths, and candlelight. The creative menu is constantly chang-ing, featuring anything from fine French cuisine to Asian delicacies. Entrees range in price from $13 to $18. Currents is very popular on weekends;

reservations are recommended. Open Friday and Saturday 5:00 to 9:00 P.M., Sunday 3:00 to 7:00 P.M.; closed from New Year's through March.

The Tritsch House, 601 South Second Street; (608) 685–4090. This rambling turn-of-the-twentieth-century inn sits on the terraced hills above the river and offers spectacular views of the Mississippi River Valley. All rooms have private baths, and breakfast is prepared for you by your host, a graduate of Le Cordon Bleu Culinary School. Rooms range from $85 to $115 per night, with reduced off-season rates.

Maiden Rock, Wisconsin

Harrisburg Bed and Breakfast, State Highway 35 at the southern end of the village; (715) 448–4500. The inn has a screened porch that looks out on Lake Pepin and provides one of the most spectacular views in the whole river valley. This homey, friendly bed-and-breakfast also features private baths and a full breakfast that includes homemade muffins. Closed January and February. Rooms range in price from $90 to $135.

Pepin, Wisconsin

Harbor View, corner of First and Main Streets; (715) 442–3893. A pale blue windswept cottage, it houses a restaurant and small bookstore. Since the mid-1980s, the Harbor View has been delighting Lake Pepin visitors with unique and tasty culinary treats. The menu changes constantly, but entrees often include Alaskan halibut, spring lamb, and fresh fish, and the Harbor View is famous for its sauces. Prices range from $10 to $20. Open seasonally Thursday through Sunday for lunch and dinner; closed from Thanksgiving until March.

Lake Pepin Inn, State Highway 35 across from the Laura Ingalls Wilder Museum; (715) 442–5400; www.lakepepininn.com. The inn is immaculately clean and outfitted with handmade Amish furniture. With their country quilts, the rooms look as if they belong in a country inn. Rates range from $50 to $65 a night; whirlpools are available.

The Pickle Factory, on the docks in the harbor off Main Street; (715) 442–4400; www.picklefactory.com. A great stop for hamburgers and onion rings. Reasonably priced. Open daily from 11:00 A.M. until business stops, usually between 9:00 and 10:00 P.M. Closed Monday and Tuesday during the fall and winter.

Stockholm, Wisconsin

Bogus Creek Deli and Bogus Creek Bakery, across a little bridge from each other on Spring Street; (715) 442–5017. Breakfast, gourmet sandwiches, soups, breads, cookies, pastries, and ice-cream treats (under $6.00) are served. Open daily April through November 9:00 A.M. to 6:00 P.M.

Pine Creek Lodge, N447 244th Street; (715) 448–3203. A modern post-and-beam-constructed home with vaulted ceilings and a northern-lodge decor, it is set in eighty acres of woods, so you can hike and cross-country ski right on the property. The tastefully decorated romantic rooms have a variety of amenities: Choose from two-person tubs, whirlpools, or private steam rooms. Rates range from $100 to $175 and include a full breakfast of your choice.

For More Information

Lake City Chamber of Commerce, 212 South Washington Street, Lake City, MN 55041–0150; (651) 345–4123 or (800) 369–4123; www .lakecity.org.

Pepin Visitor Information Center, P.O. Box 274, Pepin, WI 54759; (715) 442–3011.

Red Wing Visitors and Convention Bureau, 418 Levee Street, Red Wing, MN 55066; (651) 385–5934 or (800) 498–3444; www.redwing.org.

Wabasha Chamber of Commerce, 257 West Main Street, P.O. Box 105, Wabasha, MN 55981; (651) 565–4158 or (800) 565–4158; www .wabasha.net.

Lower St. Croix National Scenic Riverway

Past Time and Pastimes

2 Nights

The St. Croix National Scenic Riverway is more than 250 miles of protected waterway that includes the Namekagon River and the St. Croix River as it flows into Minnesota and then becomes the border between Minnesota and Wisconsin until it joins the Mississippi River at Prescott, Wisconsin. The first 200 miles are known as the Upper St. Croix, and the last 52 miles, from the dam at St. Croix Falls to Prescott, are the Lower St. Croix. The Upper St. Croix is noted for its primitive camping, moderate rapids, and the wilderness-like experience it offers canoeists. The Lower St. Croix is considered recreational, and it is popular with motorboat and sailboat enthusiasts alike.

☐ Apples

☐ Inns

☐ Fashion Shows

☐ Antiques

☐ B&Bs

For most Twin Citians, the Lower St. Croix National Scenic Riverway is simply what old-fashioned Sunday drives are all about: quaint towns, spectacular scenery, and an afternoon ice-cream cone. Like the Lake Pepin Loop (Minnesota/Wisconsin Escape Two), this getaway is more of a route through local Minnesota and Wisconsin river towns than it is an itinerary for a single destination. It's a relaxing drive that meanders through the St. Croix River Valley, happening upon little towns no bigger than a storefront or two and coming upon others that have city blocks' worth of antiques shops and restaurants and consider themselves Twin Cities suburbs. In a weekend along the St. Croix, you can count on phenomenal antiquing, abundant restaurants, amazing scenery, and charm galore.

Keep in mind that each of the little towns is fewer than 60 miles from the Twin Cities. As long as there is a place to stay (most towns offer at least one form of lodging for the night), each town is perfect for even an overnight getaway: close enough to home to get to after work, remote and tranquil enough to feel like you've gone for the whole weekend.

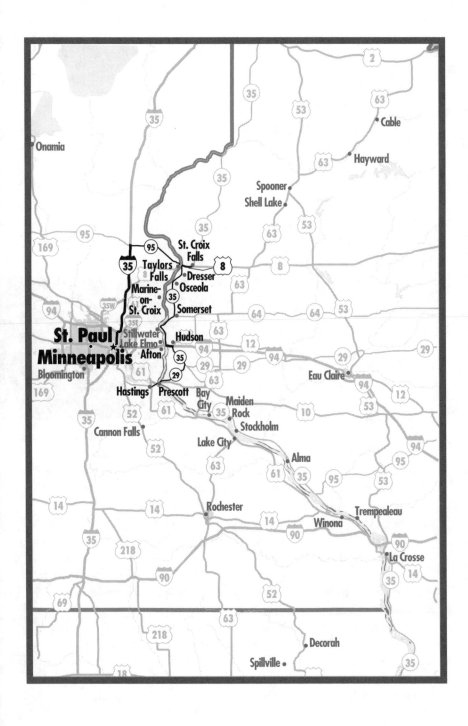

(This itinerary purposefully excludes the town of Stillwater, Minnesota. For information on Stillwater, see Minnesota Escape Eleven.)

Day 1 / Morning

Try to time your arrival in **Afton** for about 10:00 A.M.: That's when the stores open. To get to Afton, follow I–94 east, through St. Paul, past **Lake Elmo,** and all the way to the Stillwater/State Highway 95 exit. Go right and pass by another little St. Croix town, **Lakeland.** It will seem that you roll along forever through farmland and then, suddenly, there sits the village of Afton, looking like a lost Civil War town.

On a midsummer weekend it might be hard to find a parking space, but late morning on a Sunday in the fall, it might just be you, a couple of kids on bicycles, and an artist sitting on the curb, quietly sketching Main Street.

Main Street in Afton, technically St. Croix Trail, is only a couple of blocks long, consisting of the **Afton House,** an original restored hotel and restaurant, several shops, a park, and access to the marina. The shops are charming, and most smell like their delicious specialties: **Squire House Gardens** (651–436–8080), a veritable garden museum, with its blossoms and greenery outdoors and fragrances and scented candles indoors, is a shopping retreat. Even before you get there, the unmistakable aroma of homemade waffle cones coming out of **Selma's Ice Cream Parlour** (651–436–8067 or 800–235–8067) will tempt you to eat dessert long before lunch. And, especially to horse lovers, the **Afton Village Saddle Shop** (651–436–2773) will smell ruggedly good.

You probably wouldn't expect to find a designer-fashion clothing shop in such a little town, but Afton has been a fairly elite stop on the route for years, as **Baglio's of Afton** (651–436–1506) indicates. The shop specializes in casual cotton separates and unique accessories and is famous for its seasonal fashion shows that are recognized St. Croix River Valley events.

Continue south on State Highway 95 to U.S. Highway 61 south, passing the turn to Prescott, for now, into **Hastings,** the southernmost town on this route. Hastings sits just west of the confluence of the St. Croix and Mississippi Rivers, and sometimes it's hard to know where to place this historic town in the scheme of things: Its identity is half Great River Road and half St. Croix National Scenic Riverway. It's 100 percent worth it, though, if you have any interest in antiques, architecture, or good food! After you cross the bridge into town, take an immediate right and wind under the bridge onto Second Street, which is the town's main street. Preservation is not a new concept to Hastings: Restoration activities have been going on since the 1970s. Today this part of downtown looks much like it did one hundred years ago; it has sixty-two buildings on the National Register of Historic Places.

LUNCH: Park downtown and walk toward the river to **The Levee Cafe,** 100 Sibley Street. This is fine dining in a sleek cafe atmosphere. Lunch specials change daily, but you can count on a bowl of homemade chicken wild rice soup (about $3.15) or, better yet, what it's locally famous for: chicken a la king (about $6.75). Wine and cocktails are also available. Open Monday through Thursday 11:00 A.M. to 9:00 P.M., Friday 11:00 A.M. to 10:00 P.M., Saturday 8:30 A.M. to 10:00 P.M., and Sunday 8:30 A.M. to 8:00 P.M. Sunday brunch is served from 10:00 A.M. to 2:00 P.M. Call (651) 437–7577.

Afternoon

Pick up a Hastings-area antiques guide in any of the antiques stores on Second Street. There are hours' worth of antiques and collectibles browsing within walking distance of your car. The guide should take you west on Second Street under the bridge to more antiques stores. A fringe benefit of this walk will be a view of an octagonal house, a popular design in the mid-1800s. It is a private dwelling, but the owners and neighbors are accustomed to sightseers passing by. There are also several other gift shops on Second Street, not to mention **Professor Java's** coffee shop (202 East Second Street) or **Treat Me Sweet** candy and snack shop (118 East Second Street) if you need to take a break. Call Professor Java's at (651) 438–9962 and Treat Me Sweet at (651) 480–2144.

Return to your car. From Second Street backtrack across the bridge and go north on U.S. Highway 61/State Highway 95 to U.S. Highway 10. Go east for a couple of miles to County Road 21, turn left, and follow the signs to the **Carpenter St. Croix Valley Nature Center.** The mission of the nature center is environmental education, but it attracts outdoor lovers to its 10 miles of summer hiking and winter snowshoe trails. High on a bluff, the center offers great views of the St. Croix River Valley. It is open daily all year from 8:00 A.M. to 4:30 P.M. Call (651) 437–4359.

Backtrack to U.S. Highway 10 and continue into **Prescott.** You're now on the Wisconsin side of the St. Croix River. Prescott is another charming river town with an ambling main street full of good shopping, yet more antiques stores, restaurants, and lodgings.

Continuing on State Highway 35, the long way, will take you into **River Falls,** one of the homes of the University of Wisconsin and summer training grounds for the Kansas City Chiefs. College towns have a charm all their own, and River Falls is a nice town, but if you're pressed for time, follow County Road F through rolling farmland to **Hudson.** This route to Hudson will take you past an entrance to **Kinnickinnic State Park,** County Road F, about 10 miles south of Hudson, known for its excellent trout fishing. Call (715) 425–1129. However you arrive in Hudson, you will first need to get on I–94 and then leave it at exit 1, a continuation of State Highway 35, to get to downtown, the historic part of Hudson. Highway 35 turns into Second Street, the main street.

Hudson is an old wealthy town. The main street is long, the storefronts are full, the riverfront is bustling, and the neighborhoods abound in beautiful nineteenth-century residential architecture.

DINNER: Dine by candlelight at **Mama Maria's,** 800 Sixth Street North, North Hudson. It is such a quaint Italian restaurant, with murals of the canals on the walls and soft Italian music playing in the background, that you will feel as if you are in Italy. This little restaurant is exceedingly popular, and one bite of the champagne chicken breast (about $10) will explain why. Although Mama Maria's specializes in Italian food (featuring both red and white sauces), steak and seafood are also served. Arrive early; while Mama Maria's is known for its excellent food, reservations are not accepted. Open Tuesday through Friday 11:00 A.M. to 9:00 P.M., Saturday 11:00 A.M. to 10:00 P.M., Sunday 3:00 to 9:00 P.M. Call (715) 386–7949.

LODGING: There are not enough superlatives to describe the **Phipps Inn Bed and Breakfast,** 1005 Third Street. This Queen Anne "Grande Dame" Victorian mansion is easily the most elegant, most exquisitely decorated, most gracious bed-and-breakfast inn in the St. Croix River Valley. The home once belonged to William Henry Phipps, lumber baron, businessman, politician, and local philanthropist. The legendary philanthropy continues, too. Instead of feeling like a customer, you will instantly feel like a welcome guest of the home: pampered, fed, and even entertained by the magnificent Cable Crownstay baby grand player piano in the parlor. From wicker furniture and flowers to brass beds and ornate wallpapers, every room is enticingly decorated, and each has a beautiful modern bath with a whirlpool tub. Some of the rooms also have fireplaces.

If you are familiar with the watercolors of Steven Hanks, the house may even look familiar. Hanks has painted more than one of his pieces in this home. Rates for two, including breakfast, range from $169 to $209 per night, with slightly reduced rates midweek. Smoke free. Call (715) 386–0800; www.phippsinn.com.

Day 2 / Morning

BREAKFAST: A full four-course breakfast is included with your room at the Phipps Inn, and breakfast here is as delicious as your surroundings. You may choose to be served in the dining room, on the porch (weather permitting), or in your room. Entrees change regularly, ranging from heart-shaped waffles to crepes to ham-and-cheese-stuffed crescent rolls, but breakfast always includes homemade pastries, fresh fruits, and an assortment of coffees and teas.

Don't leave Hudson too quickly. The town publishes a list of fifty things to do in the Hudson area, which is way too much for a weekend, let alone a morning, but Hudson is worth exploring.

Staying at the Phipps Inn puts you directly across the street from **The Historic Octagon House,** 1004 Third Street. Eight-sided homes began in New York, and the rage spread westward but never fully caught on. Fortunately there are several surviving octagonal homes scattered around the Upper Midwest (estimates count twelve in Wisconsin alone), but most are private homes and simply fun to spot in a neighborhood among other, more traditional houses. (Additions to one or more of the sides frequently make the structures hard to recognize.) The Octagonal House in Hudson belonged to four generations of the Moffat family and only one other family before being acquired by the St. Croix County Historical Society. It is now a beautifully maintained mid-nineteenth-century home with exceptional collections, including furniture, dishes, and toys. The Carriage House and the Garden House also include exhibits. Open May through October, Tuesday through Saturday 10:00 to 11:30 A.M. and 2:00 to 4:30 P.M., Sunday 2:00 to 4:30 P.M., with additional hours for the Historic House Tour in November and Christmas tours in December. Admission: adults $3.00; seniors over 65, $2.00; students 13 to 19, $1.00; children 12 and under 50 cents. Call (715) 386–2654.

If you decide not to go hot-air ballooning (one of the fifty things), at least go for a walk on the riverfront. You can walk through the historic **Hudson Arch** on the promenade walkway at the corner of First and Locust. It's a restored abandoned toll bridge that goes over—but not across—the river and back.

The Historic Hastings Courthouse, Hastings, Minnesota

Follow the main street north out of town through North Hudson to **Somerset.** Somerset sits on the Apple River and is noted for turning tubing (riding down the Apple River in an inner tube) into a local summer industry.

LUNCH: You're bound to be hungry by the time you reach **Osceola.** Stop anywhere along Cascade Street (Osceola's main street), browse the charming shops, and then have lunch at **Mainstreeter's,** 102 Second Avenue, a friendly family cafe from yesteryear furnished with antiques— complete with tin ceilings. Hamburgers start at $3.00. Open Monday through Saturday at 5:45 A.M., it closes at 2:00 P.M. on Monday, 7:45 P.M. Tuesday through Thursday, and 9:45 P.M. on Friday and Saturday. Sunday hours are 9:00 A.M. to 2:00 P.M. Call (715) 755–3663.

Afternoon

Continue north on State Highway 35 through **Dresser** to **St. Croix Falls** (where you'll find more restaurants, shops, and a live theater company) and cross the river on U.S. Highway 8, back to **Taylors Falls,** Minnesota. The always beautiful scenery along the St. Croix will now be spectacular as you enter glacial wonderlands and forests cutting through Wisconsin and Minnesota's **Interstate State Park.**

Taylors Falls is a familiar name because of the park, but its charm as a river town is a well-kept secret. Get ready for some arduous walking; the town is spread up and down the rugged hills and has a Swiss village look to it in the winter. It's almost easier to get around on foot, to avoid stopping and parking every couple of blocks, but even the narrow streets that go up the hills are drivable. Main Street has antiques stores, gift shops, restaurants, and historic sites. Browse the shops before they close, and take the time to walk up the hill on the west edge of town to the historic **Angel Hill** district and visit the **Old Schoolhouse.** The schoolhouse, built in 1852, is the oldest existing public school in Minnesota. Be sure to look at the photograph taken of Taylors Falls in 1865 that shows the school's flag at half mast to honor President Lincoln after his assassination. The museum is free, open seasonally, and run by volunteers; donations are appreciated.

Farther up the hill and around the corner is **The Folsom House,** 272 West Government Street. Built in the mid-1800s, this lovely house was the home of lumberman W. H. C. Folsom and his family. It is a fine example of the popular architecture of the day, a combination of Federal and

Greek Revival styles sought by many of the transplanted New Englanders. The home is especially interesting because it contains so many furnishings and belongings of the Folsom family, including Civil War uniforms and family portraits. Open daily Memorial Day through mid-October 1:00 to 4:30 P.M. Also open for "Christmas in Taylors Falls." Admission: adults $3.00; schoolchildren $1.00. Call (651) 465–3125 or (888) PAST–FUN; www.mnhs.org.

DINNER: Cross the bridge going east from St. Croix Falls and follow State Highway 35 south, about 4 or 5 miles, to the **Village Pizzeria** in Dresser, Wisconsin. This is a family restaurant with a country look, serving pizza, of course, but also pastas, sandwiches, and steaks. The mouthwatering deluxe pizza with Canadian bacon, sausage, pepperoni, and green olives serves four or five people for about $17. Other entrees range in price from $8.00 to $15.00. Open Monday through Thursday 11:00 A.M. to 10:00 P.M., Friday and Saturday until 11:00 P.M., and Sunday 8:00 A.M. to 10:00 P.M. Call (715) 755–2900.

LODGING: By now you've probably passed **The Old Jail Company Bed and Breakfast,** the pretty white house and adjacent cottage up on the hill at 349 Government Street. The buildings have had many uses over the years and now house charming suites decorated with antiques and collectibles and accented with red everything, from elves to Burma Shave signs. Each suite has its own sitting area and kitchen. Rates range from $120 to $140. Open all year. Call (651) 465–3112; www.oldjail.com.

Day 3 / Morning

BREAKFAST: A complete breakfast is delivered to your room whenever you're ready to eat. A typical breakfast includes fresh-squeezed juice, fresh fruit, baked goods right out of the oven, turkey sausage, and pancakes.

After breakfast walk down into town and follow the far sidewalk down the hill, under the bridge, and into the **Interstate State Park.** (Do not cross the highway above on foot.)

Interstate State Park has some of the most incredible geologic formations in North America, including the world's deepest explored glacial pothole. The potholes were formed by whirlpools that were created as glaciers melted and the rivers swiftly cut though the rocky terrain.

Just beyond the visitor center is a paved path to the edge of the St. Croix River. It offers a great view of the jagged cliffs and some of the more accessible potholes. Although you may see a lot of swimmers and cliff-divers here, keep in mind that these activities are prohibited due to the unpredictable river currents and rugged river bottom. Kayaking and canoeing, however, are allowed.

This part of the park is wheelchair accessible, but the paths along the limestone terraces are steep, uneven, and can be dangerous. (The park has 4 additional miles of hiking trails.) Open 9:00 A.M. to 7:00 P.M. Call (651) 465–5711.

LUNCH: This time you need to get into your car to properly enjoy your lunch. Right on the main drag, just north of town, sits the **Drive-In,** State Highway 95, complete with carhops and trays that hook onto your window. Order homemade root beer and classic drive-in food and rest assured that the fifties are alive and well. Seasonal. Call (651) 465–7831.

Afternoon

From Taylors Falls continue your tour of the Lower St. Croix by heading south on State Highway 95, past **Scandia** to **Marine-on-St. Croix.** The highway splits the town in half: Main Street will be on your left, and the residential area will be on your right as you head south.

Marine-on-St. Croix has been the film location of many movies, including scenes from *Grumpier Old Men, The Cure,* and *Beautiful Girls.* And with good reason: This quaint town is picture-book pretty, with its handful of little white buildings downtown (including a gazebo) and a waterfall that runs behind them. Get an ice-cream cone at **The Village Scoop** (seasonal, 651–433–3030) and wander the town before you continue south again to Stillwater, where you can pick up State Highway 36 or I–94 and head back to the cities.

There's More

Amusements. Wild Mountain, just north of Taylors Falls, Minnesota; (651) 465–6315 or (800) 257–3550. The park offers two alpine slides, go-carts, and a water park. Open daily Memorial Day through Labor Day.

Apple Orchards. Two nearby pick-it-yourself orchards are Afton Apple Orchard (14421 South Ninetieth Street, Afton, Minnesota; 651–436–8385) and Fischer's Croix Farm Orchard (12971 St. Croix Orchard, Hastings, Minnesota; 651–437–7126).

Biking. The Gandy Dancer Trail has 98 miles of multirecreational use trails for everything from hiking to snowmobiling. Burnett County, (800) 788–3164; Polk County, (800) 222–POLK.

Camping. Afton State Park, 6959 Peller Avenue South, Hastings (651–436–5391); Interstate State Park, 12 U.S. Highway 8, Taylors Falls (651–465–5711); and William O'Brien State Park, 16821 O'Brien Trail North, Marine-on-St. Croix, Minnesota (651–433–0500), have camping. A vehicle permit is required. For reservations call (866) 85PARKS or visit www.stayatmnparks.com. Greenwood Campground, 13797 190 Street East, Hastings (651–437–5269), is a private campground with a swimming pool, rec room, showers, and a convenience store. Wildwood RV Park and Campground, P.O. Box 235, Taylors Falls, MN 55084 (651–465–7161, 651–257–3550, or 800–447–4958), is a private campground with a pool, minigolf, game room, showers, and full hookups. Full hookups for a family of four are about $27 per night.

Canoe Rentals. Canoes and organized outings are available through Taylors Falls Canoe Rental, Taylors Falls; (651) 257–3550 or (800) 447–4958. The most popular trips are from Taylors Falls to Osceola, about three hours, and from Taylors Falls to the canoe landing at William O'Brien State Park, about five hours. A shuttle bus from your car, parked at your final destination, is also available. One canoe for two people, with life preservers, runs about $25 per day. Rentals are also available within Interstate State Park, 12 U.S. Highway 8, Taylors Falls (651–465–5711), and at William O'Brien State Park, 16821 O'Brien Trail North, Marine-on-St. Croix (651–433–0500).

Golf. Afton Alps Golf Course, 6600 Peller Avenue South, Hastings (651–436–1320), offers eighteen holes, rentals, a bar, and a pro shop in a scenic setting. Bellwood Oaks Public Golf Course, 13239 210 Street East, Hastings (651–437–4141), is a challenging course offering eighteen holes, a putting green, and a snack bar. Hidden Greens Golf Course, 12977 200th Street East, Hastings (651–437–3085), offers eighteen holes, carts, a clubhouse, and a driving range. Clifton Highlands Golf Course, North 6890 230th Street, Prescott, Wisconsin (715–262–5141 or 800–657–6845), offers eighteen holes on rolling hills overlooking the lush river valley. Other amenities include a lounge and pro shop.

Live Entertainment. The Phipps Center for the Arts (109 Locust Street, Hudson, Wisconsin; 715–386–2305; www.thephipps.org) features performances of anything from chamber music to dancers and drama and has regularly changing art exhibits. Admission: adults $11 to $13; children $1.00 less. The St. Croix Festival Theatre (Auditorium Theatre, P.O. Box 801, St. Croix Falls, WI 54024 715–483–3387) season runs from July through December and includes a broad range of performances from the classics to comedies and mysteries. Professor Java's (202 East Second Street, Hastings; 651–438–9962) presents concerts in conjunction with the Minnesota Bluegrass and Oldtime Music Association. Cover charge.

Museums. The Afton Historical Museum, Afton City Hall, Afton; (651) 436–8895. First a church and then city hall, the museum has displays of local farm life and a collection of photographs documenting life in this ever-pleasant town. Open May through October 1:00 to 4:00 P.M. Free. The Gammelgarden Swedish Settlement, Scandia, Minnesota; (651) 433–5053 or (651) 433–3430. The settlement has six nineteenth-century structures, including one of the oldest log churches and log parsonages in the state. Open May through October, Friday through Sunday noon to 4:00 P.M. Admission: adults $3.00; children under 12, $2.00. The Stone House Museum, Oak and Fifth Streets, Marine-on-St. Croix; (651) 433–2061. The museum was originally the township hall. Exhibits include household items, period clothing, and a Swedish kitchen showing what life was like for the early settlers. Open July 4 through Labor Day or by appointment. Free, but donations appreciated.

Train Rides. Tour the St. Croix on a vintage train via the Scenic Osceola & St. Croix River Valley Railway, Osceola, Wisconsin; (651) 228–0276 or (715) 755–3570; www.trainride.org. Riders board at the Historic Osceola Depot on Depot Street just off State Highway 35, south of the railroad bridge. Trains run Saturday, Sunday, and holidays from late May through October. Routes vary, and round-trips are either forty-five or ninety minutes long. Trains depart at 11:00 A.M. and 1:00 and 2:30 P.M. Fares, from Osceola to Dresser, are $10.00 for adults and $5.00 for children 5 to 15, with a $25.00 family maximum.

Tubing. Apple River Campground, State Highway 35, Somerset, Wisconsin (800–637–8936); Float-Rite Park, Somerset (800–826–7096); River's Edge, 2 miles east of Somerset on State Highway 64 (715–247–3385); and Somerset Camp, Somerset (715–247–3728). All are seasonal.

Winter Alternatives

Cross-country Skiing. Lake Elmo Park, County Roads 17 and 10, Lake Elmo, Minnesota; (651) 731–3851. Afton State Park, 6959 Peller Avenue South, Hastings, Minnesota (651–436–5391), has 18 miles of trails, and William O'Brien State Park, 16821 O'Brien Trail North, Marine-on-St. Croix, Minnesota (651–433–3500), has 11 miles of trails.

Downhill Skiing. Afton Alps, 6600 Peller Avenue South, Afton, Minnesota (651–436–5245 or 800–328–1328), has thirty-two runs, tubing, four chalets, rentals, and lessons. Trollhaugen, State Highway 35 and County Road F, Dresser, Wisconsin (651–433–5141 or 800–826–7166), has forty-one runs, a chalet, rentals, and lessons. Wild Mountain, County Road 16 off State Highway 95, Taylors Falls, Minnesota (651–465–6315 or 800–257–3550), has twenty-three runs, a chalet, rentals, and lessons.

Special Events

May. Front Porch Festival, Hastings, Minnesota; (651) 437–6775 or (800) 612–6122. Includes a rocking chair marathon and dances around the maypole.

July. Rivertown Days Festival, Hastings; (651) 437–6775. Includes parades, water-ski shows, music, arts and crafts, and various competitions.

Wannigan Days, Taylors Falls, Minnesota, and St. Croix Falls, Wisconsin. Food, street dances, and more. Call (800) 851–4243.

July to August. Polk County Fair, St. Croix Falls.

August. The Scandia Speilmansstamma (Swedish Fiddler's Gathering), Scandia, Minnesota; (651) 439–7700.

North Hudson Pepperfest, Pepperfest Park, North Hudson, Wisconsin; (715) 386–8411 or (800) 657–6775. An Italian celebration that includes music, a parade, food, and activities.

September. Art in the Park, Afton, Minnesota; (651) 439–7700.

Main Street Festival, Hastings. A harvest celebration that includes bake sales, flea markets, and fruit from local orchards.

Marine Art Fair, Marine-on-St. Croix, Minnesota; (651) 439–7700.

Prescott Daze, Prescott, Wisconsin; (715) 262–3284 or (800) 474–3723.

Festivities include a parade, food vendors on the street, and sidewalk sales.

Osceola Wheels and Wings and Community Fair Weekend, Osceola, Wisconsin; (715) 755–3300 or (800) 947–0581. A collectible car show, arts-and-crafts fair, air show, parade, and carnival rides.

November. Christmas Lighting Fest (6:00 P.M. the day after Thanksgiving) and Historic House Tour, Taylors Falls, Minnesota; (800) 851–4243.

Other Recommended Restaurants and Lodgings

Afton, Minnesota

The Afton House Inn, 3291 South St. Croix Trail; (651) 436–8883; www.aftonhouseinn.com. The inn offers charming rooms, intimate dining, and peaceful surroundings. Each of the fifteen rooms boasts antique furnishings and a private bath; some have double whirlpool baths and gas fireplaces. Rooms range from $65 to $275 per night and include a continental breakfast, with homemade rolls, juice, and coffee. The Afton House is also well known for its cuisine. Whether you dine elegantly in the Wheel Room, choosing shrimp scampi (about $22) and flaming bananas Foster ($5.50); enjoy a simple meal such as a hamburger (about $6.50) or homemade pizza in the Catfish Saloon; or come just for the famous Sunday gourmet brunch, you'll be pleased. Wheelchair accessible.

Hastings, Minnesota

Mississippi Belle, 101 East Second Street; (651) 437–4814. A tradition since 1942, it offers a varied menu, specializing in seafood and Black Angus beef. Entrees, such as Cajun orange roughy and blackened catfish, start at $15. Open Tuesday through Friday for lunch from 11:00 A.M. to 2:30 P.M. and for dinner from 5:00 to 9:00 P.M. Open for dinner only Saturday, 5:00 to 9:00 P.M.

The Thorwood and Rosewood Inns are two of Minnesota's premier bed-and-breakfast inns, known for their incredible style, decor, furnishings, sunken bathrooms, superb food (gourmet dinners for two are available), and a variety of personalized amenities and packages for a memorable weekend. Between the two inns there are fifteen rooms from which to choose, each richly decorated and each offering something special, whether it's a private porch swing or a see-through fireplace. A two-night minimum stay is required on the weekends, except for the suites. Rates range from about $97 to about $277 per night and include an evening snack and a full breakfast. Smoke free. The Thorwood, an 1880 French Second Empire design, is located at 315 Pine Street. The Rosewood, an 1880 Queen Anne design, is located at 620 Ramsey Street. Call (651) 437–3297; www.thorwoodinn.com.

Lake Elmo, Minnesota

The Lake Elmo Inn, 3442 Lake Elmo Avenue, between State Highway 36 and I–694, is an old stagecoach stop turned award-winning restaurant. With stained-glass windows, white tablecloths, and all the charm of the turn of the twentieth century, the inn provides an elegant setting, friendly atmosphere, and delicious food. The service, which includes warmed hand towels after dinner, is unsurpassed. The menu features a variety of vegetarian items, salads, and soups. Dinner entrees range from a wild rice pasta sautéed with vegetables, cashews, and julienne duck ($11.95) to roast duckling ($16.95) to Cajun pork chops ($18.50). The extensive dessert menu changes constantly and includes a different torte every day—all prepared by the inn's award-winning pastry chef. The inn is open 11:00 A.M. to 1:30 P.M. and 5:00 to 10:00 P.M. Monday through Saturday, 10:00 A.M. to 1:30 P.M. (for brunch) and 4:30 to 8:30 P.M. on Sunday. Reservations are recommended, especially on weekends and holidays. Call (651) 777–8495. Wheelchair accessible.

Marine-on-St. Croix, Minnesota

Asa Parker House Bed and Breakfast Inn, 17500 St. Croix Trail North; (651) 433–5248 or (888) 857–9969. Sitting majestically on a hill overlooking the St. Croix River Valley, the inn is filled with antiques, adorned with flowers, and nestled in private gardens. The Asa Parker House provides the ultimate retreat from the hustle and bustle of city life. All the rooms have private baths (some have whirlpools), and one has a gas-burning fireplace. This winner of awards, both for food and accommodations, is bound to win your heart, too. Rooms range from $125 to $179 per night, with a 10 percent discount midweek, and include a full breakfast featuring items such as French toast Grand Marnier or baked peach pancakes.

Taylors Falls, Minnesota

Pines Motel, 543 River Street; (651) 465–3422. A charming motel with standard amenities, but it feels like a country inn with its decor, gazebo, and creek running through the property. Within walking distance of the river and downtown. Rates are about $49 per night.

Hudson, Wisconsin

Barker's Bar and Grill, 413 Second Street; (715) 386–4123. If you feel the need for a good hamburger, head to Barker's. It features hamburgers and assorted sandwiches at reasonable prices. Open daily from 11:00 A.M. to 11:00 P.M.

The Grapevine Inn Bed and Breakfast, 702 Vine Street; (715) 386–1989; www.grapevineinn.com. The room names alone at this charming country inn make it enticing: Bordeaux and Buttercream, Champagne and Roses, and Chardonnay and Emeralds. Each room is professionally decorated and has a private bath; one has a gas fireplace. Guests are invited to share the home and the private swimming pool. Rooms range in price from $120 to $149 per night (with a two-night minimum) and include a full breakfast with a gourmet entree, baked fruit, and homemade muffins. Rates are reduced midweek.

The Jefferson-Day House, 1109 Third Street; (715) 386–7111; www.jefferson dayhouse.com. The oldest bed-and-breakfast in Hudson, its motto is "Arrive as a guest, leave as a friend." The lovely Italianate structure dates from 1857, but the amenities surpass modern expectations. Each spacious room has a queen-size bed, a gas fireplace, a whirlpool tub for two, and complimentary cocktails. Common areas include the living room and library (including the keyboard of the baby grand piano). Rooms range from $139 to $199 per night, with reduced rates midweek, and include a four-course breakfast. Smoke free.

San Pedro Cafe, 426 Second Street; (715) 386–4003; www.sanpedro cafe.com. A taste of the Caribbean in downtown Hudson, this bright cafe serves breakfast, lunch, and dinner and also has an espresso bar in a smoke-free atmosphere. Their slogan says it all: "No Burgers! No Butts!" The menu ranges from hearty breakfasts to wood-fired gourmet pizzas and a good variety of Caribbean-inspired dishes such as jerk-rubbed chicken, Yucatán pork stew, and vegetable linguini. Dinner prices range from $9.95 to $16.95, salads and sandwiches from $7.95 to $9.95. Open Monday through Thursday 10:30 A.M. to 10:00 P.M., Friday 10:30 A.M. to 11:00 P.M., Saturday 8:00 A.M. to 11:00 P.M., and Sunday from 8:00 A.M. to 10:00 P.M.

Osceola, Wisconsin

Pleasant Lake Inn, 2238 Sixtieth Avenue; (715) 294–2545 or (800) 294–2545. Few bed-and-breakfast inns have the beautiful wooded lake-view setting of Pleasant Lake. There are four rooms, and each has a private bath (three have whirlpool tubs). Rates range from $89 to $149 per night and include a hearty breakfast. Smoke free.

Prescott, Wisconsin

The Arbor Inn, 434 North Court Street; (715) 262–4522; www.thearbor inn.com. This lovely red-brick turn-of-the-twentieth-century home offers that era's hospitality. The house is furnished with antiques, the beds are covered with custom hand-pieced quilts, and each of the three rooms has a private bath (all have whirlpool tubs). Rates range from $145 to $179 per night and include a four-course breakfast. Smoke free.

The Steamboat Inn, base of the U.S. Highway 10 bridge; (715) 480–8222 or (800) 262–8232. A St. Croix River tradition, the Steamboat Inn offers casual dining, a full bar, live entertainment on weekends, and beautiful views of the river. Dinner entrees include roasted Wisconsin duckling and, on occasion, hickory-smoked prime rib in a maple lager au jus ($15 and up). Open Monday 4:30 to 9:00 P.M., Tuesday through Saturday 11:30 A.M. to 2:00 P.M. and 4:30 to 9:00 P.M., and Sunday 10:00 A.M. to 9:00 P.M.

For More Information

Afton Business Association/Stillwater Area Chamber of Commerce, 423 South Main Street, Stillwater, MN 55082; (651) 439–7700. Information on Afton, Bayport, Lakeland, Lake Elmo, Marine-on-St. Croix, and Scandia.

Dresser Business Association, 710 State Highway 35 South, St. Croix Falls, WI 54024; (715) 483–1410 or (800) 222–POLK. Information on Dresser and St. Croix Falls.

Hastings Area Chamber of Commerce, 119 West Second Street, Hastings, MN 55033; (651) 437–6775; www.hastingsmn.org.

Hudson Area Chamber of Commerce and Tourism Bureau, 502 Second Street, Hudson, WI 54016–0438; (715) 386–8411 or (800) 657–6775; www.hudsonwi.org.

Interstate State Park, 12 U.S. Highway B, Taylors Falls, MN 55084; (651) 465–5711; Wisconsin, (715) 483–3747.

National Park Service, 401 Hamilton Street, St. Croix Falls, WI 54024; (715) 483–3284; or 117 South Main Street, Stillwater, MN 54024; (651) 430–1938.

New Richmond Area Chamber of Commerce, 150 West First Street, New Richmond, WI 54017–1742; (715) 246–2900.

Osceola Business Association, P.O. Box 251, Osceola, WI 54020–0251; (800) 947–0581 or (715) 755–3300.

Prescott Area Chamber of Commerce, 233 Broad Street North, Prescott, WI 54021; (715) 262–3284.

River Falls Area Chamber of Commerce, 109 West Walnut Street, River Falls, WI 54022–2244; (715) 425–2533.

Somerset Area Chamber of Commerce, P.O. Box 357, Somerset, WI 54025–0357; (715) 247–3366.

Taylors Falls Chamber of Commerce, P.O. Box 235, Taylors Falls, MN 55084; (651) 257–3550 or (800) 447–4958; www.taylorsfalls.com.

William O'Brien State Park, 16821 O'Brien Trail North, Marine-on-St. Croix, MN 55047; (651) 433–0500.

WISCONSIN
ESCAPES

Bayfield and Madeline Island

Sailboats and Superior Scenery

2 Nights

It's no surprise that Bayfield, Wisconsin, was named the "Best Little Town in the Midwest" by the *Chicago Tribune*. Bayfield is about as close as we come in this region to an eastern seaboard village. The town sits on a hill that gently rolls toward the shore of Lake Superior, and most of the homes and buildings have clapboard siding and come in assorted blues, yellows, and pinks. So it even looks friendly. There is a special charm to the windswept look of the shore-front buildings of not only Bayfield but also La Pointe on Madeline Island. It means hard work, endurance, and pride.

- ☐ Water Sports
- ☐ Ferry Rides
- ☐ Lighthouses

And Bayfield feels like a secret: the secret you want to tell the world but keep to yourself forever. This kind of secret makes Bayfield's restaurants and lodgings hard to get into, yet keeps it quaint.

Along with Bayfield comes access to Madeline and about twenty other islands that make up the Apostle Islands National Lakeshore. This is boat country: Whether you sail or ride on the ferry or just encounter boat relics in the antiques stores, they are a constant part of the great lake's scenery.

Day 1 / Morning

Bayfield is about a four-hour drive north of the Twin Cities. Follow I–35 north through Duluth to U.S. Highway 53, which takes you through Superior, Wisconsin, to U.S. Highway 2 east. A couple of miles west of Ashland, turn left (north) on State Highway 13, and follow it to Bayfield. Highway 13 takes you through the very nice town of Washburn. By now you have seen the signs with the circus tent on them that read BIG TOP CHATAUQUA and wondered what it means. The Big Top is a tent that houses live entertainment all summer long and has featured artists such as Garrison

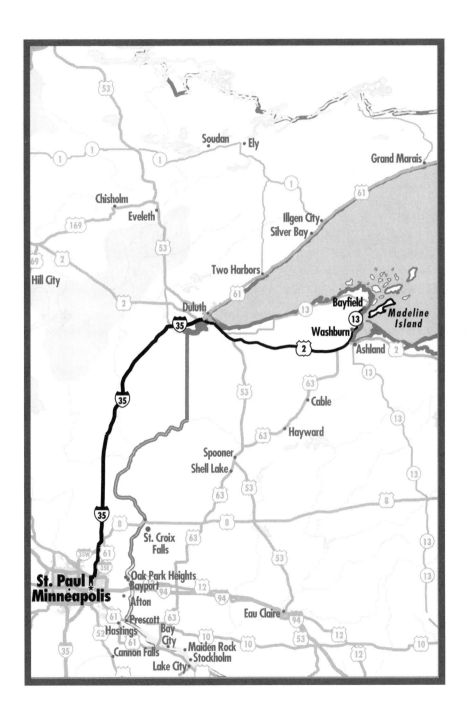

Keillor, Leon Redbone, and the Kingston Trio. Call (715) 373–5552 or (888) BIG–TENT; www.bigtop.org. Stop in **Chequamegon Book & Coffee Co.,** 2 East Bayfield Street (715–373–2899), for the Big Top newsletter (there may be a show going on tonight). You'll probably also find yourself browsing the shelves of this used- and fine-book dealer and maybe even helping yourself to a cup of coffee in the sunny room next door. Across the street is the **Washburn Historical Museum** (715–373–5591), an old turn-of-the-twentieth-century brownstone. The building alone is magnificent, and there are historical exhibits of local industries and founding families—definitely worth the stop—and a place where you can buy Big Top tickets. Open April through December 10:00 A.M. to 4:00 P.M.; January through March open by appointment only. Donations are suggested. Continue on State Highway 13 to Bayfield. The highway winds its way into town and becomes Rittenhouse Avenue. Rittenhouse continues all the way down to the shore.

LUNCH: Gruenke's First Street Inn, 17 Rittenhouse Avenue, is a great introduction to the fun and diversity of Bayfield. The restaurant is decorated with all kinds of memorabilia, including an authentic Wurlitzer jukebox, and offers breakfast until 2:00 P.M., because it's so good. Don't miss the Bayfield raspberry pancakes when in season (about $5.25), served with real whipped cream. The rest of the extensive menu includes hamburgers, salads, hot turkey sandwiches, and barbecue ribs, but it's famous for the fish, particularly the Friday-night fish boils (in summer, weather permitting) that include coleslaw, potatoes, rolls, and a dessert for about $12 per person. Call (715) 779–5480 or (800) 245–3072.

Afternoon

Take some time to drive the streets of Bayfield and get acquainted with this delightful town before you park and wander the streets and wharf on foot. You'll discover some great shops, and the wharf, where the ferry arrives and departs, is a great place for taking pictures. Don't miss **The Candy Shoppe,** 217 Rittenhouse Avenue, as you sightsee. It has really good homemade fudge, toffee, peanut brittle, and other goodies.

Now's the time to put your name on the list for dinner at Maggie's (before you get too hungry), and then keep shopping.

DINNER: Way ahead of its time, the rehabbed cottage housing **Maggie's** restaurant, 257 Manypenny Avenue, has been a popular destination for over twenty years. With its bright pink exterior and its funky decor, Maggie's is like a piñata full of surprises. The first surprise, especially on a weekend, is the up-to-two-hour-long wait. But the second surprise is that it's worth it! From hamburgers (about $5.50) and pasta to Mexican pizza (about $11.00 for the 12-inch size), every morsel is delicious. The fresh Lake Superior whitefish served with black beans and rice (about $13) is a well-known favorite. Open all year, 11:00 A.M. to 11:00 P.M. on weekdays (until midnight on weekends) in the summer and 11:00 A.M. to 9:00 P.M. in the winter. Call (715) 779–5641.

LODGING: Consider this a romantic getaway, and plan to splurge and be pampered for two nights at the **Old Rittenhouse Inn,** the magnificent Victorian home on the corner of Third Street and Rittenhouse Avenue. Operating for well over twenty years, the Old Rittenhouse has a superb reputation and is probably one of the finest inns in the nation; the hospitality is as gracious as the decor is exquisite. Each guest room is filled with antiques and has a private bath and fireplace. A lake-view room with a queen-size bed and a whirlpool runs about $179 per night for two and includes a continental breakfast of fruit or juice and homemade breads. Call (715) 779–5111 or (800) 779–2129; www.rittenhouseinn.com.

Day 2 / Morning

BREAKFAST: The Old Rittenhouse Inn.

After breakfast step down from the veranda onto Rittenhouse Avenue and go to the dock to catch the **Madeline Island Lake Superior Ferry** to **Madeline Island** for the day. The ferries run daily from "breakup" to "freeze up," but how frequently depends on the season. During the summer the ferries leave Bayfield every half hour from 9:30 A.M. to 6:00 P.M., then on the hour until 11:00 P.M. There is a fee for every person, vehicle, motorcycle, trailer, and bicycle, so keep in mind that just about everything you'll want to do you can do on foot. Besides, bikes and mopeds are available for rent on the island. Midsummer one-way ferry rates: adults $4.00; children 6 to 11, $2.00. An empty car is $9.25. (Getting across will probably be the most expensive thing you do on the island.) The crossing from Bayfield to La Pointe takes fifteen to twenty minutes and will be a highlight of the weekend. Call (715) 747–2051 or visit www.madferry.com.

Once across, head straight up the wharf to the stockadelike fence, the site of the **Madeline Island Historical Museum.** This superb museum beautifully interprets the history of the island as an integral part of the fur trade and how it evolved into a settlement and then a tourist attraction. How families could survive a winter on the island, then and now, is fascinating. The main building is a composite of original log structures from the island; the central building is an original warehouse built by the American Fur Company in 1835. Allow at least an hour to tour the museum and see the presentation. Open daily Memorial Day weekend through the first weekend in October 10:00 A.M. to 4:00 P.M. (until 6:00 P.M. mid-July through mid-August). Admission: adults $5.00; seniors $4.50; children 5 to 12, $2.25. Call (715) 747–2415.

LUNCH: Walk down the street to **Grandpa Tony's** for a great hot sandwich on homemade bread. Choose from sub sandwiches, the famous garlic burger (made with green olives, mozzarella cheese, and a secret garlic sauce), and homemade pizzas. Made-to-order fresh salads are also available. Prices range from $2.50 for a hot dog to $10.00 for a 14-inch pizza. Open daily seasonally, 7:00 A.M. to 9:00 P.M., with some extended hours Friday and Saturday. Call (715) 747–3911.

Afternoon

You can spend your afternoon wandering around on foot and browsing the gift shops, or choose a more adventuresome approach to exploring Madeline Island. Mopeds and all types of bikes are available for rent at **Motion to Go,** just off Main Street on Middle Road; (715) 747–6585. There are no designated bike paths on the island, but cars are used to sharing the road here, and the 15-mile round-trip to **Big Bay State Park** is a pleasant ride. The bikes are available during the tourist season; rates depend on the type of bike requested and length of use. Canoes and rowboats are also available for use in **Big Bay Town Park** through **Bog Lake Outfitters.** Call (715) 747–2685 for canoe rental rates. Swimming beaches are located in both **Big Bay State Park** (715–747–6425 or 715–779–4020) and Big Bay Town Park. Big Bay State Park is open from 6:00 A.M. to 11:00 P.M.; admission stickers are required on motorized vehicles.

DINNER: Allow yourself enough time to freshen up for your dinner in the elegant dining room of the Old Rittenhouse Inn. Then spend at least two hours savoring the ambience and each course of the five-course gourmet dinner presentation. The menus are verbal, and entrees change nightly, depending on the evening's chef, but there are always fish, steak, and poultry dishes offered. A steak could be a perfectly done filet mignon or an enhanced filet filled with oysters. One of the best desserts is the chocolate, chocolate, chocolate, chocolate cake, that is, of course, made with four different kinds of chocolate. The fixed dinner price is about $45 per person.

Day 3 / Morning

BREAKFAST: On this morning you might want to opt for a choice of eggs, omelettes, or pancakes from the Rittenhouse menu (about an additional $5.00 per person) so your breakfast holds you for your morning cruise around the Apostle Islands.

There are several cruises, but the **Inner Island Shuttle** allows you to tour the **Raspberry Island Lighthouse** and the surrounding gardens. So eat heartily, put on your walking shoes, and head to the **Lake Superior Boatmen's Memorial Dock** on the wharf. This cruise leaves at 10:30 A.M. and returns at 1:15 P.M. Offered late-June through September. Fare: adults $30; children 6 to 12, $17. Call the Apostle Islands Cruise Service for reservations, (715) 779–3925 or (800) 323–7619.

Back on the mainland, grab lunch at Gruenke's before you head home.

There's More

Camping. Some of the best camping around is in Big Bay State Park, Madeline Island. Call the Wisconsin Department of Natural Resources, (715) 779–4020 or (715) 747–6425. For camping reservations call (888) 947–2757.

Casino. The Isle Vista Casino, Red Cliff Indian Reservation, 3 miles north of Bayfield on State Highway 13. Bowling, bingo, and a beach are offered in addition to standard casino games. Call (715) 779–3712 or (800) 226–8478.

Golf. The Apostle Highlands Golf Course, County Road J west of Bayfield; (715) 779–5960. The club offers eighteen holes and a great view of Lake Superior.

Kayaking. Trek and Trail, 222 Rittenhouse Avenue, Bayfield; (715) 779–3595 or (800) 354–8735; www.trek-trail.com. The company offers lessons and kayak adventures.

Sailboat Rides. Sail the inland sea with the Animaashi Sailing Company on a 34-foot yacht. Full- and half-day trips are offered, starting at $45 per person. Call (715) 779–5468 or (888) 272–4548; www.animaashi.com.

Winter Alternatives

Dogsledding. Trek and Trail, 222 Rittenhouse Avenue, Bayfield; (715) 779–3595 or (800) 354–8735. Wolfsong Adventures in Mushing, HC64 Box 107, Bayfield; (715) 779–5561 or (800) 262–4176; www.wolfsong adventures.com.

Ice-skating. Skate for free, skates included, at the base of Broad Street, Bayfield.

Skiing. Mt. Ashwabay (715–779–3227) is 3 miles south of Bayfield on State Highway 13 and has thirteen downhill runs and 40 kilometers of cross-country trails. It also offers lessons for both. Mt. Valhalla (715–373–2667), 8 miles west of Washburn on County Road C, offers cross-country trails for skating and traditional styles.

Snowmobiling. There are 550 miles of groomed trails in Bayfield County. Call (715) 373–6125 or (800) 472–6338.

Special Events

February. Madeline Island Sled Dog Race, Madeline Island; (715) 747–2801.

July. Red Cliff Traditional Pow Wow, Red Cliff Indian Reservation, 3 miles north of Bayfield, State Highway 13; (715) 779–3700. Singing, dancing, and traditional foods.

Bayfield Festival of the Arts, Memorial Park, Bayfield; (715) 779–3335 or (800) 447–4094. Includes fine arts, music, and children's activities.

August. Bayfield Wooden Boat Rendezvous, City Dock, Bayfield; (715) 779–5995. Visiting builders of kayaks and canoes, plus a nautical flea market.

September. Lighthouse Festival, Bayfield; (715) 779–3335 or (800) 447–4094.

Schooner Days, Bayfield; (715) 779–3335 or (800) 447–4094. Schooner races, bagpipers, and pirates.

Apple Festival

October. Bayfield Apple Festival, Bayfield; (715) 779–3335 or (800) 447–4094. Apple everything, from pies to mustards, to sample or take home, an art fair, and street performers.

Other Recommended Restaurants and Lodgings

Gruenke's First Street Inn, 17 Rittenhouse Avenue; (715) 779–5480 or (800) 245–3072; wwwgruenkesinn.com. Not only a fun place to eat, it is also a reliably good place to stay. The original hotel dates from 1863, making the rooms exceedingly charming. Each one is different, and the amenities vary from old-fashioned with shared baths to rooms with private baths, including one with a big-screen television. A room with a private bath runs from $55 to $130 per night and includes a continental breakfast.

The Isaac Wing House, 17 South First Street; (715) 779–3907 or (800)

382–0995; www.isaacwinghouse.com. This is the unique restored home of Isaac Wing, a humble philanthropist. With its barn-red exterior and an inviting front porch, the inn offers a country retreat in the heart of Bayfield. The pleasant suites rent for $85 to $110 per night.

The Island Inn is a pleasant modern motel with a country feel. The adjacent **Old Le Pointe Inn,** a country house, also has rooms for rent. Both are located within walking distance of the Madeline Island Ferry, La Pointe, Madeline Island. The Island Inn rooms have televisions and refrigerators. Three of the Old Le Pointe rooms share a bath upstairs; the downstairs suite has a private bath. Rates run about $98 a night for the Island Inn, with reduced rates in the winter; rates run about $95 a night at the Old Le Pointe Inn. Call (715) 747–2000; www.ontheisland.com; for the Island Inn and for the Old Le Pointe Inn, (715) 747–2628; www.lapointeinn.com.

Portside Restaurant, a couple of miles south of town on State Highway 13; (715) 779–5380. Be sure to ask for a window seat—the restaurant looks out at the marina with its multitude of sailboats—for a terrific backdrop to an equally terrific dinner. The menu includes fish, depending on what's in season (from $10) to kabobs, pastas, and a center-cut New York strip steak (about $18). Open May through mid-October, dinner only.

Reiten Boatyard Condominiums, 320 South Wilson Avenue; (715) 779–3621 or (800) 842–1199; www.apostleislands.com. Accommodations are completely furnished and outfitted. Open all year, with reduced rates October 16 to May 14, except for Christmas and New Year's Eve, which call for standard rates. A one-bedroom suite, accommodating up to four people, runs about $125 per night during peak season.

Seagull Bay Motel, State Highway 13, on the right-hand side just before you get into town; (715) 779–5558. This very clean and pleasant motel offers all the standard amenities, in addition to great views of Lake Superior, for very reasonable prices. An unpaved biking/walking trail is just below the motel and follows the old railroad grade 3 blocks into town, coming out at Maggie's restaurant, or about 2 miles south to Port Superior Marina, where the Portside Restaurant is located. The motel is also on the snowmobile trail that runs through town. Open all year, with reduced rates from October 16 to May 15. Some units have kitchens, but a standard room for two runs about $60 per night.

The Silvernail Guest House, 249½ Rittenhouse Avenue; (715) 779–5575. Diminutive even in its address, it's big in charm and hospitality. The rooms are elegant, and each one has a double-whirlpool bath and a shower. Rooms rent for $109 per night, with reduced rates in the winter. A continental breakfast of gourmet coffees and homemade breads is included. Smoke free.

For More Information

Bayfield Chamber of Commerce, 42 South Broad Street, Bayfield, WI 54814; (715) 779–3335 or (800) 447–4094; www.bayfield.org.

Madeline Island Chamber of Commerce, P.O. Box 274, La Pointe, WI 54850; (715) 747–2801 or (888) 475–3386; www.madelineisland.com.

Washburn Chamber of Commerce, 109 West Bayfield Street, Washburn, WI 54891; (800) 253–4495; www.washburnchamber.com.

The Hayward Lakes Area

Fun and Fish Stories

2 Nights

The Hayward Lakes area of Wisconsin is parallel to the Brainerd Lakes area of Minnesota; both are three hours from the Twin Cities. Despite their proximity and matching latitudes, however, there is a remarkable difference in the appearance of these two resort areas. Some say it's the hills, which make Wisconsin look greener as you dip and wind through the country-side; some say it's the trees (Wisconsin has more hardwoods); while others say it's the way the trees and grasses grow right to the edge of the water alongside the Wisconsin lakeshores. Whatever the reason, the Hayward Lakes area seems woodsier, more remote, more rustic, and maybe even heartier.

☐ Resorts
☐ Muskies
☐ Wilderness
☐ Lumberjacks

There are more than 200 lakes and flowages in these Wisconsin North Woods. In 1923 when Northern States Power dammed the Chippewa River and instantly created the Chippewa Flowage, Wisconsin's largest wilderness lake, it also instantly created a recreational mecca for hunting, fishing, and vacationing, and hundreds of resorts sprang up almost as fast.

Along with the largest wilderness lake, Hayward lays claim to the largest of many attractions, from muskies to powwows to ski races. That means there's something for everyone—and a lot of it to go around.

Day 1 / Morning

The drive to Hayward is an easy one. Follow I–94 east through St. Paul and across the state line to Hammond, Wisconsin, where you pick up U.S. Highway 63 and go north all the way to Hayward. Once off the freeway, at Hammond, the drive becomes a very pleasant one as it rolls through lush farmland dotted with old town halls, antiques stores, and vegetable stands.

Unless it's the dead of winter, be sure to watch for the **Country Lane** produce stand on your right near Clear Lake. You will first be in awe of the little stone cottage with curlicue shutters (straight out of a fairy tale),

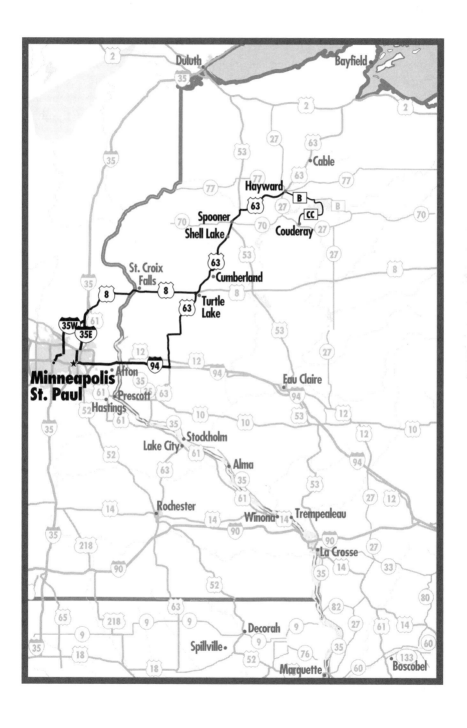

and then be delighted that flowers, fruits, and vegetables are for sale. The owners work artistic wonders decorating the grounds and ruins of an old barn with flowers and vines, and the organically grown fruits of their labors are delicious. Whether it's strawberry, raspberry, squash, or pumpkin season, it will be hard to depart empty-handed. Country Lane is open daily at 9:00 A.M. during the growing season. Call (715) 263–2105.

As you continue on U.S. Highway 63, the route takes you through smaller resort communities such as **Turtle Lake** (home of the **St. Croix Casino and Hotel;** it sits right on the highway, flanked by gift shops and antiques stores) and then **Cumberland.**

LUNCH: Cumberland is only a couple of hours out of the Twin Cities, so this may be an early lunch, but the **Tower House Restaurant,** on the highway in the heart of the business district, is worth the stop. Ahead of its time in the course of remodeling and reuse of old buildings, this restored Victorian mansion, once the family home of a local lumber baron, has been a restaurant since 1951. There are the traditional lunch offerings of hamburgers (starting at $2.50) and numerous sandwiches, from BLTs to turkey (about $2.65), but the Tower House is famous for its Italian dishes ($6.00 to $8.00), most notably for its sauce, available "to go." Of course, the breads, pies, cakes, and cookies are homemade, so if it is early, a bowl of soup ($1.85), a warm homemade roll, and a cookie may just hit the spot. Open daily, except Christmas, 8:00 A.M. to 10:00 P.M., Sunday to 9:00 P.M., with reduced hours in winter. Call (715) 822–8457.

Afternoon

Just up the road in **Shell Lake** is another Wisconsin boast, the world's largest **Museum of Woodcarving,** a collection carved by one man. This is the work of Joseph Barta, who spent thirty years carving one hundred life-size religious figures depicting various Biblical stories and numerous miniature carvings, primarily of animals. Open daily May through October 9:00 A.M. to 6:00 P.M. Admission: adults $4.00; children 4 to 11, $2.00. Call (715) 468–7100.

The next stop is **Spooner.** Like many other resort communities, Spooner was first a major railroad junction during the logging era, and then the railroad also brought tourists. Befitting its history, two of Spooner's best attractions revolve around trains: the **Railroad Memories Museum,** Island Lake Road, and the nearby, but independent, **Wisconsin Great Northern Railroad,** which offers historic railroad excursions. The museum is an exceptional display of railroad artifacts and memorabilia at home in the old Spooner depot. Open daily Memorial Day through Labor Day 10:00 A.M. to 5:00 P.M. Admission: adults $2.00; children 6 to 12, 50 cents. Call (715) 635–2752 or (715) 635–3325. The train runs daily mid-June through late October, with a variety of departure times and rides, including the special Pizza Train and Dinner Train. The standard excursion is a 14-mile trip from Spooner to Trego and back, lasting about ninety minutes. Fare: adults $15; children 2 to 12, $10. Call (715) 635–3200 or (888) 390–0412.

Continue north through Hayward, and turn right on County Road B. You will soon agree that just driving through this lakes area can be an adventure, as you quickly find yourself deep in the woods and the road names become single- and double-letter codes. You also have a good chance of spotting bears, so keep your eyes open.

DINNER: Follow County Road B east 17 miles to the classic **Dun Rovin Lodge.** Dun Rovin captures the essence of the Hayward Lakes area with its rustic, although almost elegant, interior adorned with a tremendous collection of wildlife trophies, including the world record muskie, (seventy pounds, four ounces), another Hayward claim to fame, caught more than forty-five years ago.

The menu is another legitimate boast: It is one of the best in the region. Perfectly balanced between seafood, pasta, and flame-broiled steaks, there is something for all tastes. Of course, nothing seems more appropriate than fish in this region, so the Canadian walleye may be the best choice. Broiled or pan-fried, with garlic peanut oil, white wine, and lemon, the walleye, like all other entrees, comes with soup, salad, homemade sorbet, choice of potato or rice, a fresh vegetable, and bread. All entrees range from $13 to $20. Open for dinner every day Memorial Day through Labor Day and Wednesday through Sunday the rest of the year, 5:00 to 10:00 P.M. Lunch is served from 11:30 A.M. to 4:00 P.M. every day except during November, December, March, and April. Call for reservations, (715) 462–3834.

Back on County Road B, backtrack west about 1.5 miles to County Road A and turn right (north). Continue on County Road A for several miles until you come to State Highway 77, turn left, and follow it west to Murphy Road (if you see County Road OO, you've gone too far). Take a right on Murphy Road and follow it for about 5 miles, all the way to the big log lodge.

LODGING: The big log lodge is **Spider Lake Lodge Bed & Breakfast,** 6,000 square feet of North Woods heaven. Built in 1923 as a resort, Spider Lake Lodge now houses seven guest rooms, all with private baths. Consider its cathedral ceiling, fieldstone fireplaces at each end of the living room, and a 1,296-square-foot dining room with endless windows that look out at the lake and the woods, and you'll know that just setting foot in the door will take your breath away. It's also filled with rustic furniture, creating the ultimate lodge ambience. Some of the furniture and even some of the animal trophies are original, adding to the lodge's historic charm. Pick the room with the cast-iron stove, and snuggle in for the night. Rooms rent all year between $110 and $145 a night. Call (800) 653–9472 or (715) 462–3793; ww.spiderlakelodge.com.

Day 2 / Morning

BREAKFAST: The lodge's breakfast menu changes every day, but it's always five to seven courses long and certain to please. You can count on fresh fruit and homemade muffins, and then hope you're lucky enough to be there the morning they serve old-fashioned oatmeal topped with butter, brown sugar, and sautéed apples. On the other hand, the blueberry pancakes, asparagus egg casserole, or eggs Benedict won't disappoint you. Enjoy your breakfast, maybe even a game of checkers, and the morning view of the lake, which will probably lure you to its shore for a ride in the waterbike or canoe, before you depart for some unique sightseeing.

Later, retrace your steps on County Roads A and B to County Road CC and turn left (south). Now wind your way through the woods and the Chippewa Flowage to Couderay and **The Hideout,** the modern name for the gift shop and restaurant complex that includes gangster Al Capone's country retreat. "Aim" your arrival for noon, when the restaurant opens, and start with lunch.

LUNCH: It's definitely fine dining at The Hideout, in an elegant atmosphere of a bygone era, but it caters to vacationers and dress is casual. The Hideout exploits its claim to fame and serves Chicago-style deli sandwiches and northern Italian specialties, along with steaks, chicken, and seafood (from $10 to $25). The notorious hamburgers (about $8.00) draw tourists and locals from miles around. If you have any room after lunch, stop at **The Fancy Flapper Ice Cream Emporium** for a sundae or just a cone to go. The Hideout restaurant is open daily, with varying hours, Memorial Day through September and on weekends October through

May. The house and museum tours, and treats at the ice-cream emporium, are available May through October only, noon to 7:00 P.M., with reduced hours after Labor Day. Call (715) 945–2746.

Afternoon

By the time you finish lunch in the 1920s, you'll be ready to see what life was like for Al Capone in this era on his *country* estate; there were no woods here in the 1920s. (Of course, you've had quite a taste of luxury cabin living already at Spider Lake Lodge.)

About the time that the Northern States Power Company was altering the terrain of this part of Wisconsin to harvest electrical power, Capone, one of Chicago's most powerful gangsters, was seeking refuge in it. The "Boss" chose this scenic spot of 400 acres overlooking Cranberry Lake and built a stunning cottage that combined rustic decor (its fieldstone fireplace and log interior) with the elegance of city life (a state-of-the-art bathroom and a matched pair of hand-carved mahogany spiral staircases leading to the second floor). It's not surprising that there are so few windows in the home of this notorious mobster, or that the stone walls are a foot and a half thick, or that the balcony provides a lookout on all sides, but it makes for a unique architectural and historical experience. And your introduction to this secret world doesn't stop with the house. Also on the grounds are the original garages (part of the restaurant complex) with gun slots along the roofline, a jail cell, a doghouse, maintenance buildings, and some left-to-rust, but pertinent, automobiles. New to the site is a Roaring Twenties museum with minimal items from the era, including clothing and a restored car, but not Capone's. The pride and joy of the museum, hidden behind the green curtain, is a melodramatic reenactment of the St. Valentine's Day Massacre of 1929 with taped dialogue and battered mannequins, but it doesn't hold a candle to the real exhibits that offer insight into the life of a mobster.

Allow yourself a good couple of hours to take the tour, wander the grounds, and peruse the gift shop, which includes antiques and a lot of interesting photographs and related gangster artifacts.

DINNER: After fine dining and country living, sometimes you need some basic home cooking or a pizza. If you or the kids have a craving for pizza, head to **Coops Pizza Parloure,** 10588 California Avenue. Coops offers a variety of pizzas, from vegetarian to something for the serious carnivore, and everything in between. And if you don't feel like pizza, they have a wide selection of sandwiches, salads, and pasta. Prices are reasonable, and the restaurant also has a respectable beer list. Open from 11:00 A.M. to 10:00 P.M. Call (715) 634–3027. If pizza doesn't interest you, perhaps some good old home cooking followed by a piece of pie baked on-site will. **Norske Nook Restaurant and Bakery,** 10436 State Highway 27, is the type of place locals know of but travelers might drive by without stopping. Located in a small building decorated in Scandinavian style, the restaurant serves the type of food you might find your grandmother serving, such as roasted turkey, hot beef sandwiches, and the like. And because Norske Nook is also a bakery, you can't beat their pies, cookies, and other baked goods. The tough part is saving room for dessert. Open Monday through Saturday 5:30 A.M. to 8:00 P.M., Sunday 8:00 A.M. to 8:00 P.M. Call (715) 634–4928.

LODGING: Spider Lake Lodge Bed & Breakfast.

Day 3 / Morning

BREAKFAST: Spider Lake Lodge Bed & Breakfast.

After breakfast head into downtown Hayward for a little souvenir shopping before you head home. There are several gift shops and two delectable places to stop. The **Hayward Bakery and Cheese Shop,** 10565 Main Street, specializes in European breads, Wisconsin cheeses, and all of the ordinary bakery items, except that here they're *extraordinary.* Call (715) 634–2428 or (800) 266–2428. **Tremblay's Sweet Shop, Inc.,** 122 Main Street, is just doors away, with a fantasyland interior of old-fashioned candy, lollipops, hand-dipped chocolates, fudge in the making, and live ragtime piano music in the background. Call (715) 634–2785 or (800) 40–FUDGE.

LUNCH: Shop until you work up an appetite—or at least walk off the candy—and stop for lunch at **The Angler's Bar & Grill,** 133 Main Street. This is an interesting place that dates from the 1930s and has its original four-lane bowling alley inside. Sit outside, if weather permits, and enjoy a homemade pizza, a taco salad, or a bowl of homemade soup or chili. Prices hover around $6.00, except for the pizzas; pizza prices depend on the size and toppings. Open daily all year from 10:00 A.M. to 2:00 A.M., serving food from 11:00 A.M. to 10:00 P.M. Call (715) 634–4700.

For a uniquely scenic route home, if you have the time to meander a little, follow U.S. Highway 63 south to Turtle Lake, then take U.S. Highway

8 due west through St. Croix Falls to Taylors Falls on the Minnesota side of the St. Croix River. Then follow State Highway 95 south, through Stillwater, to either I–36 or I–94, which will take you west back into the Twin Cities.

There's More

Biking. The CAMBA (Chequamegon Area Mountain Bike Association) mountain bike trail offers single- and double-track dirt or gravel surfaces on several trails in Cable, Wisconsin. Call (800) 533–7454 for maps; www.cambatrails.org.

Camping. Lake Chippewa Campground (715–462–3672; www.lake chip.com) has tent and trailer sites, a boat landing, and rentals. Primitive camping is available in Chequamegon National Forest (715–634–4821), with many lakefront locations.

Casino. Lac Courte Oreilles Casino Lodge and Convention Center, 4 miles east of Hayward on County Road 5; (715) 634–8574 or (800) 526–5634.

Golf. Hayward National Golf Club, Route 6, Hayward (715–634–6727), has eighteen holes, rentals, and a driving range. Hayward Golf and Tennis, downtown Hayward (715–634–2760), has eighteen holes, a driving range, pro shop, restaurant, and bar. Roynona Creek, U.S. Highway 63 north, Hayward (715–634–5880), has nine holes, a clubhouse, and pro shop.

Museum. The National Fresh Water Fishing Hall of Fame, corner of State Highway 27 and County Road B; (715) 634–4440; www.freshwater-fishing.org. The museum is a tribute to sport fishing and displays reels, lures, fishing trophies, and antique motors. A highlight is the World's Largest Muskie, an exhibit hall full of prize-winning mounts, with an observation deck in its mouth. Wheelchair accessible. Open daily April 15 through October 31 10:00 A.M. to 5:00 P.M. Admission: adults $5.00; children 10 to 18, $3.50; children under 10, $2.50.

Winter Alternatives

Cross-country Skiing. There are several trails in the area, including the 52K Birkebeiner that starts in Telemark, Wisconsin; (715) 634–5025.

Downhill Skiing. Mount Telemark, Cable, Wisconsin, 18 miles north of

Hayward on State Highway 63; (715) 798–3811 or (877) 798–4718. The ski resort has complete facilities, including lodging.

Snowmobiling. More than 600 miles of trails are in the area. Call (715) 634–8662 or (800) 533–7454 for maps.

Special Events

February. American Birkebeiner, aka "the Birkie";(715) 634–5025 or (800) 872–2753; www.birkie.com. The largest cross-country ski race in North America.

Winterfest Snowmobile Races. Includes world-class drag races and speed runs.

May. Fishing Has No Boundaries, Lake Chippewa Campground, Hayward; (715) 634–3185. Event precedes the muskie season opener and is held for disabled persons.

June. The Annual Musky Festival, Hayward Area Lakes; (715) 634–8662.

July. Lumberjack World Championships, 2 blocks east of Hayward on County Road B; (715) 634–8662.

Honor the Earth Pow Wow, Pow Wow Grounds, 6 miles east of Hayward on County Road B; (715) 634–8934. The largest traditional powwow in North America.

September. Chequamegon Fat Tire Festival. The largest off-road bike race in North America.

October. Muskies Inc. Chapter Challenge Muskie Tournament. Fishing contest.

Other Recommended Restaurants and Lodgings

Country Inn Suites, southern edge of Hayward on State Highway 27; (800) 456–4000 or (715) 634–4100. The inn has an indoor pool and a full-service restaurant and bar. Rooms run about $98 a night on the weekends and include a continental breakfast.

Famous Dave's BBQ Shack and Grand Pines Resort, 8.5 miles east of Hayward on Round Lake; (715) 462–3352 (restaurant), (715) 462–3564 or (888) 774–3023 (resort); www.grandpines.com. A combination of the

North Woods, the Southwest, and country living, this spectacularly furnished resort offers luxurious two- and three-bedroom cabins with whirlpools and fireplaces. Available for rent by the week in the summer (starting at $1,600 a week) and by the weekend in the winter. This is also the home of the original Famous Dave's restaurant, serving award-winning barbecue ribs (by the bone, $13 to $18) with corn on the cob and cornbread muffins. Country breakfasts are also served (about $10).

Robin's Nest Restaurant, 11014W County Road B; (715) 462–3132. A great place to stop on your way to ride the CAMBA trails or after a morning of cycling. Open 7:00 A.M. to 2:00 P.M. for breakfast and lunch. Excellent omelettes and sandwiches.

Whiplash Lake Resort, on the Spider Chain; (715) 462–4302. Three-bedroom, two-bath lake homes by the week in the summer and by the night in the winter are offered. The cabins run about $1,400 to $1,700 a week in the summer and from $120 to $185 a night in the winter.

For More Information

Cable Area Chamber of Commerce, P.O. Box 217, Cable, WI 54821; (800) 533–7454 or (715) 798–3833; www.cable4fun.com.

Hayward Lakes Area Chamber of Commerce, P.O. Box 726, Hayward, WI 54843–0726; (715) 634–8662 or (800) 724–2992.

Hayward Lakes Resort Association, P.O. Box 1055, Hayward, WI 55843; (715) 634–4801 or (800) 724–2992; www.haywardlakes.com.

Spooner Area Chamber of Commerce, 122 North River Street, Spooner, WI 54801–0406; (715) 635–2168; www.washburncounty.com.

IOWA
ESCAPES

Decorah, Spillville, and McGregor

Country Roads

2 Nights

The trip to Decorah, Iowa, is one to be shared among generations: Grandparents should take their children and grandchildren, or vice versa, especially if there is the slightest bit of Norwegian in the family tree. Decorah is a conservative Iowa farming and industrial community and home to both Luther College, a liberal arts college of the Evangelical Lutheran Church of America, and the internationally and justly famous Vesterheim Norwegian–American Museum.

- [ ] Ancestors
- [ ] History
- [ ] Burial Mounds
- [ ] Hand-carved Clocks

On the other hand, the round-trip, including Spillville and McGregor, offers something for everyone: The hikers and history buffs will enjoy following in the footsteps of Laura Ingalls Wilder to Burr Oak or in those of ancient Indian tribes among the burial mounds. Pastry connoisseurs will be raving about the kolaches in Spillville for years. And sightseers will enjoy the scenery along the Mississippi and the peacefulness of the little river town of McGregor. Besides, this part of Iowa calls itself a melting pot of immigrants, and Decorah is self-named "The City of Friendly People." So no matter what your heritage is, *velkommen*.

Day 1 / Morning

Decorah, is only about three hours southeast of the Twin Cities on U.S. Highway 52, but get an early start, and don't plan on being there in time for lunch. The route takes you past Cannon Falls, Rochester, and Harmony, and you will be hard-pressed to drive straight through without stopping in southern Minnesota.

Shortly after you cross the border between Minnesota and Iowa you will see a sign for Burr Oak, where the **Laura Ingalls Wilder Park and**

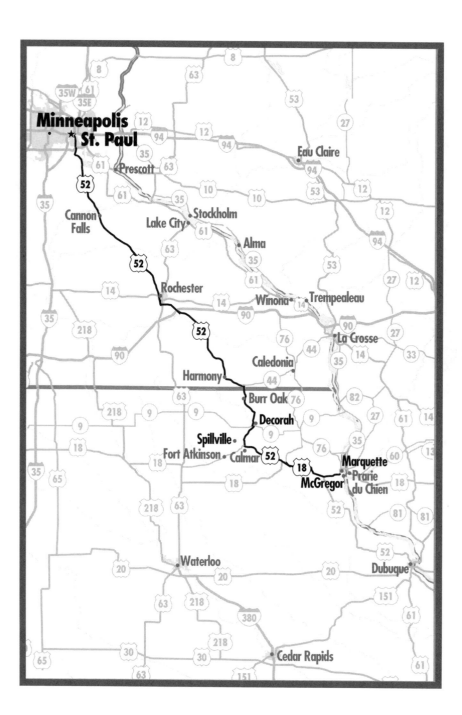

Rolling Iowa farmland

Museum is located. Go left for a couple of blocks and then left again into town. The historic site is actually the old **Masters Hotel,** 3603 236th Avenue, where Mary, Laura, and Mrs. Ingalls worked before moving back to Walnut Grove, Minnesota. It is the only childhood home of Laura's that is still standing on its original site. It is referred to as the "missing link" in the Ingalls Wilder history because the Ingalls family lived here during the year that came between the books *On the Banks of Plum Creek* and *By the Shores of Silver Lake.* Exhibits include period clothing and furnishings, but nothing that belonged to the Ingalls family because they had "lost everything," prompting the move to Burr Oak. Recent acquisitions include clothing and a trunk belonging to the girls' teacher, William Reed, and the Advent Christian Church, which was being built when the Ingalls family lived there. Open Monday through Saturday, June 1 through August 31 9:00 A.M. to 5:00 P.M.; September 1 through May 31 10:00 A.M. to 4:00 P.M. Admission: adults $5.00; children 6 to 17, $3.00. Groups should make reservations. Call (563) 735–5916; www.lauraingallswilder.us.

LUNCH: If you haven't had lunch yet, there's good news and bad news. The bad news is there are no restaurants near the park and museum (the only one closed several years ago). The good news is that Decorah is only 10 miles away south on U.S. Highway 52. A good bet for lunch in Decorah is **Burl's**, 1101½ Montgomery Street. This restaurant has a nice selection of homemade soups, breads, desserts (including pies), and sandwiches. Open daily 6:30 A.M. to 3:00 P.M. Call (563) 387–0167.

Afternoon

From Burl's it's an easy drive to the **Vesterheim Norwegian-American Museum.** Just follow Montgomery Street until it turns left and becomes Water Street, and continue to the museum at 523 West Water Street. (Water is the main street that runs east and west through town.) Consider the Vesterheim to be the "rest of your day"; you'll need at least two to three hours to enjoy this incredible museum.

Established in 1877, the Vesterheim is considered the most comprehensive museum in the United States dedicated to a single immigrant group. There are four floors to the main museum, a restored nineteenth-century redbrick hotel, and more than a dozen additional buildings that include reconstructed immigrant cabins, a church, and a mill. Especially interesting are the textiles exhibit with fine examples of hardanger embroidery, tatting, and knitting; hand-carved (and hand-painted) furnishings; and the actual Tradewind sailboat that crossed the Atlantic in time for the Century of Progress Exposition in Chicago in 1933, sailed by Harald and Hans Hamran. There is a Barne Klubb, or children's room, with music, games, and crafts. Parents and children will also appreciate that everything in the outdoor exhibits is "touchable." The complex, which includes a gift shop stocked with embroidered wool sweaters and accessories decorated with rosemaling, as well as the **Dayton House,** a cafe serving authentic Norwegian food, takes up most of a city block. Open daily May 1 through October 31 9:00 A.M. to 5:00 P.M. Admission: adults $5.00; seniors 65 and over, $4.00; children 7 to 18, $3.00. Open every day except Monday November 1 through April 30 10:00 A.M. to 4:00 P.M. Admission: adults $4.00; seniors 65 and over $3.00; children 7 to 18, $2.00; children under 7 are free. (Also ask about family and group rates.) Call (563) 382–9681; www.vesterheim.org.

DINNER: Walk down Water Street about 4 blocks to **Mabe's Pizza,** 110 East Water Street. Mabe's, now handed down through three generations, is the neighborhood "place to be." The sign says PIZZA, and Mabe's is famous for it, but you can get just about anything, from fajitas (about $4.25) to pastas (about $6.00). Mabe's also has bar service offering beer, wine, wine coolers, and some mixed drinks. Open daily 11:00 A.M. to somewhere around midnight. Call (563) 382–4297.

LODGING: This will have been a long day, especially if you are traveling with children, and it will be a relief to check into the new, clean, and cozy **Country Inn Decorah,** 1202 State Highway 9 West. Go south on Mechanic Street (which is between River and Mill Streets and intersects Water Street), curve right onto Short Street, and the Country Inn will be on your right-hand side as you go right on State Highway 9. The large parking lot is in front of the building. The rooms are comfortably furnished and have an elegant country feel to them. A room for two with a king-size bed is $67 and includes a continental breakfast. A heated indoor pool and whirlpool are also available. Call (563) 382–9646 or (800) 456–4000.

Day 2 / Morning

BREAKFAST: This is definitely a continental-plus breakfast, atypical of chain accommodations. Breakfast includes English muffins, baked muffins, bagels, fruit, cold cereals, juice, tea, and coffee.

After breakfast take a right out of the parking lot onto State Highway 9, follow it west to the intersection with U.S. Highway 52, and go left, continuing south. About 9 miles south of Decorah, before you get to Calmar, take a right on State Highway 325 and go 4 miles to **Spillville** and the **Bily Clocks** exhibit. The Bily Clocks are the complete collection of wooden clocks hand-carved by Frank and Joseph Bily, who spent their summers farming and their winters designing and carving clocks. They never traveled more than 35 miles away from home, but their clocks, influenced by religious and historical events, show a voracious appetite for reading and knowledge. Between 1913 and 1958 they carved more than forty clocks and two models. Each clock has a theme, such as the American Pioneer History Clock, with mechanical figures and intricate carvings.

As you travel into town, you will notice that you are on the Antonín Dvořák Memorial Highway, and you will soon pass **Riverside Park** on your left. Take a few minutes and drive into the park. You will find the **Innwood Pavilion,** a dance hall where the likes of Lawrence Welk and big bands used to play, and a memorial to Antonín Dvořák, the famous

Czech composer, who used to walk along the banks of the Turkey River to commune with nature for musical inspiration.

Dvořák was head of the New York Conservatory of Music in 1893 and was so tired of the big city and so homesick for his country that when he heard about the Czech community of Spillville, Iowa, he moved there for the summer. It was in Spillville that he was inspired to write *Humoresque* and made the final touches to his *New World Symphony*. He also played the organ regularly for masses held at the **St. Wenceslaus Church** in town.

It's unusual that such a little town would have two unique aspects to its history and fame. Although the Bily Clock Museum and the Antonín Dvořák Exhibit are housed in the same building, the men had nothing to do with each other. In fact, the Bily brothers were mere boys when Dvořák spent his summer in Spillville. The Bily Clocks are downstairs, and the Dvořák exhibit is upstairs. The museum is open daily April through October 8:30 A.M. to 5:00 P.M. (with reduced hours in April); on weekends only March and November 10:00 A.M. to 4:00 P.M.; and "on call" the rest of the year. Admission: adults $3.50; children 7 to 12, $1.25; under 7 free. Wheelchair accessible. Call (563) 562–3569.

LUNCH: The town is enough like a fairy tale drawing that you can almost see the curling aroma of *kolaches* and other fresh Czech specialties wafting through the air from the **Old World Inn,** drawing you in for lunch. Inside you'll find a charming country setting complete with red-and-white checkered tablecloths. This is homemade cooking in the old-world tradition true to its name. Favorites include roast pork and *knedlicky* (dumplings), goulash, and *jitrnice,* a traditional pork and barley sausage. If you don't like Czech food, though, you can opt for the chicken, fish, roast beef, or a hamburger. Entrees range in price from $7.00 to $10.00. Czech and Iowa beers are also featured. Open all year; call (319) 562–3767 for hours.

Retrace your steps to U.S. Highway 52 and follow it south to Postville. At Postville the highway will connect with U.S. Highway 18 east that eventually leads, via the business exit, into **McGregor.** This drive will take about an hour, with little more than teeny towns and farmland in between, but within this hour you will travel from rolling farmland to bluff country along the Mississippi River.

McGregor is a great little river town chock-full of gift shops, antiques stores, and bed-and-breakfast inns. You'll arrive in time to wander the shops before closing.

DINNER: Make your way to the old redbrick hotel on the corner, **The Alexander Hotel,** 213 Main Street. The Alexander has a lot to offer: rooms for rent, two bars, a cafe, and the **Lotus Room** for fine dining. The weekend specials of cod or catfish are the way to go, but you can also choose from prime rib, steaks, chicken, and chops. Dinner entrees range in price from $7.00 to $17.00. Open Tuesday through Thursday 6:30 A.M. to 8:00 P.M., Friday and Saturday until 10:00 P.M., and Sunday and Monday until 3:00 P.M. Hours are reduced in the winter. Call (563) 873–3838.

The hotel's **Ringling's Pub** is a must-see. Named for the Ringling brothers of circus fame (two of the brothers were born in McGregor), the pub has a circus motif with numerous mementos, artifacts, and photographs from the Big Top days.

LODGING: You can have an authentic but well-modernized log cabin all to yourself at the **Little Switzerland Inn,** 126 Main Street, at the east end of the street. Set back from the sidewalk, the lot allows for a "butterfly garden" out front. If you are lucky enough to be there at the end of September, and if the weather cooperates, you may have a chance to catch the spectacular sight of monarch butterflies as they migrate south to Mexico. The cabin has a fireplace and a small whirlpool tub and runs about $125 for two to $175 for six per night. Other rooms are available next door in the restored building that once housed Iowa's oldest weekly newspaper. Call (563) 873–2057.

Day 3 / Morning

BREAKFAST: The Little Switzerland offers a full breakfast of fruit, pastries, and an entree, delivered to your door along with the morning paper, so eat heartily before you head off for your morning hike.

About 5 miles north of McGregor, following State Highway 76, is the **Effigy Mounds National Monument** and visitor center. Allow at least a couple of hours to view the video, browse the museum, and hike up the bluff to see the mounds. The conical mounds are the oldest, dating from 450 B.C., and there are three of them just beyond the visitor center. To see any of the effigy mounds shaped like bears and birds, you need to hike deep into the park, and it's all uphill! The first group of effigy figures requires a forty-five-minute round-trip hike from the center; longer hikes are also routed for you and include great views of the river. This is still sacred ground, and no picnicking or camping is allowed. Only the visitor center is wheelchair accessible. Open daily (except New Year's Day,

Thanksgiving, and Christmas) 8:00 A.M. to 5:00 P.M., with increased hours during the summer season. Admission: adults $2.00; children 17 and under are free; maximum carload $4.00. No fees are charged in the winter. Senior citizens should consider purchasing a Golden Age Passport for $10; it's good for a lifetime at all national parks and national monuments. Call Effigy Mounds National Monument, (563) 873–3491.

It's about a four-hour drive back to the Twin Cities from this point. You can cross the river to Prairie du Chien, Wisconsin, follow Wisconsin State Highway 35 north until you cross the river back to Minnesota at Red Wing, and continue into the Twin Cities. Or take Iowa State Highway 76 north through the farm fields to Caledonia, Minnesota (for some spectacular scenery). At Caledonia pick up State Highway 44 and go east to La Crescent; follow U.S. Highway 61, the Great River Road, north along the Mississippi through Red Wing and on into the Twin Cities. In any case, you'll be ready for lunch by the time you get to Winona.

LUNCH: To continue making good time, stop at **The Green Mill,** 1025 U.S. Highway 61, inside the Holiday Inn complex. The Green Mill's famous deep-dish pizza makes a great lunch, but the large menu offers something for everyone (from $6.00 to $11.00). Open daily 6:30 A.M. to 10:00 P.M. Call (507) 452–0500.

There's More

Burr Oak

Willowglen Nursery, 3512 Lost Mile Road, just south of Burr Oak on U.S. Highway 53; (563) 735–5570. This is a beautiful getaway out in the country where perennials grow like wildflowers! The plants are available to buy or just admire as you walk the grounds, and someone is always available to answer gardening questions. Watch for the signs just south of Burr Oak. You'll have to travel about 5 miles down a gravel road to get there. Open 10:00 A.M. to 6:00 P.M., May and June, Tuesday through Sunday; July and August, Tuesday through Saturday; and September through mid-October, Tuesday through Friday.

Calmar

Biking. Bike or walk along the Prairie Farmer Recreational Trail, 18 miles of abandoned Milwaukee Railroad bed. The unpaved limestone-chip trail starts at the Calmar Depot and runs west through native prairie areas and woodlands to just south of Cresco. Call the Winneshiek County Conservation Board; (563) 534–7145.

World's Smallest Church. Follow State Highway 150 south from Calmar to Festina. The chapel, measuring 14 feet by 20 feet, was built to keep a family promise to thank God and is maintained by descendants of the Gaertners and Hubners, who built it more than one hundred years ago.

Decorah

Canoeing and Tubing. Upper Iowa River Canoe Rentals, 3084 Spring Water Road (Pulpit Rock Road); (563) 382–2332.

The Porter House Museum, 401 West Broadway; (563) 382–8465. This is not just another Victorian home tour. This is the lifelong collection of world traveler and naturalist Bert Porter, with carefully arranged displays of two of his passions: winged insects and rocks. You'll know you're there when you spot the sparkling rock fence around the property, designed by Porter himself, which includes geodes, agates, quartz, amethyst, and numerous minerals. The tour does include living areas of the home with many original furnishings and Oriental rugs from the early 1900s, but it's the moths, butterflies, and rock collection, including lamps constructed from rocks and coral, that will keep you spellbound. Open May through December, Saturday and Sunday only, noon to 4:00 P.M. Groups should call for special times. (*NOTE:* The house is supposed to be haunted; volunteers decorate it and dress up on Halloween to pass out candy to the trick-or-treaters.) Admission: $3.50 per person or $10.00 for a family.

Seed Savers Heritage Farm, 5 miles north of Decorah on Winn Road, just off U.S. Highway 52; (563) 382–5990. Here is another unusual concept for a museum: endangered vegetables, fruits, and cattle. The grounds include rare vegetable varieties, a historic apple orchard, and a 300-head herd of Ancient White Park cattle. Open daily Memorial Day through Labor Day 9:00 A.M. to 5:00 P.M.

Ft. Atkinson

Ft. Atkinson, State Highway 24, southwest of Calmar; (563) 425–4161. A reconstructed fort, Atkinson was originally built in 1842 to protect the Winnebago Indians from the Sioux, Sauk, and Fox Indians and from white enemies. Open Saturday and Sunday Memorial Day through Labor Day noon to 5:00 P.M.

Marquette

Isle of Capri Riverboat Casino, U.S. Highway 18; (800) 4–YOU–BET. Slots, poker, roulette, a marina, and all-you-can-eat smorgasbords at the Captain's Reef Buffet. Open twenty-four hours.

McGregor

Spook Cave and Campground, 6 miles west of McGregor on U.S. Highway 18; (563) 873–2144; www.spookcave.com. Full hookups, swimming, and a thirty-five-minute underground boat tour of Spook Cave. The cave is open Memorial Day through August. Camping is available May to October. Fees are charged for each.

Winter Alternatives

Cross-country Skiing. The Prairie Farmer Trail, Calmar; (563) 534–7145. The trail converts to cross-county skiing in the winter.

Downhill Skiing. Nor Ski, 1.5 miles north of U.S. Highway 52 and State Highway 9, Decorah; (563) 382–4158. Five slopes, a chalet, and rentals.

Ice-skating. Wayside Park, Decorah; (563) 382–3990. Outdoor rink with a warming house.

Snowmobiling. There are several trails in and around Decorah. Call (563) 382–3990 for maps.

Special Events

May. Spring Arts/Craft Festival, Triangle Park, McGregor; (563) 873–2186 or (800) 596–0910.

June. Laura Ingalls Wilder Day, Burr Oak; (563) 735–5916. Includes a pancake breakfast, children's games, and a "Little Miss Laura" contest.

July. Woodcarver's Show, Spillville; (563) 382–3782.

Crazy Daze, sidewalk sales in both Marquette and McGregor; (563) 873–2186 or (800) 896–0910.

Nordic Fest, Decorah; (800) 382–FEST. Scandinavian food, music, games, and costumes.

September. Lumberjack Festival, McGregor; (563) 873–2186 or (800)

896–0910. Includes lumberjack shows, arts and crafts, food vendors, a beer garden, and more.

October. Fall Arts and Crafts Fest and the Leaves Arts and Craft Festival, Triangle Park, McGregor; (563) 873–2186 or (800) 896–0910.

Other Recommended Restaurants and Lodgings

Calmar

The Calmar Guest House, as you enter town on U.S. Highway 52; (563) 562–3851. This is the only place to stay in this little town. Decorated with some antiques and abundant religious prints and statuary, this clean, huge Victorian house offers small-town hospitality, a full homemade breakfast, and a shared bath. Rooms rent for $53 a night.

The Train Station Restaurant, 202 North Maryville; (563) 562–3082. A full menu with old–fashioned prices. Here you can get a grilled cheese sandwich or a tossed salad for a little more than $1.00, a bowl of chili for $1.75, or splurge and order a rib-eye steak for about $9.00. Daily specials are also featured. Open Monday through Thursday 6:00 A.M. to 10:00 P.M., Friday and Saturday until 11:00 P.M., Sunday 10:00 A.M. to 2:00 P.M.

Decorah

The Dayton House Cafe, next door to the Vesterheim on Water Street; (563) 382–9683. The cafe is run by the Vesterheim Museum. It offers authentic Norwegian food like *lefse, krumkake* (50 cents), and *lapskaus,* a beef and pork stew ($4.50), in a setting scrubbed as clean as Norwegian white linens. Open daily 11:00 A.M. to 4:00 P.M.

Magpie Coffee House, 118 Winnebago Street; (563) 387–0593. Espresso, coffee drinks, soups, sandwiches, fresh-baked breads, and desserts are served Monday through Wednesday 8:00 A.M. to 5:00 P.M., Thursday and Friday 8:00 A.M. to 8:00 P.M., and Sunday 9:00 A.M. to 3:00 P.M.

T. Bock's, 508 West Water Street; (563) 382–5970. A sports bar best-known for its incredible selection of specialty-topped hamburgers ($2.50 to $4.00) and its wide variety of domestic, imported, and specialty beers, it is open Monday through Saturday through football season, 8:00 A.M. to midnight, Sunday 11:00 A.M. to midnight; closed Sunday the rest of the year.

McGregor

The Alexander Hotel, 213 Main Street; (563) 873–3454; ww.alexanderhotel.net. Rooms with full and shared baths start at $50, with reduced rates in the winter. Although it dates from the mid-1800s, all the rooms are air-conditioned, heated, have cable television, and are newly refurbished. Shuttle service to Isle of Capri Riverboat Casino is included.

The American House Inn, 116 Main Street; (563) 873–3364. These bed-and-bath suites offer a great lodging alternative for groups and families. As a hotel, it housed such famous guests as Mark Twain and Ulysses S. Grant. The two suites can accommodate two people (about $90 a night) to as many as eight (about $200 a night).

The White Springs Supper Club, U.S. Highway 18 as you come into town from the west; (563) 873–9642. The club has people lining up outside its door on the weekends. It's been a neighborhood fixture for many years and is the kind of place that has country-western music wailing from the jukebox, a bathroom sink in use in the hall, and staff chatting at the tables until the customers arrive. But the tangy barbecue sauce (smothering hickory-smoked ribs, $7.75) and French dressing are secret recipes, the hamburgers are made fresh to order ($1.75), and you can't beat the home-made potato salad—it's just like Mom's. Open Monday through Saturday 11:00 A.M. to 11:30 P.M., Sunday 4:00 to 9:30 P.M.

Spillville

The Old World Inn, Main Street; (563) 562–3767. The Old World Inn has a restaurant downstairs, guest rooms upstairs. All four rooms have private baths and are furnished in a country motif. One room has a sitting area and a kitchenette and is designed for families. Rates vary but include a complete Czech breakfast of sausage, eggs, rye toast, and a bowl of fruit.

The Taylor-Made Bed and Breakfast, 330 Main Street; (563) 562–3958. A charming vernacular-style home with sunny, sparsely furnished rooms, it offers a beautiful bath to share (private bath available) and the smell of freshly baked breads—the owner bakes for the Old World Inn! A lower-level room has a private bath and is wheelchair accessible. Rooms are $69 per night and include an enormously good breakfast. The Taylor-Made also offers its converted "woodshed," a delightful private cottage with a kitchen, for $95 per night.

For More Information

Decorah Area Chamber of Commerce, 111 Winnebago Street, Decorah, IA 52101; (563) 382–3990; www.decorah-iowa.com.

Iowa Division of Tourism, 200 East Grand Avenue, Des Moines, IA 50309; (515) 242–4705 or (800) 345–IOWA; www.traveliowa.com.

McGregor–Marquette Chamber of Commerce, P.O. Box 105, McGregor, IA 52157; (563) 873–2186 or (800) 896–0910; www.mcgreg-marq.org.

Okoboji

The Other Great Lakes

2 Nights

What the Northern Lakes area is to Minnesota, Okoboji is to Iowa. Okoboji is the catchall term for the Iowa Great Lakes recreation area that comprises five interconnected glacial lakes spanning more than 3,600 acres. The most popular lake is 134-foot-deep West Okoboji, which is rimmed with little towns, resorts, cottages, restaurants, and shops.

Like the history of many resort areas, tourism in Okoboji followed in the wake of the railroads that enabled people to travel and vacation far from home. More than one hundred years ago, vacationers discovered Okoboji to be a cool oasis in the midst of prairie and farmland heat, and grand hotels sprang up almost immediately.

☐ Resorts

☐ Recreation

☐ Amusements

Today the lavish hotels are gone, but the charm is not. Imagine Nisswa, Minnesota, fifty years ago, or imagine Lake Minnetonka more recently, when Excelsior Amusement Park was still popular and you could see the roller coaster and the lake in the same picture. That's what the Okoboji area is like today, and thrill seekers can still ride one of the thirteen wooden roller coasters left in the United States.

This classic resort area offers recreation galore. Aside from the standard lake fun, there are water and amusement parks, antiques stores, and good shopping. Then, of course, there is all the fun of the University of Okoboji.

The University of Okoboji could almost be called a state of mind university. Begun on a whim in the early 1970s, the U of O celebrated its centennial in 1978. Yes, the University of Okoboji is a concept as made up as its date of origin, but the "college" events, including soccer and rugby tournaments and even homecoming (in July, no less), are very, very real. This is a "college" boasting everything from a campus bookstore (the souvenir shop) to student housing (hotels, resorts, and campgrounds) and a motto, "Where fun in life is your degree." So head to lake country by going south for a change—you may even pick up an honorary degree (a T-shirt?) just for having a good time.

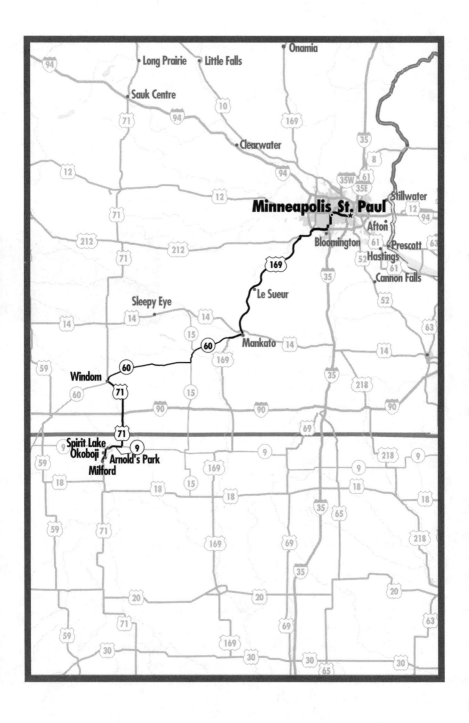

Day 1 / *Morning*

The trip to Okoboji is an easy three-hour drive. Follow U.S. Highway 169 south to Mankato. From Mankato, take State Highway 60 west to Windom, where you pick up U.S. Highway 71 and follow it south, through Jackson and across the Minnesota–Iowa border to Spirit Lake, Iowa, the town at the top of the chain of lakes. Stay on U.S. Highway 71, and it will take you through the heart of the tourist attractions.

LUNCH: If you leave in the morning, you'll be in the Okoboji area for lunch. A great way to get a feel for the small-town charm that lingers in this resort community is to eat lunch at the **Koffee Kup Kafe,** on U.S. Highway 71 just before you get to the stoplights in **Arnold's Park.** (Arnold's Park is the name of the town as well as the name of the amusement park.) The Koffee Kup is known for its breakfasts, particularly its homemade cinnamon rolls. For lunch a multitude of homemade specialties is offered: breaded pork tenderloins (about $5.00), cream of potato or vegetable beef soup (in a homemade bread bowl to boot), and hot-beef sandwiches with real mashed potatoes (about $4.00). Open Tuesday through Sunday, all year, from 6:00 A.M. to 2:00 P.M. Call (712) 332–7657.

Afternoon

Just to get your bearings, continue on U.S. Highway 71 to **Boji Bay Water Park,** take a right on State Highway 86, and then follow it as it turns north along the west side of **West Okoboji Lake.** Although there are a few resorts and restaurants tucked back in here, the countryside quickly reverts to farmland as you cut through cornfields to the northern tip of the lake. Turn right on State Highway 9, follow it east to U.S. Highway 71, and then turn south again. It's obvious that the strip between West and East Okoboji Lakes has most of the action. Although this stretch of Highway 71 has been widened, it can be very congested on a summer weekend, so it's a good idea to know where you are headed (take note of the locations of various attractions). This is also a good time to explore the antiques stores and other fun shops along the highway.

DINNER: Why not splurge right off the bat? Treat yourself at **Yesterday's,** 131 West Broadway, 2 blocks west of the stoplights in Arnold's Park. This is easily one of the best restaurants in the area. Yesterday's specializes in seafood, including live Maine lobster. It's definitely upscale, but casual clothing is acceptable all over this resort town. Open April through

September for lunch and dinner, through December for dinner only. If it's midsummer, reservations are a good idea. Call (712) 332–2353.

LODGING: As you near Arnold's Park from the north, watch for the Kum & Go gas station and take a right, heading west. This road will turn into Lakeshore Drive and take you to **The Inn,** 3301 Lakeshore Drive, about 1 mile west of U.S. Highway 71. With all the updates, there is almost no evidence of the hotel/resort that occupied this spot one hundred years ago, except for the old-fashioned hospitality. Along with the hospitality comes a 500-foot lakefront, tennis courts, and a private nine-hole golf course. Speedboats, water skis, and Jet Skis are also available for rent. A standard double-occupancy room at the inn is about $140 to $150. Open mid-May through mid-September. Wheelchair accessible. Call (712) 332–2113 or (800) 831–5092; www.theinnatokoboji.com.

Day 2 / Morning

BREAKFAST: Have your breakfast at the **Stars and Stripes Cafe,** The Inn's own restaurant overlooking the pool. Waffles, eggs, and omelettes are made to order (about $5.00 to $8.00). Then spend the morning indulging in resort life: swimming, sunning, or boating.

After your leisurely morning, head south on U.S. Highway 71 to **Arnold's Park Amusement Park.** Well over one hundred years old, Arnold's Park is considered the "oldest amusement park west of the Mississippi." Little has changed over the years because of the park's high regard for its own history. In fact, the entire town recently rallied together and, through its "Save the park through all ages for all ages" campaign, Arnold's Park Amusement Park has been spared destruction. Although go-carts and miniature golf have been added (not included in the pass), the amusement park is all the fun and nostalgia from yesteryear; it's more like a Coney Island of the Midwest than it is a Valley Fair of Iowa. The wooden roller coaster is one of the twenty oldest in the United States. The Majestic Roller Rink, which had lost its popularity by the 1980s, was not torn down but instead restored as the **Majestic Pavilion,** preserving its floors and charming interior for picnics, dinners, and wedding receptions.

This is a fun-filled day for children and adults, who will enjoy the rides as much as just holding hands and walking through the park along the lakeshore. Be sure to look for the **Nutty Bar Ice Cream Shop,** in the same location since the 1940s and still serving the original ice-cream bar coated with cracked peanuts.

Arnold's Park Amusement Park

Open Memorial Day through Labor Day, weekends only while school is still in session. Hours are Monday through Friday 1:00 to 9:00 P.M., Saturday noon to 10:00 P.M., and Sunday noon to 6:00 P.M. Admission is by height: over 48 inches, $15.95; 36 to 48 inches, $11.75; under 36 inches, free; observer rate, $5.50. Call (800) 599–6995 or (712) 332–2183; www.arnoldspark.com.

LUNCH: There is only one lunch at an amusement park: hot dogs (under $2.00), slushes, and cotton candy for dessert.

Afternoon

Adjacent to the amusement park is the new Iowa Welcome Center, known as the **Okoboji Spirit Center.** This bright yellow building houses the local chamber of commerce as well as the **Iowa Great Lakes Maritime**

Museum, which documents the maritime history of the region. The concept of maritime history in the middle of cornfields is an amusing concept to some, especially since the community is so small, but every resort area has a maritime history. A hundred years ago the trains brought the tourists to the lakes, but there were no roads, so steamships were used to ferry vacationers to their resorts and from resort to resort just to visit. The museum offers a presentation on the geology of the region, artifacts from the old resort days, and a collection of restored wooden boats (there were several boat builders in the area). A highlight includes the once-sunken wreck of one of the speedboats used at Arnold's Park Amusement Park for "thrill rides" during the 1940s. Open Monday through Saturday 9:00 A.M. to 9:00 P.M., Sunday 10:00 A.M. to 6:00 P.M. Suggested donation: $2.50 per person or $6.00 per family. Call (712) 332–5264.

A perfect end to your nostalgic day will be a ride on the *Queen II*. Built in 1986, the *Queen II* is a replica of the steamship *Queen* that once traveled these waters. The ninety-minute cruise will take you on an 18-mile narrated tour of West Lake Okoboji. (And just play along when the captain points to buildings in the distance and tells you they are on the campus of the University of Okoboji.) Board at the *Queen II* dock in Arnold's Park Amusement Park. Fare: adults $8.50; seniors 62 and over $7.50; 36 to 48 inches $6.50; children under 36 inches free. Family package rates are also available. Call (712) 332–5159.

DINNER: Mrs. Lady's, on the corner of U.S. Highway 71 and Broadway in Arnold's Park, has great Mexican food. Using homemade dough for tortillas, it features the usual quesadillas and chimichangas, but it specializes in its very own "insane taco"—it's loaded! Entrees range from $5.50 to $9.00. Open Tuesday through Sunday 11:30 A.M. to 9:00 P.M. Call (712) 332–7373.

LODGING: The Inn.

Day 3 / Morning

BREAKFAST: Start your morning at the Koffee Kup Kafe so you don't miss out on one of their breakfasts. Go for the French roll, a cinnamon or caramel roll dipped in French-toast batter and then fried; the Boji omelette, a Western omelette with hash browns inside (under $6.00); or simply one of the homemade cinnamon rolls heaped with white frosting (about $1.50). Then head south on U.S. Highway 71 to **Milford.** This is a roundabout way back to the Twin Cities, but you can't come all this way and miss the home of the University of Okoboji.

Milford is 1 mile south of West Lake Okoboji on the highway, and the famous store, **The Three Sons,** where you're heading now, is "1 block east of the bank stoplight." The Three Sons is the headquarters of the U of O, every tourist's alma mater, and one of the friendliest shops you'll ever encounter. You can get your T-shirt here, along with a number of designer fashions, including shoes. Open all year Monday through Saturday 10:00 A.M. to 5:00 P.M. and Sunday noon to 4:00 P.M. Call (712) 338–2424; www.threesons.com.

Wander the town, shop Okoboji Avenue, and then have lunch before you turn toward home.

LUNCH: Bird House Cafe, 919 Okoboji Avenue, Milford, is a great place to stop for the home cooking that small towns are known for. Open daily 7:00 A.M. to 2:00 P.M. Call (712) 338–2700.

There's More

Amusements. The Ranch Amusement Park (U.S. Highway 71, Okoboji; 712–332–2159) has Kat Karts, bumper boats, and miniature golf. Open daily from 10:00 A.M. Memorial Day through Labor Day. Admission charged. Boji Bay Water Park (intersection of U.S. Highway 71 and State Highway 86; 712–338–2473) has a wave pool, waterslides, children's pool, concessions, showers, and free life jackets. Open daily Memorial Day through Labor Day 11:00 A.M. to 8:00 P.M. Admission charged.

Arts. The Lakes Arts Center, U.S. Highway 71, Okoboji; (712) 332–7013; www.lakesart.org. The center offers exhibits, original art for sale, and foreign film showings. Free. Open Memorial Day through Labor Day, Monday 9:00 A.M. to 8:00 P.M., Tuesday through Thursday 9:00 A.M. to 4:00 P.M., and Friday through Sunday 1:00 to 4:00 P.M.

Biking. The paved Spine Bike Trail (712–332–2209, 800–270–2574, or 888–OKOBOJI) runs about 13 miles from Milford through Spirit Lake. The trailhead is 1 block east of Okoboji Avenue on County Road A–34.

Camping. RV camping with full hookups is available at Crow's Nest Resort (East Okoboji, Arnold's Park; 712–332–2221) for about $20 per night. Gull Point State Park (712–337–3870) and Emerson Bay (712–337–3805), both north of Milford on State Highway 86, and Marble

Beach (712–336–4437), north of U.S. Highway 71 in Orleans, offer camp-grounds with beaches. All are wheelchair accessible. Call Iowa Department of Natural Resources for more information; (515) 281–5145.

Golf. Okoboji View Golf Course (State Highway 86, Spirit Lake; 712–337–3372) offers eighteen holes, putting greens, carts, a restaurant, and a lounge. Indian Hills Golf Course (2 miles west of the junction of State Highway 9 and U.S. Highway 71, Spirit Lake; 712–336–4768) offers nine holes, carts, snacks, and a lounge.

Parasailing. Extreme Water Sports, Arnold's Park Amusement Park, next to the *Queen II* dock; (712) 332–5406. Ski boat and Jet Ski rentals are also available.

Winter Alternatives

Cross-country Skiing. Kettleson Hogsback Wildlife Area, a few miles northwest of Spirit Lake on County Road 276.

Downhill Skiing. Riverside Hills, Estherville; (712) 362–5376. A small ski resort about 15 miles east of Okoboji.

Sliding. Horseshoe Bend, 3 miles south of Milford on U.S. Highway 71; (712) 338–4786. Rentals available.

Snowmobiling. The Spine Bike Trail converts to a snowmobile trail in the winter. The trailhead is 1 block east of Okoboji Avenue on County Road A-34, Milford. Snowmobiling is also available in most of the city and state parks throughout the Iowa Great Lakes area. Call (888) OKOBOJI or (800) 270–2574.

Special Events

January. University of Okoboji Winter Games; (712) 338–2424.

February. Estherville Winter Sports Festival, Town Square; (712) 362–3541.

May. Blue Water Music Festival, Spirit Lake; (712) 336–3564. University of Okoboji Three on Three Basketball Tournament; (712) 338–2424.

June. University of Okoboji Tournaments: Tennis, Soccer, Rugby, Women's Softball, and Cycling Classic Campus Ride; (712) 338–2424.

July. University of Okoboji World Tennis Classic, Homecoming, Marathon, Half Marathon, Triathlon, 10K, and Environmental Clean-Up Drive; (712) 338–2424.

Milford Pioneer Days, Milford; (712) 338–4712.

August. Ritz Charity Golf Classic, Emerald Hills Golf Course; (712) 332–7100. University of Okoboji Men's Softball Tournament; (712) 338–2424.

Other Recommended Restaurants and Lodgings

Crescent Beach Lodge, 1620 Lakeshore Drive, State Highway 56, on the west side of West Okoboji Lake; (712) 337–3351 or (800) 417–1117; www.crescentbeachlodge.com. The lodge is a family resort and one of the "best restaurants in the state" according to the *Des Moines Register*. The restaurant offers elegant dining and is well known for its Sunday champagne brunch, 10:00 A.M. to 2:00 P.M. (about $14 per person). All rooms have the modern amenities of air-conditioning, cable television, and telephones. Open May 15 through mid-September. Rates vary; a parkside room is about $100 per night, and a lakefront room with a kitchenette, for four, runs about $230 a night midseason. A three-night minimum is required.

O'Farrell Sisters, Smith's Bay, 1109 Lakeshore Drive, Okoboji; (712) 332–7901. A classic diner featuring homemade food and specializing in pies. The buttermilk pancakes are great! Reasonably priced. Open seasonally.

The Ramada Limited, intersection of State Highway 9 and U.S. Highway 71 in Spirit Lake; (712) 336–3984 or (800) 272–6232. The inn offers an indoor pool, exercise room and spa, and a continental breakfast. A standard double-occupancy room is about $95 a night.

The Ritz, U.S. Highway 71, Arnold's Park; (712) 332–2777. The restaurant is notorious for its pizzas and fishbowl drinks. Try the taco pizza! Open May through September.

Sandbar Beach Resort, 11302 270 Avenue Place, on Big Spirit Lake; (712) 336–0538 (summer), (972) 596–8645 (winter); www.sandbarbeach.com. For a change of pace from chain motels and fancier resorts, nothing beats staying at a cottage at a family resort. All cottages are housekeeping units and range in size from one bedroom to four bedrooms. The resort is open

May through September, and rates range from $425 to $850 per week during peak season.

Time Out Bed and Breakfast, 250 West Maple Drive, Hartley; (712) 728–2213; www.nwiowabb/timeout.htm. If you need a break from the amusement park, tourist shops, and busy atmosphere of Okoboji, this appropriately named bed-and-breakfast should fit the bill. Located about 30 miles south of Okoboji in the small town of Hartley, Time Out has four rooms (two with private baths, two with a shared bath) in a 1927 mission-style prairie bungalow. Rates are $55 per night for two people, which includes a full Iowa breakfast.

Tweeter's, U.S. Highway 71, Okoboji; (712) 332–9421. A sports bar considered to be "Hawkeye Headquarters," it's famous for its "Oscars," chicken or beef medallions on an English muffin topped with asparagus and hollandaise sauce (about $10). Open all year 11:00 A.M. to 11:00 P.M., until midnight on weekends.

Village East, U.S. Highway 71, north of Okoboji; (712) 332–2161 or (800) 727–4561. Village East offers luxury accommodations, fine dining at Minerva's, and a multitude of recreational activities, including tennis and golf. Rates run about $175 a night for two. Winter packages are also available.

For More Information

Iowa Division of Tourism, 200 East Grand Avenue, Des Moines, IA 50309; (515) 242–4705 or (800) 345–4692; www.traveliowa.com.

Okoboji Tourism Association, U.S. Highway 71, Okoboji Spirit Center, Arnold's Park, P.O. Box 215, Okoboji, IA 51355; (712) 332–2209, (800) 270–2574, or (888) OKOBOJI; www.okoboji.com. or www.vacation okoboji.com.

The Amana Colonies

Blood, Sweat, and Prayers

2 Nights

With a history that began during the Renaissance, the German-born Amana Church in America is the result of hundreds of years of religious persecution. Officially known as the True Inspirationists—members of the Community of True Inspiration, who believed in their inspired leaders as well as in the Bible—these religious refugees fled Germany, first settling in America in Ebenezer, New York, and established their communal way of life in the 1840s. By the 1850s the community had outgrown its holdings in New York and searched for a new, larger location.

☐ Arts and Crafts

☐ German Food

☐ Wine Tasting

☐ History

It was the lush Iowa River Valley that attracted the True Inspirationists' leaders to Homestead, Iowa, and its surrounding land in 1855. The rolling hills, protecting and isolating the colonies the way they did 150 years ago, enhance the modern-day visit to this uniquely preserved bit of history. And the biblical name Amana, the "fixed or true" mountain referred to in the Song of Solomon, holds fast.

There are seven villages scattered across the hills like tumbled gemstones: South Amana, West Amana, High Amana, Middle Amana, Amana (or Main Amana), East Amana, and Homestead, the little town the True Inspirationists bought. Set 1 to 3 miles apart, each colony operated independently. Each had its own church, furniture factory, woolen mill, tinsmith, communal gardens, kitchen, and bakery. But as part of the whole, each acted under one law: *"Bleib Treu; remain faithful, tilling and grazing one earth."* Today each village offers a glimpse into the communal life of the Amana colonists that survived for nearly one hundred years.

In 1932, after a disastrous fire at one of the woolen mills and adjacent flour mills, and due to a growing discontent among the members, communal living came to an end. It was then that the Amana Society, as the corporation is known today, established itself and continued to regulate land use and run the farms and businesses. But for the first time, and smack

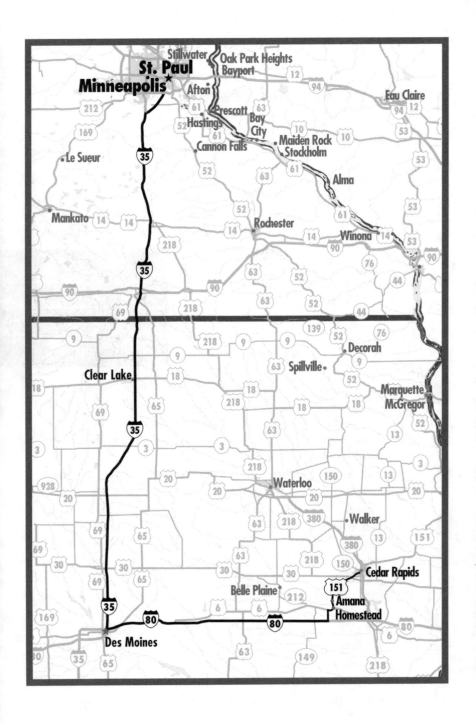

in the middle of the Depression, the members were faced with new concepts such as wages, taxes, and meals at home in their own houses. Yet they fared well. The colonies have produced numerous entrepreneurs, including the man who started the Amana Appliances corporation by betting he could make a cooler that would work reliably.

There were many religious groups that sought refuge in the United States during the 1800s, and the settlers in Amana are often confused with the Amish, who followed a similar route to religious freedom. But the True Inspirationists are due special recognition in our history. After all, they established the prototype for corporate farms, giant inventories, and day-care centers for preschoolers that allowed the mothers to tend to their work, albeit communal. It is clear why today's descendants are proud to recall their ancestors as a progressive people.

There are about 600 direct descendants who have remained in the colonies. Some still operate their families' original businesses or simply conduct the tours through them, perpetuating history. The Amana community, comprised of the descendants and about 1,200 newcomers, is a mix of heritage, pride, craftsmanship, and tourism. The woolen mill is still a woolen mill, but communal kitchens have become bed-and-breakfasts and museums, houses have become shops, and meat-curing barns have become restaurants. It all blends so well, though, that it's sometimes hard to tell the new from the old. That is, until the church bell rings on Sunday morning, the women don their shawls and bonnets, and families stroll across the lawns to church, where you are welcome to join them.

Day 1 / Morning

The Amana Colonies nestle themselves into hillsides about five hours southeast of the Twin Cities. The drive goes very quickly, however, following I–35 south through picturesque farm fields, especially if you stop for a break at the halfway point in the congenial town of **Clear Lake,** Iowa.

Clear Lake is a sunny little community on the edge of a crystal-clear 3,600-acre lake with a main street full of restaurants and antiques and gift stores. Downtown is so complete that shops include a Ben Franklin, the Corner Drug Store (that serves phosphates and malts at the counter), and the Lake Theatre, a restored opera house that shows first-run movies and boasts the "largest screen in Northern Iowa."

Park on the street, wander the shops, and stay for lunch.

LUNCH: There are several restaurants in town (and fast-food stops near the highway), but Clear Lake is the kind of town that calls for wicker baskets and gingham picnic cloths. With that in mind, a lunch "to go" from the **Backyard Deli,** 300 Main Avenue, is the perfect choice. Choose from bagels, hearty sandwiches, homemade soups, or one of the special combos (about $5.00)—and don't forget the potato salad! Open daily 8:00 A.M. to 5:00 P.M., with reduced hours in winter. Call (641) 357–2234. Cross the street to the city park, pick a table, watch the kids play on the swings, and enjoy your lunch near the lake.

Afternoon

If you're tempted to stay, there are several bed-and-breakfast inns and motels in Clear Lake, but if you're planning to eat dinner in the Amana Colonies, it's almost time to hit the road. You can't leave town without a visit to the **Surf Ballroom,** 460 North Shore Drive (just follow the shoreline north), famous as the site of Buddy Holly's, Richie Valens's, and the Big Bopper's last concert. It is so perfectly restored to its 1940s magic that it looks like a movie set, and it is still bringing to its stage such famous names as Creedence Clearwater Revisited and Styx. Formal tours are available for a small fee, but feel free to drop in and browse when you're in town. The nostalgia will sweep you off your feet. Open daily. Call (641) 357–6151 for information on special events.

Backtrack to I–35 and continue following it south. Near Des Moines, pick up I–80 and follow it east all the way to the **Amana Colonies.** Take exit 225 north to U.S. Highways 6 and 151. Go left (east) 3 miles. The collection of redbrick and sandstone houses and farm buildings is **South Amana,** the first Amana Colony on this route. Follow the country highway north 3 miles and you will curve past **West Amana** onto 220th Trail, which will take you east (and eventually south) through the rest of the colonies. By now the colonies are beginning to make sense: small clusters of ancient houses and farm buildings dispersed among the lush green hills of the Iowa River Valley.

The colonies are situated 1 to 3 miles from each other. In addition to reliable hospitality, each has something a little different to offer. For example, **High Amana** has an old-fashioned general store and the **Amana Arts Guild Center,** and **Middle Amana** has the only functioning Amana church, an original bakery, and the **Communal Kitchen Museum.** The village known strictly as **Amana** is, admittedly, where most of the "action" is. The largest of the seven colonies, it is home to

Traditional Maifest in the Amana Colonies

the bulk of the restaurants, shops, and artisans.

You can start your tour in any one of the villages and work your way around the circle (allowing for a stop at the visitors bureau 1 mile west of Amana), but you may want to save all the tourist activity for tomorrow; dinner and a whirlpool soak probably sound pretty good right now.

Evening

DINNER: Entrees like veal piccata and pasta tossed with grilled chicken in a Riesling wine sauce aren't exactly standard Amana fare, but dinner at **The Smokehouse,** South Amana, is not to be missed. The chef, who has "been in the business since he was ten" and recently relocated from the locally famous Collins Plaza in Cedar Rapids, takes pride in his remarkable creations while his business partners and the rest of the staff take pride in their service. This solid, restored 1856 smokehouse provides great atmosphere for dinner and makes a perfect introduction to the colonies and their knack for blending the old with the new. Entrees range in price from $13 to $20, and the hefty portions hold their own against those of the traditional German family-style restaurants. Open Monday through Thursday 11:00 A.M. to 9:00 P.M., until 10:00 P.M. on Friday and Saturday, and Sunday 11:00 A.M. to 7:00 P.M. The restaurant is closed Sunday and Monday from September 1 through May 1. Call (319) 622–3750 or (888) 622–6246.

LODGING: Enjoy live music in the bar at the Smokehouse before you continue to Middle Amana for a peaceful sleep at **Dusk to Dawn Bed and Breakfast,** 2616 K Street. What looks like modern post-and-beam architecture is really the original sturdy construction of timber, brick, and plaster that's over 150 years old. Here the rooms are private, pleasant, and quiet. In keeping with communal life, the guest rooms share a sitting area replete with books and magazines. All the rooms have private baths; a separate cottage is perfect for groups or families. The large whirlpool tub amid the gardens and under the stars is the perfect ending to a long day. Rates range from $60 to $70 a night. Call (319) 622–3029 or (800) 669–5773.

Day 2 / Morning

BREAKFAST: Dusk to Dawn Bed and Breakfast. Your breakfast of fresh fruits, pastries, juice, and coffee or tea is included in the price. Any dietary needs will be catered to upon request.

It would be hard to thoroughly cover every Amana colony in a weekend, but a few "must visits" will give you a taste of the area. The "musts" in Middle Amana are **Hahn's Hearth Oven Bakery** and the **Communal Kitchen Museum.** (Addresses aren't used much in the colonies; just watch for the little white signs, barely bigger than labels, that point your way.) Hahn's Bakery has been in the same family for a century and a half. Although the original hearth oven now burns natural gas instead of firewood, it still turns out hearty loaves of bread (up to 140 at a time), *kolaches,* and more. Hahn's is open April through October, Tuesday through

Saturday; March, November, and December on Wednesday and Saturday; and on Saturday only in January and February. The bakery doors open at 7:30 A.M. and close when everything is gone. Be sure to get there early if you're anxious to buy something; they sell out fast.

Next door is the communal kitchen for Middle Amana, where, until 1932, thirty to forty farmhands would have been fed several times a day. Tours are self-guided, but your knowledgeable hosts and hostesses, some of them direct descendants, are full of memories, stories, and anecdotes.

NOTE: All Amana museums are open May 1 through October 31, Monday through Saturday 9:00 A.M. to 5:00 P.M. and Sunday noon to 5:00 P.M. Admission: adults $5.00; children 8 to 16, $1.00; children 7 and younger are free. The price covers admission to all four of the museums of the Amana Heritage Society.

Also in Middle Amana is the colonies' only original church still in operation. Visitors are welcome to attend the Sunday services. The early service is in German; the 10:00 A.M. service is in English.

From Middle Amana follow 220th Trail to Amana, the commercial hub of the colonies. Park your car along the street or in specified lots, and enjoy the village on foot. The streets are lined with shops that have everything from arts and crafts to woolens, including Christmas ornaments, fudge, and leather goods. There are so many restaurants that when it comes time to eat, you can practically close your eyes and point and not go wrong.

LUNCH: The Colony Inn, at the east end of the main street in Amana, is the epitome of family-style dining in the Amana Colonies. With its blue-and-white checkered tablecloths, aproned servers, and tall wooden booths, it's homey, friendly, and good. Traditional choices are Amana pork sausage, Wiener schnitzel, and sauerbraten. All entrees include bowls heaped full of mashed potatoes (fried potatoes are served at night), lots of gravy, a vegetable, and a slice of pie. Prices hover in the $12.00 range, but "plate lunches" (smaller, individual portions) are available for about $8.00 each. American favorites are also on the menu. Open daily 7:00 A.M. to 8:00 P.M., Sunday until 7:30 P.M. Call (319) 622–6270 or (800) 227–3471.

Afternoon

As you continue to wander the shops, don't miss the **Amana Woolen Mill,** the **Amana Furniture Shop** (both Amana Society businesses), and the open-air beer garden, the **Millstream Brewing Company,** which serves its own root beer. Each offers demonstrations of the production process plus a chance to buy their fine finished products.

Also in (Main) Amana, at the west end of the main street, is the **Museum of Amana History.** It gives a comprehensive overview of Amana life, from Germany through the disbanding of the colonies, and includes a stunning collection of black-and-white photographs by Amana photographers that depict, with rare insight, the lifestyle within the colonies.

DINNER: The menu at **Zuber's** in Homestead is familiar—Amana bratwurst, country-style chicken, Wiener schnitzel, and sauerkraut—but the story is unique. The restaurant's namesake, Bill Zuber, was a boy who grew up in the colonies in the 1920s. Like most boys his age, he longed to play baseball, but the game, along with many other pastimes, was banned by the church. With the end of communal living in sight, however, the colonies formed competing teams, and in 1930, at age seventeen, Bill was discovered by C. C. Slapnicka, a Cleveland Indians baseball scout. Bill Zuber not only got to play ball, he made it to the Major League, playing for the Yankees and pitching in two World Series. In 1949, after an injury, Bill retired from baseball and went home to the Amana Colonies, where he purchased the old Homestead Hotel that now houses the restaurant. The interior is covered in Bill Zuber baseball memorabilia that, combined with Amana hospitality, creates an atmosphere as charming as his story. Entrees range from $10 to $16 and include coleslaw, cottage cheese, applesauce, and potatoes. Open Monday through Saturday 11:00 A.M. to 2:00 P.M. and 4:30 to 8:00 P.M., Sunday 11:00 A.M. to 2:00 P.M. Call (319) 622–3911 or (800) 522–8883.

Evening

Don't pass up the opportunity to see a performance by **The Old Creamery Theatre Company.** Productions vary season to season—from comedy to vaudeville—except for its traditional rendition, *Christmas Carol with the Creamery*. Performances are held on the Pine Creek Stage at the **Amana Colonies Visitor Center,** 0.5 mile west of Amana off Highways 220 and 151. Shows run May through December, Wednesday, Friday, and Saturday at 8:00 P.M., with a 3:00 P.M. matinee on Thursday and Sunday. Admission is charged. Call (319) 622–6194 or (800) 35–AMANA or visit www.oldcreamery.com.

LODGING: Dusk to Dawn Bed and Breakfast.

Day 3 / Morning

BREAKFAST: Dusk to Dawn Bed and Breakfast.

This will be a day filled mostly with driving, but there is time to take in a couple more sights before you head home. Consider the **Communal Agricultural Museum,** 505 P Street, South Amana. The giant barn, one of Amana's oldest, houses a collection of farm implements and a photo-essay on communal farming in Amana. Another option is the **Amana Community Church** at 4210 V Street in Homestead. Both museums are included in the pass for the museums of the Amana Heritage Society. Or you can continue to check out the shops or pay a visit to one of the many wineries throughout the colonies.

LUNCH: Depending on how long you decide to stay in the Amana Colonies, and whether you want one more schnitzel before you head home, you may decide to eat lunch in one of the villages. Otherwise, the logical stop on the way home will be Clear Lake. This time try **Ge-Jo's by the Lake,** 12 North Third Street. It's a bustling little Italian restaurant with a service bar, outdoor seating, and a view of the lake, serving home-made pizzas and all the traditional pastas such as spaghetti, lasagna, rigatoni, and more, plus Italian sandwiches. Prices range from $6.00 to $10.00 per person. Open Wednesday and Thursday 4:00 to 9:00 P.M., Friday 11:30 A.M. to 2:00 P.M. and 4:00 to 10:00 P.M., Saturday 11:30 A.M. to 10:00 P.M., and Sunday 11:30 A.M. to 8:00 P.M. Call (641) 357–8288.

There's More

The Amana Colonies

Biking. The Kolonieweg Recreational Trail is a 3.1-mile hard-surfaced trail that runs between Middle Amana and Amana. It also connects to more than 20 miles of lightly traveled roads frequented by bicyclists. All patrons should use caution; it is shared by both bicyclists and pedestrians.

Camping. The Amana Colonies RV Park, 1 mile west of Amana near the visitor center off Highways 220 and 151 (319–622–7616), has sites for everything from tents to RVs, with electrical hookups, propane, showers, a store, and a playground. Open April 15 through October 31.

Golf. The Amana Colonies Golf Course, north of Middle Amana on Twenty-seventh Avenue; (319) 622–6222 or (800) 383–3636; www.amana

golfcourse.com. The course offers eighteen holes, a dining room, and a full-service pro shop.

High Amana General Store, 1308 G Street, High Amana; (319) 622–3567. The store has been perfectly preserved through three generations of the same family, right down to its glass display cases. Open daily June 15 through October 31, Saturdays only in November and December.

Hiking. The Amana Colonies Nature Trail, U.S. Highways 151 and 6, Homestead, offers 1- and 3-mile hikes through wildlife and Indian mounds.

Krauss Furniture and Clock Shop, on U.S. Highway 6 just east of South Amana, has been making walnut, oak, and cherry furniture for five generations. The shop offers tours of the factory, as well as its furniture, wooden gifts, and clocks for sale. Open all year Monday through Friday 8:00 A.M. to 5:00 P.M., Saturday 9:00 A.M. to 5:00 P.M., and Sunday, May through December, 1:00 to 4:00 P.M. Call (319) 622–3223; www.krauss furniture.com.

Tanger Outlet Mall, on I–80 in Williamsburg, just west of the Amana Colonies, offers clothing and home fashions from more than sixty brand-name manufacturers at huge savings. Open daily all year. Call (319) 668–2885.

Wineries. The Village Winery, Main Amana; (319) 622–3448 or (800) 731–7142. Features an assortment of fruit wines created in Colony tradition; open daily. Ehrle Bros. Winery, Homestead; (319) 622–3241. The oldest winery in the Amana Colonies; tours of the wine cellar and wine tastings are offered. The Ackerman Winery, South Amana (319–622–3379), and the Heritage Wine and Cheese Haus, Amana (319–622–3564), offer two locations for the same award-winning wines. Open daily.

Clear Lake

Cerro Gordo Wind Farms. The windmills are visible from across the lake at the end of Main Avenue. More than 10 miles away, the 265-foot turbines look like children's toys, and the magical lure they have lends an understanding of *Don Quixote.* You could crisscross the Iowa cornfields by car forever and would still need a telephoto lens to capture the image: The wind farm spans more than 2,100 acres.

Coffman's Carts, north side of U.S. Highway 18; (641) 357–4118. Coffman's has go-carts, water balloon games, miniature golf, and a video arcade. Fees for each are charged. Open daily late May through Labor Day and on weekends in April, May, September, and October.

Golf. The All Vets Golf Club, 2000 North Shore Drive; (641) 357–4457. The public is welcome at this eighteen-hole golf course that features bent-grass greens, a golf shop, and a snack bar.

Lady of the Lake, Sea Wall, downtown Clear Lake; (641) 357–2243. This stern-wheeler that once navigated the Mississippi River now offers cruises to visitors. The *Lady* departs Monday through Thursday at 7:00 P.M., Friday at 7:00 and 9:30 P.M., and Saturday and Sunday at 2:00, 4:30, and 7:00 P.M., with an additional Saturday night cruise at 9:30 P.M. Fares: adults $12.00; children under 12, $6.00.

State Parks. Clear Lake State Park, 2730 South Lakeview Drive (641–357–4212), has opportunities for picnicking, camping, fishing, and swimming. There are 215 campsites, 95 with electrical hookups, and the beach is 900 feet long. Showers and flush toilets are also available. McIntosh Woods State Park is on the northwest shore of the lake and has fifty campsites (forty-five with electrical hookups), showers, and a playground.

Winter Alternatives

Cross-country Skiing. The Amana Colonies Nature Trail, with up to 3 miles of trails, is open to cross-country skiers.

Ice-skating. Marian Park, Second Avenue North and Second Avenue Northeast, converts to a public ice rink in the winter. A warming house is open Monday through Friday evenings 6:30 to 9:00 P.M. and Saturday and Sunday 1:00 to 5:00 P.M.

Snowmobiling. Trails crisscross the lake, the state parks, and McIntosh Woods near Clear Lake. Snowmobiles are also permitted in downtown Clear Lake.

Special Events

February. Buddy Holly Dance Party, Surf Ballroom, Clear Lake; (641) 357–6151.

May. Maifest, Amana; (319) 622–7622 or (800) 245–5465. Includes food, music, crafts, and the traditional dance around the maypole.

June to July. Municipal Band Concert, City Park, Clear Lake; (641) 357–2159 or (800) 285–5338.

July. Lake Fest, Clear Lake; (641) 357–2159 or (800) 285–5338.

August. Festival of the Arts, Middle Amana Park; (319) 622–7622 or (800) 245–5465. Features arts and crafts, ethnic food, and entertainment.

September. Antiques in the Park, Clear Lake; (641) 357–2159 or (800) 285–5338.

October. Oktoberfest, Amana; (319) 622–7622 or (800) 245–5465. Includes the traditional beer tent, German food, music, and a parade.

Other Recommended Restaurants and Lodgings

The Amana Colonies

The Amana Barn Restaurant, (Main) Amana; (319) 622–3214 or (800) 325–2045. The restaurant sits on the site of one of the original Amana community cattle barns. Its menu features traditional family-style German fare, with a number of standard American favorites, but the atmosphere, with its red tablecloths and intimate lighting, brings a touch of elegance to the colonies' country setting. The Amana Barn is a full-service restaurant that offers holiday specials, theater/dinner packages, and even tours of the colonies.

Die Heimat Country Inn, Homestead; (319) 622–3937 or (888) 613–5463; www.dheimat.com. Boasting "no frills," its decor is as traditionally Amana as possible. The rooms are painted in pale Amana blue and furnished with hand-hewn Amana pieces, including canopy beds, and the floors are covered in the timeless handwoven rugs. This meandering inn, with nineteen rooms, was the original stagecoach stop for the colonies and was later used as a communal kitchen. All rooms have air-conditioning, television, and private baths. Rates range from $50 to $70 and include a breakfast buffet of scrambled eggs, French toast, pastries, and fruit served in the common area, the original "lobby."

Guest House Motel/Motor Inn, 4712 220th Trail, Amana; (319) 622–3599 or (877) 331–0828. In the heart of Main Amana, this ancient sandstone home with a new addition offers accommodations for both the historic- and modern-minded visitor. All rooms have private baths and cable television. Rooms run about $50 a night.

Holiday Inn Amana Colonies, I–80, exit 225, Amana (319–668–1175 or 800–633–9244; www.amanaholidayinn.com) has a lounge, restaurant, and a "Holidome" with an indoor pool, hot tub, exercise room, and spa. A standard room for two runs about $85 a night.

Rawson's Bed and Breakfast, Homestead; (319) 622–6035 or (800) 637–6035; www.amanacolonies.com/rawson/. Once a communal kitchen, as a B&B it offers 10,000 square feet of Amana hospitality, including an antiques and gift shop in the restored cellar. Rooms are air-conditioned, all have private baths, and many have whirlpools. The inn is open all year. Rates range from $69 to $119 a night and include a full breakfast.

Rose's Place B&B, Middle Amana; (319) 622–6097 or (877) 767–3233; www.amanacolonies.com/rosesbb/. Built in 1872, Rose's was once the Sunday school in Middle Amana. Its whitewashed, sunny interior is especially inviting, and you're welcome to play the old Sunday school piano located in the dining room. All rooms have private baths. The hearty breakfast includes Amana ham, an egg dish, blueberry muffins, and beverages. Rates are $55 to $65 a night.

Clear Lake

Larch Pine Inn, 401 North Third; (641) 357–7854; www.larchpine inn.com. A grand yet friendly Victorian home just 1 block from the lake, with common areas that include a guest parlor, an upstairs kitchenette, and the inviting, tree-shaded wraparound porch. Rates not only include a full breakfast of fruit, homemade rolls, and a mouthwatering entree served on the porch, but also an evening dessert. Rooms rent for $75 to $99 a night.

Martha's, 305 Main Avenue; (641) 357–8720. Serving fantastic breakfasts, daily lunch specials, and homemade pies for dessert, this is also a great place to grab a sandwich and a bowl of soup (about $4.00). Open Monday through Saturday 5:30 A.M. to 3:00 P.M. and Sunday, Memorial Day through Labor Day, 5:30 A.M. to 12:30 P.M.

For More Information

Amana Colonies Convention and Visitors Bureau, 39-38th Avenue, Suite 100, Amana, IA 52203; (319) 622–7622 or (800) 579–2294; www.amana colonies.com and www.amanaheritage.org for information on historical sites.

Clear Lake Area Chamber of Commerce, 205 Main Avenue, Clear Lake, IA 50428–0188; (641) 357–2159 or (800) 285–5338; www.clear lakeiowa.com.

Iowa Division of Tourism, 200 East Grand Avenue, Des Moines, IA 50309; (515) 242–4705 or (800) 345–4692; www.traveliowa.com.

INDEX

C